GUIDE TO
CATALINA
AND CALIFORNIA'S
CHANNEL
ISLANDS

FIFTH EDITION

GUIDE TO CATALINA

AND CALIFORNIA'S CHANNEL ISLANDS

FIFTH EDITION

CHICKI MALLAN

PHOTOS BY
OZ MALLAN

GUIDE TO CATALINA
AND CALIFORNIA'S CHANNEL ISLANDS

Published By
PINE PRESS
P.O. Box 3151
Paradise, CA 95969 USA

Printed By
Colorcraft, Ltd. Hong Kong

Please send all comments,
corrections, additions,
amendments, and critiques
to:
Guide To Catalina
Pine Press
P.O. Box 3151
Paradise, CA 95967, USA

PRINTING HISTORY
1st edition ....January 1984
2nd edition.........March 1989
3rd edition ....August 1990
4th edition ...December 1992
5th edition ....July 1996

ISBN: 0-9651300-0-2
ISSN: 1087-5190

Editor: Karen Bleske
Design and Production: Tony Sanders at Avalon Studio Arts
Cartographer: Bob Race
Index: Nicole Revere

Cover Photo: Oz Mallan
Banner Art: Kathy Escovedo-Sanders
All photos by Oz Mallan unless otherwise noted.

Distributed in U.S. by Publisher's Group West
Printed in Hong Kong

To the "Cousins."
May they keep the special memories of Catalina forever bright:
The smell of the sea, hamburgers, sympathy,
French fries and love -- the back door.

ACKNOWLEDGEMENTS

Thanks to all the good people of Catalina Island for their willingness to help, their good nature, and their time. Special thanks to Editor Karen Bleske who has the quickest mind this side of the Atlantic! Kudos to researcher Patti Lange (above and below the water), to Anna Karlsson, the best "left-arm" one could ask for, and to Tony Sanders and Avalon Studio Arts for great designs and layouts. A very special thanks to Bill Newlin and all the talented folks at Moon Publications for their help with this first publication of Pine Press.

IS THIS BOOK OUT OF DATE?

Between the time this book went to press and the time it got onto the shelves, hotels have closed, restaurants have changed hands, and prices have probably gone up. Because of this, all prices herein should be regarded as approximations and are not guaranteed by the publisher or author. Because keeping this book accurate and timely means later editions, we would appreciate hearing about any errors or omissions you may encounter in Guide to Catalina. Also, if you have any noteworthy experiences (good or bad) with establishments listed in this book, please pass it along to us. If any attraction is out of place on a map, tell us; if the best restaurant in town is not included, we'd like to know. All contributions will be deeply appreciated and properly acknowledged. Address your letters to:

Chicki Mallan
%Pine Press
Box 3151
Paradise, CA
95967

CONTENTS

MAPS

CHARTS AND SPECIAL TOPICS

Santa Catalina Island

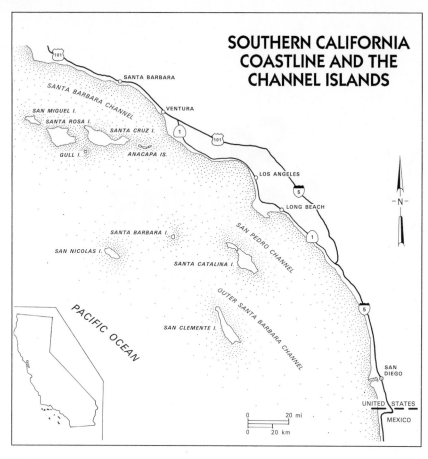

SOUTHERN CALIFORNIA COASTLINE AND THE CHANNEL ISLANDS

SANTA BARBARA

SANTA BARBARA CHANNEL

VENTURA

SAN MIGUEL I.

SANTA ROSA I.

SANTA CRUZ I.

GULL I.

ANACAPA IS.

LOS ANGELES

LONG BEACH

SANTA BARBARA I.

SAN NICOLAS I.

SANTA CATALINA I.

SAN PEDRO CHANNEL

OUTER SANTA BARBARA CHANNEL

SAN CLEMENTE I.

PACIFIC OCEAN

SAN DIEGO

UNITED STATES

MEXICO

-N-

0   20 mi
0   20 km

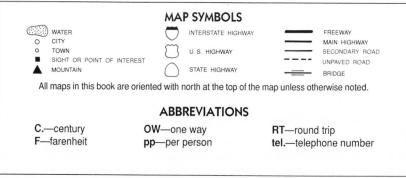

MAP SYMBOLS

WATER

CITY

TOWN

SIGHT OR POINT OF INTEREST

MOUNTAIN

INTERSTATE HIGHWAY

U. S. HIGHWAY

STATE HIGHWAY

FREEWAY

MAIN HIGHWAY

SECONDARY ROAD

UNPAVED ROAD

BRIDGE

All maps in this book are oriented with north at the top of the map unless otherwise noted.

ABBREVIATIONS

C.—century

F—farenheit

OW—one way

pp—per person

RT—round trip

tel.—telephone number

KATHY ESCOVEDO-SANDERS

INTRODUCTION

An island is a special place. A dreamlike quality clings to a bit of land surrounded by the blue sea. Birds, fish, and seals frolic in splashing ocean spray for the benefit of anyone watching--or not. Tall peaks give the sun and moon a dramatic stage on which to perform their magic each day--and the show is always different. For those who have not yet discovered their "special island," may we recommend Santa Catalina?

In Avalon, simple things bring new pleasures: walking along the beachfront's serpentine wall, watching the harbor lights when the bay is filled with boats, listening to the special music of a clinking halyard on a tall mast. Inhale fresh sea air on a breezy morning, or sit under the palm trees on Casino Point watching the sea change colors. And even if you're not a fisherman, you will rush along with the other beach-goers to see a marlin winched up to the pier's scales when the cannon booms across the harbor.

That's just part of what Catalina is about, but if that much sounds good, cross the channel and have a look. Take a hike into the interior, see untamed bison grazing on a hillside above the Pacific Ocean, study plants that have been

extinct on the Mainland for thousands of years, see California as it looked before concrete--or cars, or high-rise buildings. Crossing the channel for the first time, you'll sample a whole set of experiences that you'll remember for a lifetime: the porpoises following along, diving in and out of the ship's wake, the surprise of finding your "sea legs" while carrying coffee and a sandwich to the upper deck, meeting fellow travelers also curious about islands. But probably the most indelible memory of all is first seeing the white speck on the horizon that slowly becomes Avalon's hallmark, the great white Moorish-style Casino building on the bay. Avalon, on the crescent cove, is a Mediterranean-like village that climbs the hillsides dotted with vivid bougainvilleas. Tall eucalyptus trees line zigzag roads that circle into the cleavage of the Island. The Casino presides over it all.

Many people already know Catalina's special appeal because there's something of interest for every visitor. Boaters, hikers, campers, horsemen, cyclists, divers, anglers, sun worshipers, and jet-setters will find all they're looking for, as will historians, naturalists, archaeologists, and botanists. Vacationers can choose nonstop activities around Avalon town--or in their own boats discover the magic of a small cove and complete solitude, alone with nature's wonders. Parents can relax as their children splash happily on Avalon's beaches, or play in town-organized groups. It doesn't have to be summer; winters are mild, spring is glorious, but some swear fall is the most beautiful time of year. Come on over; once is all it takes, and Catalina will become your "special island."

KATHY ESCOVEDO-SANDERS

THE LAND

Santa Catalina Island is third largest of the eight California Channel Islands stretching along the Southern California coast. Catalina itself has a 120-million-year geological history. Early paleontologists assumed that it was once attached to the Mainland, but recent studies and modern scientific methods have raised some doubts about this theory. Catalina, only 19 miles from the Mainland at its closest point, sits on the Pacific tectonic plate, while most of California and the rest of the U.S. rest on the North American plate. Plate movements and volcanic eruptions are responsible for the formation of Catalina Island, though this is not true of all the Channel Islands. The two most common types of Island rock are the result of this formation process: igneous (volcanic) and metamorphic (usually sedimentary rock that has changed under pressure, heat, or chemical action).

The Indians of the Mainland called Catalina Island *wexaj momte asunga wow*-- "mountain ranges that rise from the sea." Most of the Island consists of mountains interspersed with meadows and valleys. Black Jack (2,006 feet) and Mt. Orizaba (2,097 feet) are the highest peaks.

Some of the coastal cliffs fall abruptly to the sea, leaving not even a path's space along the ocean, while in other areas the hills slope gently to sandy beaches below. The 21-mile-long Island lies southeast-northwest. On the western (or windward) side, the Pacific crashes against the tall, rugged coast. Off the eastern (or lee) coast that faces the Mainland, the sea is calm and placid. Catalina's widest section stretches between leeward Long Point and China Point on the windward side (approximately 7.5 miles). The Island's east and west sides nearly meet at Two Harbors--a half-mile-wide isthmus six miles from the west end--which is the narrowest point. A deep undersea ledge girdles the Island's land mass, fostering a rich habitat for marinelife. Catalina's steep canyon walls create a climate that helps sustain vegetation unique to the Island. Catalina boasts 54 miles of beautiful rugged coastline.

Although surrounded by water, Catalina lacks much of the drinkable kind. In the early days, the Indians and the first settlers relied on the few natural springs scattered over the Island, plus the few streams that still run to the sea after a

Catalina's inland roads wind around the rugged mountaintops overlooking the sea.

good wet year. Today, Avalon's high-tech desalination plant, along with a dam, reservoir, and pipeline, carry water to accommodate the Island's freshwater needs.

CLIMATE

Many people mistakenly believe that Catalina is a tropical island. Though the sun shines an average of 267 days a year, the Island's climate is similar to that of the Southern California coast. Thanks to cooling marine breezes, Catalina is generally moister and cooler in the summer than the Mainland; in winter, with help from the warm Japanese current, it's generally a few degrees milder.

In summer, the average temperature ranges from 70-76° F. In the winter, the temperature ranges from 49-63° F. The average rainfall is 14 inches per year, but the extremes can be great. Some years (as on the California Mainland), as much as 30 inches of rain fall, while the drought years of 1977-78 brought virtually none. The average sea temperature in the winter is 56-59° F, in the summer 67-70° F.

The winter almost always brings a northeastern (Santa Ana) storm or two. The Santa Ana can turn the calm Pacific into a raging sea. Its high winds are infrequent but dangerous; sometimes reaching 50 knots, they blow November to March. Fog forms in all seasons, but in winter it covers a wider area and lasts longer. In May and June, fog hovers over Catalina until about noon. Many visitors consider Catalina's biggest attraction the lack of smog, which is due to westerly winds and the Island's distance from the Mainland.

An occasional storm hits Catalina Island, pounding her placid shores with a turbulent surf.

FLORA

CATALINA PLANTLIFE

Though the plantlife is similar to the Mainland's, Catalina's resident species are slightly different. Some plants that thrive on the Island today existed on the Mainland 20,000 years ago, but as the Mainland became drier, many of those plants died out. Of approximately 600 species on Catalina, 396 are native.

Some of the wildflowers growing on Catalina are:

bright eyes
brodiaea (blue dick)
bush lupine
bush sunflower
shore heliotrope
California bindweed
California island poppy
sumac (lemonade berry)
California lilac
tree tobacco
tree poppy
everlasting flower
violet nightshade
fiesta flower
wild apple
giant sea dahlia
wild four o'clock
ground pink
wild sweet pea
Indian paintbrush
woodland star
yellow pansy

CATALINA'S ENDEMIC PLANTS

Catalina has 396 native plant types, but only nine are endemic (found nowhere else in the world but on Santa Catalina Island). The following list contains eight plants; in recent years, the ninth, the Catalina Monkey Flower, has not been collected. It's possible that it has died out.

Catalina Mahogany
Catalina mahogany is a large evergreen shrub or small tree that grows to about 15 feet. The young shoots are reddish brown. The grayish-green leaves are thick and leathery, the lower surface covered with dense furlike hair. The small whitish flowers usually grow in clusters and in great abundance. After flowering, the seeds, or fruits, grow long, hairy twisted tails that give the plant a most unusual appearance. Only 10 of these shrubs/trees occur naturally in a single canyon.

St. Catherine's Lace
St. Catherine's Lace is usually broader than it is tall and is generally thought of as an evergreen shrub. The flowers on this beautiful plant are borne on long stems well above its silvery gray-green leaves, and grow in clusters that form a flat, lacy canopy. The plant is soft grayish-white in May and June, then turns to ivory, beige, and light brown, and finally in autumn it turns a rich russet color. It grows mainly on the dry, rocky slopes throughout the Island's interior.

Catalina Manzanita
Catalina manzanita is a spreading evergreen shrub or small tree that stands as much as eight feet tall with smooth, dark red bark and bright green, hairy leaves. The leaves are oblong or elliptical and have a leathery texture. The flowers bloom from January to March in large spreading clusters at the tips of the branches; individual flowers are urn-shaped, white, fragrant and about one-half-inch long. The fruit is about three-eighths-inch thick and is pinkish-yellow when forming and usually turns from golden brown to the rich color of the bark when mature--a favorite food of the ground squirrels.

Catalina Live-Forever
This low-growing succulent rosette-type perennial has numerous slender, pencil-shaped leaves, which are bluish to light green. The yellow-white, star-shaped flowers are borne on

DIANA LASICH HARPER

SHOOTING STARS

Shooting Stars are February's flowers,
Carpeting the Deer Trail bowers,
Dainty, delicate, fragrant showers,
February's Stars.
Five petaled, bent back on the stem,
Stamens forward, nature's gem,
Hidden in a fern-filled glen,
Rose-orchid Stars.
Golden rings, the heart of you,
Bill of purple, another's hue,
Beauty's crown, climber's view,
Long-stemmed treasures.

MARIPOSA LILY

Three-petaled, dainty
Flush of the dawn,
Velvet red heart of you,
Slender stem long,
Bearing another bud,
Unfolds to light,
Mariposa Lily,
Lovely and bright.
Growing in wild oats,
Planted by God,
Speaking of Love divine,
Ne'er of the sod.

CATALINA ISLAND MUSEUM

Ann-Cloud Reynolds in 1951

ANN CLOUD REYNOLDS

From the 1920s into the '50s, Ann was a familiar sight in Avalon with her walking staff, floppy straw hat, rucksack, and beach towel around her shoulders heading into Catalina's hills. She reveled in nature's offerings, from Cottonwood Canyon to Silver Peak and all in between. As others know the floor plans of their homes, Ann knew Catalina's interior, every rock, mountain, valley, and wildflower. She wrote three small books, all including poetry and a feeling that she was one with the land and with the Indians from the past. Ann (now deceased), always referred to "Hiker" in her books. Hiker was Ann. Hiker found Indian caves with ancient markings, spent nights under the stars long before most, fed the ravens, spoke to the goats, took pictures of wildflowers, and sang from the hilltops:

> Echoing across the years,
> Comes the call,
> Brings the tears,
> Of joy, to know the Indians all,
> Listen ever for the call -- *Yo te hoy!*

verses by
Ann Cloud Reynolds

DIANA LASICH HARPER

St. Catherine's Lace

fleshy pink stalks that are five to 15 inches long. It blooms in May and June. This is the only Catalina endemic that's a succulent; it grows on the slope of the Wrigley Memorial.

Catalina Ironwood
Catalina ironwood is a handsome slender-crowned evergreen tree that grows 50-70 feet tall with a single trunk or with a number of stems arising from the ground. The dark green leaves are three to six inches long and are generally entire or whole with an occasional tendency toward a fernlike dissection. It has reddish-brown stringy bark. The small white flowers, borne in large flat-topped clusters four to eight inches across, mature in June and July. Unique to Catalina, it grows nowhere else.

Yerba Santa
This evergreen shrub has shredding bark and a pungent fragrance. It has an open, sprawling growth habit. The leaves are grayish-white and woolly, usually toothed and mostly crowded toward the ends of branches. The whitish-purple flowers cluster on the branch tips and bloom in May and June.

Catalina Bedstraw
This plant is a perennial herb with four-angled slender woody stems and branches. This dense, low-growing under-shrub with inconspicuous whitish flowers blooms from April through July.

Catalina Bush Mallow
This coastal sage scrub grows upright with thick pink blossoms and dense foliage. Though the flowers are quite small (an inch across), they're similar to the garden hibiscus.

TREES

Though accounts by miners and settlers mention an abundance of pine trees, the pines introduced in recent years haven't thrived on Catalina because of the frequent dry seasons. Thanks to Philip Wrigley's conservancy program, introduced in 1972, hikers to the interior can see 10 adult mahogany trees in an obscure canyon.

Island cherry, island oak, and **ironwood trees** grow on California's offshore islands. One of the most unusual of nature's quirks is a stand of **Torrey pines** on Santa Rosa Island. This is the only example of these pines outside Torrey Pines State Park, north of San Diego. These,

shaggy bark of the ironwood tree

along with the **Santa Cruz Island pine,** are remnants of an archaic Pleistocene forest that have survived a multitude of climatic changes over thousands of years.

Some of Catalina's trees are:
California holly (toyon)
elderberry
Catalina ironwood
greasewood
Catalina manzanita
island oak
Catalina wild cherry
mountain mahogany
cottonwood
scrub oak

PLANT LORE

Culinary Uses

Indians and pioneers, as well as modern-day herbologists, have told of the culinary and medicinal uses of a number of Catalina's plant species. Some of these may be more lore than fact; others still prove useful. One is the **prickly pear,** a common edible fruit that grows on cacti, found not only in Catalina but in many other parts of the world. A deep purplish-red, this fruit is sweet and juicy when ripe, and according to some, makes a great fruit pudding. Firsthand we know it makes a great jelly. A good way to get rid of the thorns and skin without injury is to leave the fruit attached to the plant and carefully peel. Otherwise, a fork makes a good handle while peeling the nasties off.

The **Catalina cherry tree** grows well on the Island; a large grove on the west end carries the appropriate name of Cherry Cove. The reddish-black cherry has little flesh around its seed, but is quite refreshing. It's said to have been one of the favorite fruits of the Indians. **Sumac,** or lemonade berry, provides a refreshing drink called "lemonade" by the Mexicans. **Wild sage,** which also grows profusely on the Mainland, is gathered by herbologists for home remedies--it's great added to turkey stuffing and other cooks' specialties. Wild cucumber and radish, beach strawberry, toyon berry, blackberry, and wild currant were most likely eaten by the original inhabitants of the Island and are still a treat for today's residents.

Remedies

Old-timers used **wild carrot** and **rattlesnake weed** to treat rattlesnake bites, applying a poultice of the fresh leaves to the wound. If, in the course of an illness, copious perspiring was required, they made a drink from the leaves of the large **elderberry** tree *(Sambucus mexicanus). Yerba mansa (Anemopsis california)* was chewed raw for mucous membrane sickness, and it was also made into powder for knife wounds. **Snake cactus** was used to fight high fever. Anthropologists think the aborigines made a liniment remedy for rheumatism from an extract of the **white willow.**

Narcotics

Historians believe that the Gabrielino Indians practiced the Toloache religion, taking part in ceremonies involving **jimsonweed** to initiate adolescents entering manhood. The jimsonweed *(Datura metaloides)* is a highly effective narcotic. After a three-day fast, young men were given a drink made of jimson leaves. Afterward, they would dance until they passed out. Their dreams during this time were thought to be prophetic and held great significance for the rest of their lives.

Old-timers have described the **yerba santa** as having the power to induce a "gentle sleep," but it's rarely found on the Island today.

Miscellaneous

Long and coarsely fibrous, the tuberous root of the **soap plant** works well as a scrub brush. The *Chenopodium californicum,* a parsniplike root, also provides a detergent in lieu of soap. **Poison oak** grows on the Island, and if you are sensitive, contact with it can cause discomfort any season of the year. Leaves, bare branches, or even smoke from a burning bush can bring on an itchy rash.

Restoring the Land

Today, the Catalina Conservancy maintains a native plant nursery at Middle Ranch. Here seedlings of plants are coaxed along and then planted throughout the interior. This restoration is an ongoing project that some dreamers believe will eventually present the Island as it was 150 years ago.

FAUNA

LAND CREATURES

Goats

The hills of Catalina Island are lined with a network of narrow paths. Most are goat trails. Since goat bones have not been found in the Indian kitchen middens, historians assume that goats arrived after the Spanish era. Some claim Spanish explorers carried goats onboard their ships to ensure a supply of meat for their travels. Naturalists have yet to find proof for that theory. Goats were brought to the Island by early settler A.W. Timms to help keep his sheep in line. Allowed to run free for years, the goats eventually grew in number to thousands. Goats nibble every living thing, including the endemic plants on the Island; the destruction of grasses, shrubs, and trees was overwhelming. For that reason, the Conservancy has rid the Island of a lot of the feral goats.

Backpackers and hikers might still see a few running along the trails. Their coats vary from white to brown to black or a mixture of all three; the most common is the shaggy black and brown goat. Some billies' horn-spreads measure three feet and more. These ornery animals command the sheerest cliffs, and frequently climb down to the water's edge to lick salt from the ocean-sprayed rocks.

Wild Pigs

The feral pig was introduced to Catalina in the mid-1920s to hold down the rattlesnake population. These pigs are mean when cornered and have multiplied to at least two thousand. They occasionally wander into Avalon and damage the golf course by digging up the greens, but for the most part they stay in the backcountry, running loose on the roughly 47,884 acres at their disposal.

Bison

For years, the answer to the question, "How did the buffalo get to Catalina Island?", was academic. In 1924, when Western moviemaker William Farnum was filming Zane Grey's *The Vanishing American,* his crew brought 14 bison to the Island for the film. Rounding up the bison afterward proved to be difficult, so in the end they were left to roam. Recently, the erstwhile

A small herd of buffalo gathers around a waterhole.

OZ MALLAN

curator of the Catalina Island Museum, Patricia Moore, decided the museum should have a copy of the old film in its film collection. After finally finding the film, Patricia was shocked to find nary a buffalo in it. So either this old story was fiction, or the buffalo wound up on the cutting room floor, or . . .?

Actually, talking about how the buffalo got here is a good way to start an argument among some history buffs. Some say Lasky's movie studio brought the bison, some say for another old film, the *Covered Wagon.* If anyone out there in movieland knows more about this, please let us know.

Note: Catalina buffalo are really bison, but most folks refer to them as buffalo, so in this book we use the word interchangeably.

By 1934, the herd had increased to 19, and then 30 additional bison were brought from Colorado to supplement the herd. Today's population is held to 200-400--ideal for the ecosystem. When the herd gets too large, bison are culled. Many are shipped to buffalo ranches in the western U.S.; other animals are sent to the Mainland to be butchered and frozen and then shipped back as hamburger--buffalo chili and buffalo burgers are sold at the **Runway Cafe** at the Airport-in-the-Sky and in other cafes on the Island.

When an old bull is challenged by a younger one, a fierce battle generally follows. The young bull is usually sent scurrying, but in some cases the old bull is run out of the herd. Considered a rogue, it thereafter roams the hills alone. Fencing at every road entry into Avalon from the interior and a large metal bump-gate for cars ordinarily keep the animals in the hills out of town, but the exceptions are exciting. Early one morning in 1978 the town awoke to see a rogue wandering down the beach. Before anyone could react, he had trotted up Sumner St. and darted onto the brick-walled Pitch and Putt golf course (today it's the Sand Trap) adjoining Avalon's elementary school. The whole affair soon turned into a noisy roundup with cheering children and a siren-blaring police car chasing the running bull back and forth the length of the golf course, trying to guide him through the only gate, missing at least eight times. Finally, the buffalo found the opening and fled toward the peaceful environment of the interior, probably wondering why he ever wanted to know what was on the other side of that mountain!

Deer

Although anthropologist Alfred L. Kroeber briefly mentions Catalina's deer in his 1925 *Handbook of Indians of California,* many historians date the introduction of deer to the Island to 1930, when the California Fish and Game Commission brought 18 mule deer for refuge. Today historians link the findings of deer bones in ancient middens to the Catalina Indians' trading. Ar-

island fox

chaeologists have found mostly hindquarter bones, and from that they deduct that the Indians traded with Mainland Indians for food, including deer meat.

The deer adapted well to the environment, multiplying to the point where deer hunts must be organized periodically to keep the population down. In years of little rain the deer come into town to feast on rosebuds, pansy blossoms, and other garden delicacies. During one severe drought, they did considerable damage. To avert total devastation, many of the animals were trapped in huge cages, shipped to the Mainland, and set free in a wild area where ample forage was available.

Catalina Island Foxes

The small island fox living on Catalina and many of the other Channel Islands is a diminutive form of the Mainland gray fox. Its color is variegated gray, black, rust, and white. It is a nocturnal creature and seldom seen by the casual observer. However, folks say that if you study the shoreline at night when the flying-fish boat aims its powerful light toward shore, you might see a pair of glowing eyes. Fish often get confused or mistakenly follow the light beam and land on the rocky beach, stranded. They don't remain long, as the small fox with his sharp vision is also watching and waiting for just this opportunity for a fresh seafood snack. The small omnivorous

fox includes in its diet lizards, insects, fruits, and wild berries.

According to Misty Gay, Catalina's naturalist, the fox is a subspecies endemic to Santa Catalina Island. Six of the eight Channel Islands have Channel Island foxes; on each the fox has evolved into a separate and unique subspecies. It is Catalina's largest native mammalian predator.

Rodents

The plentiful **beechey ground squirrel** is also endemic to the island. This small gray-brown squirrel, which lives in subterranean tunnels, has an unmistakable clacketing chatter. Also native to Catalina are the **western harvest mouse** and **deer mouse**. The recent discovery of an **ornate shrew** on the Island stirred up a lot of excitement for the Conservancy. There were signs for some time that the small creature was an inhabitant; in 1941 a dead shrew was found, and another was found in 1983 in Cottonwood Canyon. In 1993, two live ornate shrews were found and set loose, an exciting event for the Conservancy.

Other Animals

Other animals include **birds, bats, lizards, snakes, salamanders,** and **frogs.** After a good rain, very large bullfrogs visit Haypress, and in the early morning you can enjoy a frog chorus a

the first ornate shrew found alive on Catalina Island

JESUS MALDONADO

capella. Haypress is a small pond on the left side of the road going to the interior, across the road from Toyon Junction.

Family Pets
Islanders have their share of house pets--the usual dogs, cats, canaries, and parrots. Thoroughbred Arabian horses are raised at Rancho Escondido, a 537-acre private ranch owned by the Wrigley family. At Middle Ranch, now part of the Catalina Conservancy, kids from Avalon learn to ride at the pony center; some of them travel to the Mainland to compete in horse shows.

WATER CREATURES

Sea Lions
Herds of this "circus seal," intelligent and easily trained, range the California waters and are protected by law from hunters. Some specimens in

OZ MALLAN

Catalina sea lion

the wild live as long as 18 years; in captivity they can live longer. Varying in color from tan or gray to almost black, the California sea lion cow may grow to more than six feet long and weigh more than 300 pounds, while the bulls can grow to nine feet and 1,000 pounds. A large male usually has a prominent crest on its forehead.

Though sea lions don't pup on Catalina, they do on some of the other Channel Islands. Today only the harbor seals pup on Catalina, producing a single pup in the spring.

The sea lions return to the place of their birth to mate each year in late spring or early summer. These enormous bulls battle for favorite locations for their breeding harems, even while the cows are still birthing. Pups are usually born in June, though some are born as early as May and as late as July. The pups then have the summer--a gentle season of mild weather--and an abundant supply of fish to encourage their rapid growth.

Naturalists studying Catalina report the sea lion population is on the increase. If you have any interest in the habits of these intelligent, inquisitive pinnipeds ("fin-footed" ones), the ideal way to observe their habits is from a boat and with a pair of binoculars. Watching them lolling on the rocks in the summer sun or gently nudging their pups into the water for a swimming lesson is well worth the time. You may pick the day that one of the rare pinnipeds, such as the elephant seal, visits the Island.

Whales
Although for centuries Islanders have watched mammoth gray whales in large pods pass Catalina on their way to mate in Mexico's Scammons Lagoon, the gentle giants never pause near the island.

AIR CREATURES

Birders will find close to 100 species of birds on Catalina. Each December Audubon makes a count on the Island. Catalina harbors several subspecies of birds found nowhere else in the world, including the Beuwick's wren and the Catalina quail. While exploring the Island, visitors can also expect to see the red-tailed hawk along with many species of common Mainland birds such as the sparrow, finch, warbler, hummingbird, and mockingbird. At one time there were hundreds of quail and they were legally hunted; now, you see them only when there's a good hatch (which is very rare). A surprising number of northern saw-whet owls lives on the Island, unusual since this species (one of the smallest owls) of North American owls is generally at home in forested habitats. Keep your eyes open around Haypress; a blue heron and its offspring have been reported hunting around the water. Ravens are still plentiful on the Island, but by the mid-1900s the magnificent eagles had all but vanished.

The Common Raven

The raven, largest member of the crow family, shines a deep black and sports a very large bill. You can see the raven all over the Island, and hear it, too. When a group of them gather around a dead sea mammal, or anyplace for that matter, they produce sounds from a deep croaking to cheery "laugh" to a high clear soprano bell tone. Some birders refer to their calls as the "songs of the raven." The raven loves people food as well as carrion and wild toyon berries, so if you have a picnic in the interior don't leave it unguarded.

The Catalina Indians considered the raven sacred; it represented reincarnated ancestors, their guardian spirits. Perhaps they believed this because of the raven's flying habits, which take it swiftly into the clouds (where the god Chingichnich dwells), or because of the way it appears to be suspended in the air--no movement, just magically hanging. We will never know.

The California Bald Eagle

Before DDT, these keen-eyed raptors were common sights, soaring high over the sea as they studied the water for prey. Eagles built their nests on the sheer cliffs of Catalina that overlook the sea, but by the mid-1970s nests and eagles were scarce. Illegal hunting, and the toll of pesticides on the hatch rate, rapidly decreased their numbers.

The Catalina Conservancy, the Institute for Wildlife Studies, and the California State Department of Fish and Game have undertaken the painstaking task of reintroducing the bald eagle to the Island. Beginning in 1980, a nesting platform was built and 14 eaglets were fed and

seagull

OZ MALLAN

observed until they were able to fend for themselves. Since then other eaglets have been released, making a total of 37. A recent count placed the eagle population at about 30, including at least two mating couples. Eagles mate for life. As Island naturalist Misty Gay explains, some of the eagles fly away from the Island and others die of natural causes, and one is known to have been shot.

Despite setbacks, the program is considered successful; in 1987, adult eagles built the first nest and laid eggs. None of the eggs hatched, but that first nest was definitely a good sign that the eagles were adapting to their new home on Catalina. Nesting eagles care for their young for up to five months. By then the chicks are nearly the size of an adult. The nest (of necessity) is large; one of the largest nests on record was six feet across.

The Conservancy has recently tried a new tack, introducing young eaglets into a nest where perhaps eggs are not hatching. It removed a four-week-old eaglet from a wild nest in northern California and in the brief absence of its new parents, fostered it into the Catalina nest, built 400 feet up a nearly vertical cliff. (All this was accomplished with the help of a helicopter and a nervy biologist suspended 220 feet beneath the chopper.) The eagle parents were mildly surprised to find a chick when they returned after leaving behind only an egg. But according to the Institute of Wildlife Studies and the Catalina Conservancy team, baby and proud parents were thriving!

When hiking in the interior, you may glimpse the regal bird soaring on updrafts along the cliff sides or over the sea or reservoirs watching with sharp eyes for an errant fish, an important part of their diet. Thanks to the Conservancy, these birds are the beginning of a new community of bald eagles on Catalina Island.

Raptors
Raptors are birds of prey that have the ability to spot their targets while soaring on wind currents great distances in the sky. Raptors are the notable meat-eaters of the bird community. The Catalina group includes eagles, owls, falcons, and hawks. Another bird originally native to Catalina is the peregrine falcon. The Conservancy also has begun a program to release these birds into the interior.

Sea Birds
Like most communities near the Pacific, Catalina hosts an abundance of waterfowl, including the cormorant, many varieties of seagull, the tern, grebe, and pelican. Occasionally, migrating birds find the climate and atmosphere of Catalina delightful and stay on. A white long-legged egret has taken up residence on buoy #249 just off Casino Point along with the pelicans and seagulls. Blue herons and their offspring have been reported at Haypress. If you happen to be in Cat Harbor, note the rookery, several nests of blue herons on the rocks.

Birders
Contact the Catalina Conservancy or Audubon Society to take part in the Annual Christmas Bird Count. The Conservancy has for sale in its gift shop the new *Santa Catalina Island Bird Check List*. For more information call the Conservancy office, tel. (310) 510-2595.

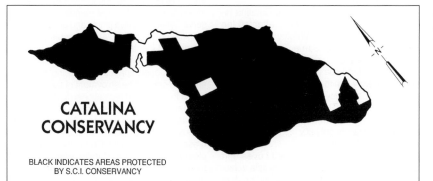

CATALINA CONSERVANCY

BLACK INDICATES AREAS PROTECTED
BY S.C.I. CONSERVANCY

CATALINA CONSERVANCY MEMBERSHIP

Fees Are Tax Deductible		Marineros	$100
Introductory	$25	Caballeros	$100
Catalina Resident	$25	Divers	$100
Student	$25	Amigos	$100

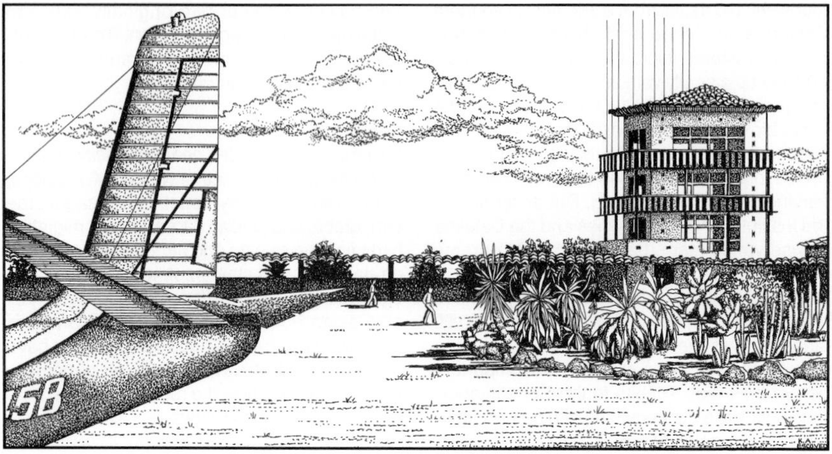

KATHY ESCOVEDO-SANDERS

SANTA CATALINA ISLAND CONSERVANCY

The Beginning

Since William Wrigley Jr. bought Catalina Island in 1919, few changes have affected the interior of the Island. Mr. Wrigley bought controlling interest in the Santa Catalina Island Company (SCI Co.) primarily because he thought the Island some day would be the last vestige of early California and that it was too precious a commodity to be subjected to massive development. The Santa Catalina Island Company turned its attention to establishing Avalon, the Island's only city, as a major resort and vacation destination.

Catalina's interior and isolated coves and bays remained unspoiled, with very little vehicular traffic but a favorite for hikers and boaters who reveled in the area's beauty.

What is the Catalina Conservancy?

In 1972, William Wrigley Jr.'s son, Philip K., created a nonprofit foundation, the Santa Catalina Island Conservancy, to ensure the continued preservation of the majority of the Island. "The property can never revert to private ownership, so the wildlands, open space, and nature areas will be there for the enjoyment of generations to come." Its legal mandate is "to preserve Catalina's native plants and animals, its biological communities, and its geological and geographic formations of educational interest. The Conservancy is charged with managing Catalina's open spaces and seeing that they are used only for the enjoyment of scenic beauty and for controlled recreational purposes." The Conservancy has grown and maintains Conservancy House in downtown Avalon at 125 Claressa Ave., tel. (310) 510-2595, mailing address Box 2739, Avalon, CA 90704. You'll find a pleasant, little gift shop, **Catalina Nature Co.,** offering a variety of publications, T-shirts, CDs, games, cards--all with a definite ecological slant. I bought a marvelous CD there (Dan Gibson's *Solitudes*) that explores nature with music. This is a vibrant world of natural sounds united with only the best music. Talk about relaxing! Investigate shelves and corners and you'll find great gifts and souvenirs to take home.

The Conservancy bears considerable financial responsibility, including maintenance of 100 miles of interior roads and trails, general land management, upkeep of the Airport-in-the-Sky, and taxes. To help pay its bills, the Conservancy solicits memberships.

Preservation

The Conservancy has worked to halt deterioration of Catalina's natural resources, enabling threatened plant and animal species to reestablish. In the 1800s and early 1900s, domestic sheep were allowed to graze and proliferate freely. Along with the goats and wild pigs, these herbivores depleted many native grasses and other plants, which encouraged the growth of cactus in their places. The restoration program has begun to replenish many of these plants, and the animal populations are kept at numbers the interior lands are able to support. The sheep were removed entirely in 1923.

AIRPORT-IN-THE-SKY

It's not all work and no play. The Conservancy strives to develop ways for the visitor to Catalina to enjoy the land and the sea under its management. The airport is becoming a fine destination rather than a pass-through utility.

Airport History

Until 1946, the only planes that landed at Catalina Island were small amphibians. Shortly before WW II, the tops of three mountains were leveled and the canyon between filled in to build an airport runway. When the war started, logs, boulders, and barbed wire were strung all across the unfinished runway to prevent its being used in case of enemy attack. Building resumed immediately after the war and the runway was finished and a lovely terminal was erected.

The Airport-in-the-Sky overlooks rolling hills to the ocean and is owned and operated by the Santa Catalina Island Conservancy, which houses some of its offices here.

United Airlines flew DC-3s from Los Angeles to Catalina from 1946 to 1954. In 1959 the airport was opened to private aircraft. Many small private planes visit Catalina every year, and the number of Islanders who commute to the Mainland in their private planes and park their planes here continues to grow. The Airport-in-the-Sky receives no federal funds (most airports do), and as prices rose it had to begin charging Airport usage fees. As of July 1995, fees are as follows: landing fee for plane and pilot $7, two people $10, three or more $15, the overnight $5 tie-down and parking fee remains the same. For more information call the airport at (310) 510-0143.

Today, several charter flights provide passenger service from San Diego and freight planes land at the Airport-in-the-Sky. The 3,250-foot asphalt runway is capable of handling planes up to and including DC-3s.

Private Planes

By far the most activity comes from the private planes that come and go frequently. Some peo-

OZ MALLAN

Small planes come and go all year long.

*History Wall
at Airport
Nature Center*

OZ MALLAN

ple just fly in for breakfast or lunch, others catch the shuttle into Avalon and spend the day or several days. As more people get into aviation, more Mainland pilots appreciate short flights to exotic destinations--isn't Catalina the best?

Note: Check out the aviation history wall in the airport and ask about a great video that gives a complete historical background about aviation on Catalina Island.

The airport, 10 road miles from Avalon (about 30 minutes), is served by a shuttle that runs frequently to Avalon and to Two Harbors. Many visitors enjoy taking an entire day to visit the airport. This is a good hiking destination, group nature tours are available (with reservations), and trekkers can visit an Indian archaeological site just 10 minutes away. Ask at the airport; the staff will direct you to the remnants of an Indian soapstone bowl quarry. Please don't deface this relic, this connection with the past. It withstood the forces of nature for centuries; let's keep it intact for our grandchildren.

Runway Cafe and Gift Shop
The Spanish-style Runway Cafe is a popular place to stop for breakfast, lunch, or a snack. Outdoor dining is on the lovely red-tiled patio with wonderful views of the hills stretching in all directions, and toward the sea. On a chilly winter day, the large stone fireplace warms the room called the Pilots Lounge. The Runway Cafe specializes in buffalo burgers and buffalo chili, along with a regular menu. And for those

who like homemade cookies, owner Sue Rikalo times the cookies to come out of the oven at noon. The Runway Cafe will reserve for large families or groups for special evening barbecues and other events.

Roundtrip fare to the airport is $13, and the first trip leaves Avalon at 7:30 a.m. The van runs frequently throughout the day; call (310) 510-0143 for schedule. Group prices for van transportation can be arranged, so if you're having a birthday party while visiting Catalina, bring a whole gang to the airport for a different experience; ask for Sue, tel. (310) 510-2196, open daily from 8:30 a.m.-4 p.m.

The gift shop carries a good collection of Catalina gifts, books, art pieces, children's goodies, and T-shirts.

AIRPORT ACTIVITIES

**Exploring in the Vicinity
of the Airport-in-the-Sky**
You'll find many ways to incorporate the airport into a day of hiking and exploring. If you don't want to make the trek from Avalon, but you want to do some hiking and looking, take the airport van as far as the Black Jack Junction and hike from there. You have several options, but first go across the road to take in the view. It's breathtaking; don't forget your camera.

You can find the Catalina ironwood tree across the road and at the end of a short hike. This tree grows nowhere else in the world, though thousands of years ago it grew profusely on the Mainland.

Another option from Black Jack junction is a 1.5-mile hike to Black Jack campgrounds, or take a well-marked path along the way to a lovely picnic area in the pine trees. You can arrange with the van driver a time to pick you up. Otherwise, it's another 2.5 miles to the airport.

Airport Nature Center

Open to the public, the Conservancy-owned and -operated airport is fast becoming the inland hub of Conservancy activities. A small nature center here displays the Indian history of Catalina, on a beautifully painted "history" wall, plus plant, animal, and geology exhibits. Catalina docents give nature programs and hikes. A great pictorial and review of the Island, "Santa Catalina, an Island Adventure," is available at the Runway Cafe Gift Shop at the airport, Sugarloaf Bookstore in Avalon, Catalina Museum Bookstore at the Casino, and many other gift shops on the Island. College-student interns assist in interpreting the Island for visitors. The Conservancy also offers guided nature hikes in the Catalina hills with previous arrangements. Allow ample time for reservations; there is no charge but a donation is always appreciated. Call at least two weeks in advance, (310) 510-0954, and ask for Misty Gay.

Flying into the Airport-in-the-Sky

For airport shuttle-bus information and general airport information, call (310) 510-0143. Private planes are welcome from 8 a.m.-7 p.m. mid-May to mid-October, 8 a.m.-5 p.m. the rest of the year.

CONSERVANCY PROGRAMS

Jeep Eco-Tour Program

The Conservancy offers several exciting tours. These very popular trips into the interior and seaward side take you into rugged areas of the Island that up until now only hardy hikers could explore. These jeep trips are private tours and include half-day and full-day trips; the newest is a two-hour East End Tour. Think of these as minisafaris. For prices and reservation information call Tina or Erica, tel. (310) 510-2595, ext. 100, or talk to any Conservancy person.

Avalon Summer Naturalist Program

The Conservancy presents summer naturalist programs in and around Avalon. The programs include nature walks and hikes, multimedia presentations and campfire talks. The programs are open to the public, very informative, and best of all they're *free.* For more information call (310) 510-2595, or drop by Conservancy House at 125 Claressa, Avalon.

Education

One of the Conservancy's extensions is the education program. In 1995 a new program brought inner-city kids to the Island for an all-day learning experience in Catalina's interior.

Kids travelled over on the boat (for some, their first boat ride) where they were shown a Conservancy video, channel history, and a marine-life talk on their way to the Island. Buses took the kids to the interior with a narration on wildlife, ecology, archaeology, plants, and natural history. They were served lunch at the airport's Runway Cafe, and then an interactive, hands-on experience at the ecological restoration program at the native plant nursery. The day ended with a trip to the Botanical Garden and Wrigley Monument. It was unanimous; their favorite subject was "Indian" lore. For more information, call (310) 510-0595.

Membership

The Conservancy support groups are organized around special interests. The Catalina Marineros is a group for people interested in boating and sailing along the Catalina coastline. Catalina Caballeros members enjoy horseback riding through the interior of the Island and they gather annually for rides. The newest group is the Catalina Divers for those who thrive in the wet world of Catalina.

A Conservancy membership is a satisfying way to ensure that the Island will remain the great untainted open space it is now.

There are many ways to get involved; classes of membership are based on contribution amounts (tax deductible; see chart on page 17).

All members receive the Catalina Conservancy newsletter and other special mailings. For more information, contact Santa Catalina Island Conservancy, P.O. Box 2739, Avalon, CA 90704, tel. (310) 510-0595.

KATHY ESCOVEDO-SANDERS

HISTORY

THE FIRST ISLANDERS

Prehistory

Catalina Island boasts a mysterious and complex history. In the last 30,000 years, no fewer than five aboriginal cultures have occupied California's Channel Islands. But the history of man is clouded; there are few definite answers to long-asked questions. For a brief period, there was wild speculation that Catalina's first inhabitants were a cultured race of white giants, survivors from a sunken continent. Old ships' logs and other written accounts refer to the "white-skinned" Indian communities on Catalina Island, but no evidence exists that whites inhabited the islands.

Anthropologists now think that during the Pleistocene Ice Age (50,000 B.C.), when the sea receded, men and animals crossed the Bering land bridge from Asia to the American continent. For nearly 50,000 years, humans trekked southward, spreading throughout North, Central, and South America until approximately 1000 B.C., when they reached Tierra del Fuego and could go no farther.

With the possible exceptions of Alaska and remote sections of Canada, the use of stone tools continued on Santa Catalina longer than anywhere else in North America. The quantities of soapstone available for making tools, cooking utensils, and ceremonial objects was unlimited, and the Island was isolated from outside cultural influences and other sources of materials.

Gabrielino Indians

Much of our knowledge about early man in the Channel Islands is based on speculation. Deep layers of excavated cultural material from middens (ancient refuse heaps) clearly establish that a sizable number of people have lived on Catalina Island for 6,800 years, but early anthropologists and archaeologists believed that they could trace the more modern Indians of the Channel Islands (referred to variously as "Gabrielino" and "Shoshonean") only as far back as 500 B.C.

Alfred L. Kroeber, an anthropologist distinguished for his studies of early California Indians, wrote that the "remains" found on the majority of the Channel Islands show all the characteristics of Chumash civilization in its most perfect state. But the Indians on Catalina called themselves "Pimugnans" (they called the Island "Pimu" or "Pimugna"), though they enjoyed a lively interaction with the Chumash. Their an-

*previous page: boating visitors to Avalon, top left: Holly Hill House, top right: Casino art,
bottom: diving with the Garibaldi*

cestors were from the early Shoshonean linguistic group that migrated from the Great Plains.

Anthropologists speculate that at the peak of their civilization, 2,500 Indians lived all over the Island with larger groups at three major sites: Little Harbor, Avalon, and Two Harbors. Hundreds of other sites have been found; some were permanent and others were temporary bases for hunting and gathering expeditions. Since the sea supplied the major part of the Indian diet, the permanent sites were near a freshwater supply that was reasonably close to the shoreline. It appears that the Two Harbors area had the largest community, and the site at Little Harbor was the oldest.

The Pimugnans were later called Gabrielinos. This and other names for natives were taken from the missions that eventually became the homes of the last survivors of the Southern California tribes: the Obispeno, from San Luis Obispo; Purismeno, from La Purisima Concepcion; and Diegueno, from San Diego. As time passed, coastal Mainland and Channel Island Indians traded, intermingled, and developed a shared culture. They have since all come to be called "Canalinos."

In an old sea log Friar Torquemada, interpreter for Friar Ascension, the adventurous missionary who accompanied the Vizcaino expedition in 1602, described the Indians as a warm, friendly people and physically hardy. The Indian houses on Catalina were described by Miguel Costanso, an engineer with the 1769 Portola expedition, as circular, thatched domes 60 feet in diameter, spacious enough to hold three to four families. The men and children usually went naked; the women wore otter-skin aprons. At night they used otter-skin robes as blankets.

The Gabrielinos or Pimugnans of Catalina were energetic traders with a flourishing stoneware trade: archaeologists have found Catalina steatite artifacts in Indian sites as far away as Nevada and New Mexico. Many artifacts were removed from the Island in the early 1900s and moved to the now defunct Heye Foundation's Museum of American Indians in New York. (The Heye Museum was to become a part of the National Museum of the American Indian in Washington, D.C.)

Religious Beliefs

Many of the Islanders' customs differed from those of the Gabrielinos on the Mainland. According to Bernice Eastman Johnston, noted author associated with the Southwest Museum of Los Angeles, the Mainland Gabrielinos found something sinister in the isolation granted their tribesmen by the rough waters of the channel. Even though brisk trading went on between them, and the Mainland Indians had absorbed many of the elements of the vigorous Chingichnich-based religion from the men of Santa Catalina, they whispered that the Islanders were fierce wizards.

Legends tell of a mysterious temple complex where the Indians from all the Channel Islands gathered once a year to worship Chingichnich. This god was meant to protect them from the intrusion of the Spanish, from the Christian religion, and from their diseases. According to legend, the Indians' highly formalized and ritualized religion involved temples called *yuva'r*, sacred open-air enclosures with elaborate poles and banners decorated in feathers. An image of Chingichnich was placed in the *yuva'r*, and only old men possessing great "power" could enter. Lengthy and involved ceremonies were performed for every important event in life: birth, puberty, marriage, and death. Offerings of food and goods were presented not only to Chingichnich but also to the owl, raven, crow, and eagle.

THE SPANISH ERA

Early Explorers

The first white explorer known to visit the Indians of Catalina was Juan Rodriguez Cabrillo, a Portuguese navigator sailing under the Spanish flag. He claimed the Island in 1542 and called it

San Salvador. Sixty years later, Sebastian Vizcaino claimed it for King Philip III. Because his arrival on Nov. 24, 1602, coincided with the Catholic feast of St. Catherine of Alexandria, Vizcaino and his men renamed the island Santa Catalina in her honor. The Indians gave the crew an enthusiastic, hospitable welcome, and the ship remained in various Catalina harbors for several days. We have learned much from their logs about the Catalina Indians. We know that they caught fish on barbless hooks and kept dogs as pets--dogs that "do not bark, but howl like coyotes."

After Vizcaino's visit, however, the Channel Islands were ignored for more than 150 years. In 1769 an expedition headed by Gaspar de Portola and Friar Junipero Serra claimed all of California for Spain. Catalina was considered as a possible mission location, but the shortage of missionaries and the Island's distance from the Mainland made this impractical. So time and outsiders continued to pass Catalina by.

Note: A new book, *Cabrillo,* adds another theory to the mix of "fact or fiction." Author Harry Kelsey declares that it's entirely possible Cabrillo was buried on Catalina.

The Sea Otter Trade

Toward the end of the 1700s the Catalina Indians still enjoyed a peaceful lifestyle, though this was not to last much longer. As Spain established presidios, missions, and pueblos along the California coast, ships discovered the safe harbors of Catalina--and the sea otter. This small, intelligent mammal furnished the most valuable fur found on the entire coast from California to Alaska. Ships and crews competed violently to monopolize the feeding grounds of these animals, which had gamboled freely for centuries in the waters of the Channel Islands. Their velvetlike skins, sold regularly to Chinese merchants in Canton, also brought exorbitant prices from Russian nobility. During the period of global development beginning in the mid-1700s, many countries cast a covetous eye to the coast of California. Russia, England, France, and America recognized its potential. However, the Spanish colonial government forbade foreign vessels to trade along the California coast. If a ship was caught, its cargo was confiscated or its crew had to pay a 100% duty.

The brig *Lelia Byrd* was the first American ship on record to anchor in Catalina waters. Captain William Shaler, his hold loaded with otter skins, had put into the Spanish harbor of San Diego desperate for food, water, and repairs. The authorities became suspicious; when they threatened to search the ship, Shaler made a run for the open sea. He limped into the Avalon Bay in May 1804. His ship, leaking badly, was careened, and with the aid of the Catalina Indians he caulked his vessel with lime and tallow. Six weeks later, Shaler sailed to the Hawaiian Islands and sold his precious cargo of skins to King Kamehameha.

Final Chapter

The end of the Indians' way of life began in 1806 when the Russian-American Fur Company, based in Sitka, Alaska, and two American traders, Joseph O'Cain and Jonathan Winship, formed a business alliance. With a captive crew of Aleuts and Kodiak Indians, the Russian trappers sailed south along the coast from their colony in Alaska to hunt the sea otter at any risk.

The frenzied hunting lasted for several years, during which the otters were all but exterminated. Some stories say the Pimugnans were looted, the women raped, and many men slaughtered. Whether or not that's true, by 1832 the population had been devastated, and the few remaining Indians sought refuge with the Mainland missionaries at San Gabriel and San Fernando. Most died within several years, unable to cope with the transition from the Stone Age to the lifestyle and diseases of a more modern civilization.

THE CHINESE

As early as 1847, a small group of Chinese immigrants entered California. Lured from poor towns in China by the stories of high-paying jobs in the gold mines, 20,000 Chinese were living in the state by 1852.

In those first years California politicians and entrepreneurs welcomed the Chinese as hardworking, dependable laborers willing to work for pennies an hour. They held the lowliest jobs in cigar factories, laundries, kitchens, private homes, railroads, ranches, and gold mines. Resentiment against the Chinese developed when, despite their low wages, with enormous frugality and perseverance they often ended up wealthier than their American coworkers.

The Chinese were subjected to a variety of indignities and violent acts ridiculing their dress, almond-shaped eyes, and food habits (Chinese ate bamboo shoots, seaweed, salt ginger, and dried duck liver). This jingoism fueled anti-immigration legislation.

The cry "California for the Americans" brought about various laws over the years. One enacted during the 1850s stated that every foreigner entering the state must pay an immigration head-tax of $50. Until then, many sea captains arranged with landowners and businessmen to pick up in China and deliver cheap laborers-- all penniless. Under the new law, the captain would have to pay the fee unless he managed to sneak past Customs. Corrupt sailing masters arriving from China would avoid Customs in the larger northern ports and continue south to Monterey. If they were unsuccessful finding buyers for their human cargo, they continued to Catalina, where the Chinese were hidden in Iron-bound Bay, Lobster Bay, or Smuggler's Cove to wait for smaller ships to transport them to San Pedro on the Mainland and new work.

Even after the laws were changed there were still periodic political "clean-ups"; Chinese operating restaurants and laundries in San Francisco were rounded up and loaded on ships supposedly destined for China. Most were simply hidden on Catalina and other Channel Islands until things settled down once more; then the captives were returned to their waiting employers.

Smugglers used Catalina as a warehouse for contraband, itinerant sheepherders tended animals on the Island, and fur traders made their secret headquarters there. In those early years, Catalina harbored both legal and illegal trade, neither of which benefited the development of the Island.

SILVER AND GOLD

George Yount, a pioneer and otter hunter in the 1830s, told stories on the Mainland of "gold-bearing" rock he'd seen on Catalina Island. In 1863, miners from everywhere flocked across the channel in anything that floated, and the purple hills of Catalina crawled with men greedy for gold. For "$2 including grub," optimistic miners traveled on boats already loaded with lumber, tools, and provisions to supply the operating mines. They never found gold but they did find silver. And the "rush" continued.

Such sloops as the *Ned Beale,* the *Anna Maria,* and the schooner *Commerce* all plied the waters between San Pedro and Catalina's Two Harbors.

Phineas Banning, who was destined to play an important part in the history of Catalina Island, advertised that his steamer *Cricket* and his schooner *San Diego* were available to those who wished to charter them for trips to the "very rich mines" on Catalina.

According to old records at the *L.A. County Recorder,* most of the miners worked in the vicinity of Cherry Valley, Two Harbors, and Silver Canyon. Although operating expenses of mining were too high to make it profitable, dreams of grandeur kept these miners groping. Names of claims were as rich as the hopes of the owners: Gem of the Ocean, Pacific Gold,

OWNERSHIP OF CATALINA ISLAND

KING OF SPAIN
Through Spanish occupation of California begun in 1769
|
MEXICO
Through successful revolt against Spain, accomplished in 1822
|
THOMAS M. ROBBINS
By grant on July 4, 1846, from Governor Pio Pico
|
JOSE MARIA COVARRUBIAS
By deed of August 31, 1850, his title being confirmed by
U.S. Land Commission and U.S. Patent
|
ALBERT PACKARD
By deed of October 13, 1853

¾	¼
JAMES RAY	EUGENE L. SULLIVAN
Deed May 14, 1864	Deed June 9, 1858
WALTER HAWXHURST	CHAS. M. HITCHCOCK
Sheriff's deed August 6, 1867	Deed Feb 4, 1864

JAMES LICK
By deeds May 23, 1864; May 23, 1865; June 27, 1866; September 16, 1867
|
TRUSTEES OF JAMES LICK TRUST
By deed June 2. 1874
GEORGE SHATTO 1887 - 1891

J.B. BANNING	Lots in Avalon sold to various
Deed Sept. 30, 1891	individuals

TRUSTEES OF JAMES LICK TRUST
By Sheriff's Sale
|
WILLIAM BANNING
By deed September 20, 1892
|
SANTA CATALINA ISLAND COMPANY
Incorporated October 16, 1894; by deed of May 7, 1896
|
The Santa Catalina Island Company now owns approximately 13%
of Santa Catalina Island.
|
Santa Catalina Island Conservancy owns approximately 86% of total land area,
by deed of February 18, 1975.
|
University of Southern California—Marine Science Center—Big Fisherman's Cove
By deeds of March 8, 1965 and January 26, 1972

Lots in Avalon sold to various individuals approximately 1%

Silver and Galena Co., Diamond Mining, James Lick's Small Hill Mining Co., Bouchette's California Land Co., and General Wright Mining Company. Curiously, the last is the name of the Union general responsible for ordering miners on the Island to abandon their claims and leave their dreams behind.

AN AMERICAN CALIFORNIA

The coast was perfect for harboring and stocking ships for the long journey to Asia. The moderate climate provided a long growing season on fertile farmlands. Mexico welcomed foreigners to California, but only those who wished to become naturalized citizens. The Mexicans encouraged trade, placed a price tag on it, but then found it difficult to collect the tariffs. As a result, many American clipper ships battled the gales around Cape Horn and made a lively profit bringing manufactured goods to the isolated *rancheros* along the California coast. The picture changed when California became a U.S. state in 1850.

A Silver Saddle

Thomas Robbins, an American from Massachusetts, first visited California in 1823. He got his first glimpse of the Catalina hills rising from the Pacific as mate on the *Rover*. After several subsequent trips to California he settled in Santa Barbara, ran a general store, and continued sailing in channel waters as captain of the schooner *Santa Barbara*. In 1834, he married Encarnacion, the daughter of a rich Santa Barbara landowner, Carlos Carrillo. Because he was known as a good friend to Mexican as well as American officials, Robbins's general store became a gathering place for seafarers who stopped at Santa Barbara.

In the service of Mexican Governor Alvarado, Robbins later commanded the government schooner *California* and came to know all the Channel Islands. In 1839, he asked the governor for possession of Catalina Island. Alvarado did not issue the grant to Robbins or to any of the other petitioners for the Island. But in 1846, before the Mexican War when American "takeover" rumors were rife, provisional Governor Pio Pico signed away Catalina Island to Robbins as a last gesture of his authority. The favorite story of the event suggests that on the 4th of July, with the Americans about to take full control, Governor Pio Pico passed through Santa Barbara on his way to meet General Castro. He gave the long-sought Catalina grant to Robbins. Fictioneers like to say it was in exchange for a silver saddle and a fresh horse. However, Pico was a

Old photo of Avalon Bay before the 1915 fire

SCI COMPANY

highly respected governor and not "fleeing" from anyone. He continued to live in and develop California as a highly respected citizen. After Robbins, many title changes affected the fortunes of Catalina Island.

Guadalupe Treaty

In 1848, with the signing of the Guadalupe Hidalgo Treaty that ended the Mexican War, Catalina was annexed to California, along with Santa Barbara, San Clemente, and the Anacapas.

Civil War

Occupation of the Island by Union Army troops during the Civil War finally put an end to mining. For years, historians maintained that the Union believed the miners were actually Confederate sympathizers who planned to seize Catalina to use as a base for piracy by Southern privateers. However, research shows that the Union Army's Commander of the Department of the Pacific, Brigadier General George Wright, ordered a company of infantry to take possession of Catalina; he had been having trouble with certain Indian tribes that refused to stay on their reservations north of San Francisco and he wanted to move them to the Island. General Wright described the condition of the Island in a letter:

From a special report which I have just received from the commanding officer on the island, I am well satisfied that it is better adapted for an Indian reservation than I at first supposed. It appears that we found on the island some 80 to 100 people, some few of them mining and the others engaged in stock raising. There are twelve or fifteen small valleys embracing an area of 1,000 or 1,200 acres of good fertile land. The island has on it a large number of wild goats estimated at 15,000, besides quail and small game. It has an abundant supply of fresh running water which can easily be conducted to any part of the island.

Army officials in Washington rejected this proposal and the plan was scrapped. From this letter it would appear that water was plentiful. However, the letter that follows says otherwise:

In continuation of my report of January 19, 1864, I can now say from personal observation that the so-called big spring has not sufficient water to attempt to lead it to this post, there being not more than half an inch of water at most. This being the case we will refer to the only living stream of any size on the island distant from the isthmus in an air line about six miles, but from the broken and rolling nature of the country will take, in my judgment, ten miles of pipe to reach the post.

Water continued to be a problem for years.

The war itself never reached Catalina, but while there, the soldiers built a barracks. The barracks still stands, and has since been transformed into a privately owned yacht club. Although Wright's letters implied that Catalina belonged to the government, in fact it was legally deeded at that time to a man named James Lick.

TITLE HISTORY

After Thomas Robbins, Catalina had several owners. Fellow Santa Barbaran Jose Maria Covarrubias bought the Island from Robbins for $10,000. Next, Albert Packard, a lawyer also from Santa Barbara, bought it in 1853 for the all-time bargain price of $1000. James Lick, eccentric founder of the Lick Observatory, was the next owner. He had arrived in San Francisco in 1847 with $40,000 in gold. While other newcomers mined, he began to buy choice pieces of city real estate. In 1861, he built the magnificent Lick House, then rented it out and lodged alone in one of its cheapest rooms. At a time when his yearly income was $200,000, he traveled around San Francisco in a dilapidated buggy pulled by an aged horse. While the public laughed, he continued augmenting his fortune.

In Los Angeles, Lick acquired Los Feliz Rancho, now the location of Griffith Park, and from 1863-67 he bought Catalina Island in quarter shares from four separate owners for $23,000 each. (See chart.) Much to his credit, he enjoyed using his money for others--he funded an old ladies' home, an orphan shelter, a library association, a society for the prevention of cruelty to animals, free public baths, and a memorial to his mother. James Lick died in 1876 and was buried beneath the dome of his powerful telescope on Mt. Hamilton near San Jose, at what is now the Lick Observatory.

The SCI Company

Lick's trustees sold Catalina in 1887 to the ambitious George R. Shatto for $200,000. Shatto was the first to create and subdivide the town of Avalon. He was unable to keep up the mortgage payments and the Lick trustees took the Island back, reselling it in 1892 to William Banning for $128,740. In 1896, he deeded the Island to the newly formed (1894) Santa Catalina Island Company (SCI Co.). The company was family-owned, the stock held by three Banning brothers--William, Hancock, and J.B.--and their two sisters--Katherine and Anna. The Banning brothers turned themselves enthusiastically to building and developing Catalina Island into a pleasure resort. The green Pleasure Pier was built in 1909. SCI made some major changes to Avalon (see "Casino Point"), but the 1915 fire that damaged a good part of the town thwarted the development plan. Progress came to a halt for lack of capital until 1918, when the St. Catherine Hotel was built and opened.

William Wrigley Jr.

In 1919, chewing gum magnate William Wrigley Jr. bought the major interest in SCI Company for $3 million, announcing that "the development of Santa Catalina Island will be one of the greatest pleasures of my life." A man of his word, he created a fabulous resort within a few short years.

Until his death in 1932, Wrigley indulged his love affair with Catalina. He invested huge amounts of money in building projects such as an enormous ballroom housed in the Casino, the first completely round structure built in Southern California. He created a bird park and invited the public to visit without charge the literally thousands of extraordinary birds that paraded around the "largest bird cage in the world" (built from the ribs of the old Sugarloaf Casino). He developed a baseball field and brought his Chicago Cubs over every year for spring training. He put in costly utility systems. And he built for his wife, Ada, the white house with green shutters that she had always wanted: the family home on Mt. Ada. Catalina soon became the favored vacation spot for the stars and celebrities of Hollywood's Golden Era, as well as an attainable vacationland for regular people . . . as it is today.

Philip K. Wrigley

In 1932, his son Philip K. Wrigley assumed control of the company and continued to improve the Island. It was Philip who saw to it that the big bands came to the Casino. Under his supervision Hamilton Cove's sea plane ramp and airlines thrived. And one of his finest gifts was the establishment of the Catalina Conservancy in 1972. Philip was active in the affairs of the Island until his death in 1977.

Catalina still rests in the hands of the Wrigleys. Philip's son, William Wrigley, sits as the SCI Company's director, and nephew Paxson Offield, who moved to the Island in the mid-1970s, is president. Offield's move to Catalina was a banner moment; it was the first time since 1919 that anyone in the Wrigley-Offield family would live full time on Catalina.

WW II

The growth cycle was interrupted by WW II, when Catalina became a training area for Merchant Marine, Army, Coast Guard, and Navy personnel, including the mysterious OSS (Office of Strategic Service). From 1941-45, tourists were not permitted on the Island. The Merchant Marine took over the St. Catherine Hotel for a cooking school. It never regained its original beauty or its popularity, and in 1965 the classic hotel was demolished. Several years passed before Catalina was "rediscovered."

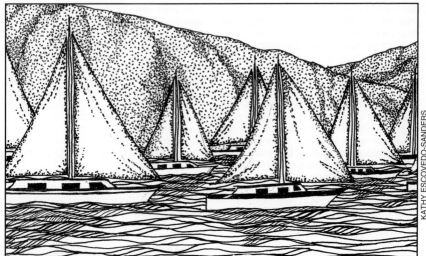

KATHY ESCOVEDO-SANDERS

CATALINA CRUISING

Catalina is unquestionably the most popular boaters' destination along the Southern California coast. An island is an obvious draw for boaters--even for those in smaller craft. If you're a boater looking for an active nightlife and other shore activities, Avalon is the harbor for your visit.

On the other hand, if it's the quiet life you're seeking, escape to one of Catalina's many small isolated coves, where the loudest thing you'll hear--aside from other boaters--is the slap of the water on your bow and maybe a squawking seagull. Most of these isolated coves show no sign of man's intrusion. All of California's Channel Islands are also perfect for day-hikes, which will bring you into direct contact with the natural phenomena of the Islands, where diving is unparalleled.

CIRCUMNAVIGATING CATALINA ISLAND

FROM AVALON TO CATALINA'S EAST END

Seal Rocks

Since pinnipeds (in this case California sea lions and harbor seals) are migratory animals, viewing them depends on the season. California sea lions don't pup on the Island, but the harbor seals do. So during the mating season, begin-

ning as early as June, the males take their harems to a private cove; in July and August they return to Seal Rocks in larger numbers to sun themselves, swim, and dive for fish.

To China Point

As you round the Island's east end you'll pass Church Rock before coming to the Palisades area, so named because of the steep mountains that drop to the sea. From the water you can see the weblike paths of the mountain goats that once roamed these hills. This is good anchorage during Santa Ana storms.

Going on, you'll pass Silver Canyon Landing, which has no moorings but which does have anchorage with some westerly protection. Going ashore is risky because of the surf, but if you plan to attempt a landing you'll find the fewest breakers on the southwest corner.

Continuing past Bulldog Rock and Salta Verde Point with its "painted cliffs" will bring you to China Point. In the 1800s, this was the location of one of the camps where illegal Chinese immigrants, supposedly being returned to China by government order, were dropped off by unscrupulous sea captains before being smuggled back to the California Mainland.

Between China Point and Ben Weston Point you may spot seals. Ben Weston Beach has no moorings, and anchorage is considered unsafe.

Little Harbor

After you round the east end of the Island and head west, you'll pass landmarks Church Rock, Binnacle Rock, the Palisades, the opening from Silver Canyon, China Point, Ben Weston and Indian Head Rocks. Beyond Indian Head Rock, you'll come to one of the Island's most picturesque harbors, which is really two individual harbors, Little Harbor and Shark Harbor. Little Harbor has no moorings, but excellent anchorage for 10-15 boats. Shark Harbor, the larger, has no moorings; anchorage is considered unsafe. Surfing, however, can be good. Little Harbor offers improved campsites for 150 people. From here, you can hike to the tops of the surrounding hills for spectacular coastal vistas, see

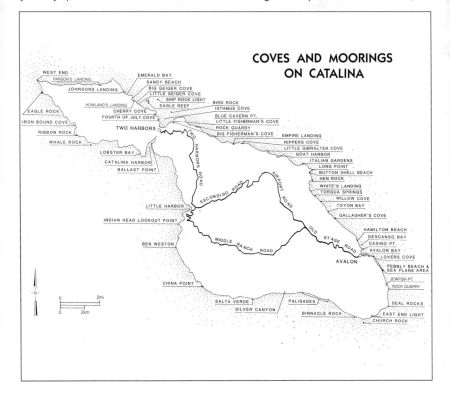

COVES AND MOORINGS ON CATALINA

wildlife, and explore the ancient location of one of the main communities of the Catalina Indians.

WEST END AND TWO HARBORS

Catalina Harbor

Following the coast toward the West End past Little Harbor, you'll come to Cat Harbor, which has 96 moorings plus anchorage for 235; onshore facilities are available for California Yacht Club members. Within the deep harbor you'll find Ballast Point, which is said to have been formed by Yankee clippers that dropped ballast here to scrape the bottoms of their ships. Firepits, good picnic facilities and toilets are available to the public for day use, but camping is not allowed at Cat Harbor.

In the days before these waters were charted, this nub of land separated by Two Harbors fooled sailors into thinking that this was another island.

Continuing around Catalina Head, you come to Lobster Bay, which, according to legend, was a pirate hideout. At Whale Rock, what looks like a whale's waterspout is only a "blowhole" formed when the tide hits the rock and forces a column of water along it and up into the air.

Ribbon Rock attracts attention with its striated layers of quartz against the high dark face of the cliff. It was here, according to Frederick Holder's story, "Adventures of Torqua" (see "Blue Cavern Point" in this section), that white settlers forever trapped a band of thieving Indians in an underground cave by sealing the exit. Iron Bound Cove has no moorings; although the anchorage is exposed, it's considered fair. From Iron Bound Cove, legend has it, Chinese immigrants left their temporary camps and hiked over to Catalina Harbor to gamble.

From Eagle Rock to Land's End

Eagle Rock is almost at Land's End, the western tip of Catalina. Until 1952, the American bald eagle used this isolated area to breed. Today, although eagles are not seen in large numbers, an occasional bird soars over the rocky cliffs--thanks to the ongoing Bald Eagle Reintroduction Program overseen by the Catalina Conservancy (see "Fauna"). Sizable numbers of brown pelicans cluster on the rocks. As you cruise around Land's End you'll see the West End Light; expect strong currents and swell.

Parson's Landing

Once around the western tip, you'll reach Parson's Landing, which has no moorings but anchorage for 10. This is a good beach for camping, with fire rings, toilets, and barbecue pits. Call Camp and Cove, tel. (310) 510-0303, for reservations. In all but very dry years, there's a freshwater spring up the canyon. At one time the home of miners and pioneers, the area was named for the twin brothers Nathaniel and Theoples Parsons, who lived here in the mid-1800s.

camping at Parson's Landing

PATTI LANGE

Beyond Arrow Point lie Johnson's Landing and Emerald Bay. Samuel Prentiss lived in a small stone house here at Johnson's Landing while he searched the Island for an elusive treasure. During the mining years of 1863-64, grandiose plans for Queen City were begun here by the rough-and-tumble miners who had set up a temporary community in the flush of the gold frenzy on Catalina. The Union Army arrived to survey the Island for a possible Indian reservation and ended the miners' dreams of riches by ordering them to leave.

Emerald Bay

Emerald Bay, with its isolation and natural beauty, is a favorite anchorage for boaters. It has 99 moorings and anchorage for 5-10 boats. Shore land has been leased to the Great Western Council of Boy Scouts for many years; leasing changes were being discussed. At one point it appeared that Jacques Cousteau's organization would build an ecological resort. However, a cry went out from those who were concerned that the balance of nature would be upset; the Cousteaus dropped out. A small dive operation started up, using existing cabins for short stays at Emerald. For more information, contact Scuba Outpost, tel. (800) 574-0900.

At present, Sandy Beach is available for day camping only.

Howland's

Just around the bend from Sandy Beach is another favorite boat harbor, Howland's Landing, with 40 moorings. High up in the canyon sits the windblown stone marker of Samuel Prentiss keeping a lonely vigil as the only marked grave outside of Avalon. Land ashore is leased to Catalina Island Camps and Los Angeles Yacht Club.

Big Geiger Cove

This spot has anchorage for 10, and the shore is leased to the Blue Water Cruising Club. **Little Geiger Cove** has one mooring and anchorage for three; the land is leased to Offshore Cruising Club.

Cherry Cove

Cherry Cove offers 103 moorings but no anchorage. The shore has been leased to the San Gabriel Valley Boy Scouts for many years. Cherry Cove was named for 77 Catalina cherry trees planted up the canyon. See "Flora."

Fourth of July Cove

Here you'll find 42 moorings but no anchorage. It's named for the holiday celebrations the Banning family held every July during their era of ownership. The land is leased to the Fourth of July Yacht Club.

FROM BLUE CAVERN POINT TRAVELING EAST

Blue Cavern Point

With its clear deep waters, this is a favorite diving spot for taking photos. Caves and other small coves invite exploration. This is the site of one of the scenes described in Frederick Holder's "Adventures of Torqua," a tale of Indian raiders who take valuables from the camps of the white man and make their way to Blue Cavern Point. From there an underwater opening leads into a tunnel that passes through to the opposite side of the Island. The Indians then exit at Ribbon Rock to escape with their loot. While the victims are bewildered at first, they eventually work out the puzzle. After discovering the Indians' method of escape, the disgruntled white men block the exit at Ribbon Rock and wait for another raid. Once again the Indians creep into camp, take what they can carry and make their way to the point, slipping silently into the black water and the even blacker cave. The white men hide and when all the Indians are inside, seal the entrance of the cave, entombing them for eternity. Fiction?

Rock Quarry

This quarry site, with a dock for emergency landing only, has operated intermittently for the last 40 years or more; it provided Island stone for building sites and breakwaters all along the Southern California coast. Empire Landing boasted one of the largest hills of soapstone on the Island. The Indians carved it into religious artifacts and everyday utensils such as ollas (for grinding acorns and other hard grains). Many fascinating artifacts were found here, including remnants of half-made ollas attached by stems of stone to the outcropping, as though the carv-

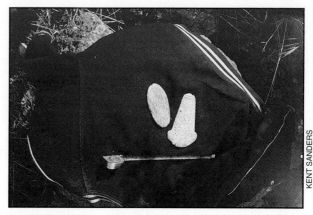

*carved Indian
Soapstone from
Empire Landing*

KENT SANDERS

er had been interrupted and left his project unfinished. During the 1950s, the soapstone was blasted and removed in the course of quarry production.

Empire Landing

Boaters will see two moorings, but they are private; however, there's anchorage for 20. On the bluff overlooking the bay are houses occupied by quarry personnel when it's in operation; at other times they are rented to those who enjoy isolation.

Rippers Cove

You'll find no moorings here, but there's an-

KENT SANDERS

Frank Machado discovering Indian artifacts

chorage for 5-10. Two beaches with crystal-clear water are fine places for swimming and diving. Look for "velvet-covered" sand dollars spinning along like miniature wheels on the sandy bottom of the bay.

Little Gibraltar

No moorings here, but there's anchorage for five to seven boats. Around Little Gibraltar to Cabrillo Beach the shore is leased to the Long Beach Boy Scouts.

Goat Harbor

No moorings here, but there's anchorage for 5-10 boats and good camping and hiking. Supplies for Middle Ranch, a working ranch in the interior, used to be unloaded from boats here and taken inland. In 1966, Explorer Scouts were breaking camp on the beach when they discovered a half-buried chest containing gold-leaf-wrapped opium. Who knows how old it was!

Italian Gardens

No moorings here, but it's a fair anchorage and a good fishing spot. Italian fishermen from San Pedro came regularly to this "sea garden" to take abundant catches of fish back across the channel.

Long Point

Folklore tells of a cave at Long Point that (still) whistles when the wind approaches from a certain direction, with an eerie sound that struck fear into the hearts of the Indians. Long Point Light warns boaters of the presence of this jutting finger of land.

Buttonshell Beach
You'll find seven moorings and anchorage for 10. The land ashore, called Camp Fox, is leased to the Glendale YMCA.

Hen Rock Cove
The cove offers 24 moorings and anchorage for 10. It's a good snorkeling area. The land is leased to the Balboa Yacht Club.

White's Landing
Here you'll find 17 moorings and anchorage for 16. The land is leased to Los Angeles Girl Scouts and part of the beach to the Balboa Yacht Club.

Here you'll see a well and the foundations of a smelter; a conveyor brought silver ore to the landing from Black Jack Mine high on the ridge above this beach.

This mine produced more silver ore than any other mine on the Island.

Moonstone Beach
This beach offers 38 moorings and anchorage for 12. This beach is leased to the Newport Harbor Yacht Club. It was named Moonstone be-cause in years past the beach was covered with small shiny rocks.

Torqua Springs
From descriptions in old ships' logs this was probably where the Indians came to get their water. For years, this was also one of Avalon's main water sources. Today, it's famed for a 100-foot-deep artificial reef built from old cars, pipes, machinery, and tanks, creating a good habitat for fish and an excellent dive area.

Willow Cove
No moorings, but there's anchorage for four boats. It's a small quiet cove; beach camping is permitted, and the swimming is good in its clear water.

Toyon Bay
You'll find nine moorings and anchorage for six boats. The shore is leased to the Catalina Island Marine Institute. Youngsters come here for a week at a time and learn about nature at its best.

Gallagher's Beach
No moorings, but there's fair anchorage for three to five boats. The shore is leased to "Campus-by-the-Sea" vacation camp. At this point you will have just about circled the Island.

BOATING PRACTICALITIES

INFORMATION

Weather
Every seaman has a big responsibility--not only for his own safety and that of his crew, but also (as most would concede) for a large financial investment. Weather plays an important part in boating, and a lot of tragedies could be averted with the use of common sense. Boat owners should take advantage of all the information available to them, and in Southern California there's a lot; monitoring the weather is of prime importance.

Even though some of the islands are not far from the Mainland (Catalina is only 22 miles

from Long Beach Harbor), the Santa Barbara/Catalina Channel is a formidable stretch of open sea. The crossing can be smooth or it can pitch waves that pound the hull and leap the gunwales. Fog can settle in anytime, but in the winter it's denser and hangs in there longer. Fog seldom forms when the air is at least 5° F warmer than the water, so visibility improves with fresh southerly winds and a steady or slow-ly falling barometer.

During the winter in the Catalina Channel, Santa Ana winds (also called northeasters) can shift swell-direction and render an anchorage unsafe. And although all coves and harbors in Catalina provide peaceful anchorage most of the time, safe boaters pay heed to the forecasts. When an advisory is in effect or a storm warning is up, they don't go out unless they are highly qualified sailors who have experience in the prevailing sea conditions--and it's an emergency trip! If already at sea, most make for home port --pronto!--or to the nearest harbor that offers protection from the predicted wind and sea direction.

Flags and lights give warnings on the mole in Avalon and at the Two Harbors Office.

Note: One red pennant or red-over-white lights mean the forecast is an 18- to 33-knot wind and/or sea, dangerous for small boats. Two red pennants or white-over-red lights mean a 34- to 47-knot gale. One square red flag with black center or red-over-red lights mean a 48- to 63-knot storm. Southern California harbormasters are always on call for a local weather report; Avalon's number is (310) 510-0535.

It's wise to know where the safe harbors and coves are in case you need to make a run in the middle of the night. The seasons generally hold true, but to eliminate any unpleasant surprises, boaters must know what's coming.

One of the biggest aids in stormy conditions is to stay calm and remember everything you ever learned about sailing. As in any emergency, panic compounds existing problems.

Radio Equipment
For about $400, boaters can buy a receiver that will pick up the weather and not take up much space or, for more money (about $1000), a ham radio rig. You must have a license to broadcast, but not to listen. Other boaters talk to each other and give good information about the weather in different areas.

Anyone interested in sailing frequently and far would be wise to get a general-class license (or higher) to have full capability to broadcast through the ham networks, which are especially helpful in emergencies.

Navigation
Accurate charts are available from most marine supply stores. Valuable books that should be on board for all sailors who cruise the channel are *Pacific Boating Almanac* and *Cruising Guide To California's Channel Islands,* by Brian M. Fagan, both published by Western Marine

Enterprises, Inc. The Chart Guide for Catalina is also handy to tuck away. For maximum convenience and safety, ask to have your name put on a free mailing list for the "Local Notice to Mariners," which provides weekly NOAA chart editions that indicate shoreline and depth changes. For this service write to: Commander, 11th Coast Guard District, 400 Oceangate, Long Beach, CA 90822.

SERVICE

Towing Assistance
Members of Boat/US (which number about 215,000) now receive a reimbursement up to $50 for boat-towing service. Membership in the nonprofit organization is $17 and entitles each member to a $50 towing reimbursement per

---

SOUTHERN CALIFORNIA COASTAL STORM WARNING DISPLAY LOCATIONS

San Diego: Ballast Point, B Street Pier, Coronado Yacht Club, Shelter Island, Mission Bay Aquatic Headquarters, Oceanside Harbor

Dana Point Harbor

Catalina Island: Avalon Pleasure Pier, Isthmus Cove

Sunset Beach

Newport Beach Harbor: Channel Entrance

Long Beach Marina: Administration Building

San Pedro: Marine Exchange Building

Redondo Beach: King Harbor on the Breakwater

Marina del Rey: Administration Building

Port Hueneme Naval Station, Oxnard: Channel Islands Harbor

Ventura Marina

Santa Barbara: Weather Signal Station

CALIFORNIA COASTAL
STORM-WARNING FLAGS AND LIGHTS

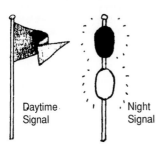

Daytime Signal | Night Signal

SMALL CRAFT ADVISORIES

One red pennant displayed by day or a red light over a white light at night indicates that winds as high as 33 knots (38 mph) and/or sea conditions considered dangerous to small-craft operations are forecast for the area.

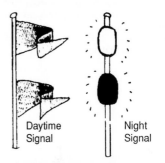

Daytime Signal | Night Signal

GALE WARNING

Two red pennants displayed by day or a white light above a red light at night indicates that winds 34-47 knots (39-54 mph) are forecast for the area.

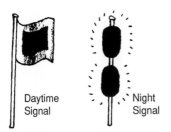

Daytime Signal | Night Signal

STORM WARNING

A single square red flag with a black center displayed during daytime or two red lights at night indicates that winds 48 knots (55 mph) and above are forecast for the area. If the winds are associated with a tropical cyclone (hurricane), the storm warning displays indicate that winds 48-63 knots (55-73 mph) are forecast.

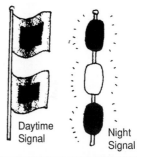

Daytime Signal | Night Signal

HURRICANE WARNING

Displayed only in connection with a tropical cyclone (hurricane). Two square red flags with black centers displayed by day or a white light between two red lights at night indicates that winds 64 knots (74 mph) and above are forecast for the area.

year. Broader towing coverage is available from Boat/US for an additional fee.

The association made this service available in 1984, when the Coast Guard turned all non-emergency towing over to commercial firms (except in foul weather or darkness). Other services and marine insurance are available through Boat/US; for more information contact Boat/US, 880 S. Pickett St., Alexandria, VA 22304, tel. (703) 823-9550.

Underwater Repair Service

If you need an emergency underwater repair, if your line gets wrapped around the prop, or if you've dropped your only prescription glasses overboard, don't panic. Avalon's Mooring & Diving Service, tel. (310) 510-0779, is available for any diving jobs you need done. Argo Diving, tel. (310) 510-2208, is also available for even the most unusual of diving needs.

AVALON

KATHY ESCOVEDO-SANDERS

INTRODUCTION

HISTORY

THE SAGA OF AVALON

Catalina's largest town, Avalon, turned 100 years old in 1987. The town has endured many changes in its first century.

A Name is a Name is a Name

When the first Spanish ships sailed to Catalina Island, the harbor now called Avalon was known by the Pimugna Indians (or so romantics like to think) as the Bay of the Seven Moons. Since then, the name has changed to reflect the changing owners, residents, and destiny of the Island. Known as Johnson's Landing under the ownership of James Lick (1867-87), it was serviced by Captain A.W. Timms, who renamed it for himself: Timms Harbor. He also controlled the harbor at San Pedro, which he called Timms Point. Thus, his three sailing vessels operated from Timms to Timms. When George Shatto bought the Island in 1887, his business agent decided to call it Shatto City. This did not sit

well with Shatto until Etta Marilla Whitney, George Shatto's 25-year-old whimsical sister-in-law, chose a new name from a phrase out of Tennyson's *Idylls of the King:*

> *To the island-valley of Avalon:*
> *Where falls not hail or rain or any*
>   *snow;*
> *Nor ever wind blows loudly; but*
>   *it lies*
> *Deep-meadow'd happy fair with*
>   *orchard lawns*
> *And bowery hollows crown'd with*
>   *summer sea . . .*

George Shatto

George Shatto dreamed of transforming the simple tent city into a dazzling, modern tourist center. Drawing up a city plan, he laid out properties and streets and auctioned them off--from

SANTA CATALINA ISLAND COMPANY

Swimming in Avalon, late 1890s. Note Sugarloaf Rock in background, later replaced by the Casino.

$150 for a 20-foot lot to $2000 for a larger bay-view site. On these small lots people pitched tents or built lean-tos that could be taken down at the end of their vacations. Small lots were also leased to summer campers for $25 yearly. What's now known as Avalon is the only land on Catalina Island ever sold to private parties. Shatto built the Hotel Metropole, a gathering spot for the social elite and for the sportsfishermen drawn to the harbor for the rich schools of game-fish that surrounded it.

Soon Avalon was well on its way to becoming the tourist attraction of Shatto's dream, with the completed Hotel Metropole and Banning's two steamers shuttling people across the channel. But they did not bring in enough money for Shatto to meet his financial obligations. After only four years, Shatto's schemes failed and he was forced to sell.

The Bannings
In 1892, the Banning family became the new owners. William Banning was the first of his family to realize Catalina's true potential and he became actively involved with Avalon. By 1894 the rest of the family followed, forming the Santa Catalina Island Company (SCI Company) to further develop Avalon as a tourist center. The town grew: beaches were dotted with more and more tents, and hundreds of vacationers swam in Avalon's clear waters, fished for their dinner,

and listened to the music of the Metropole orchestra that floated over the bay.

Visitors even enjoyed the new thrill of glass-bottom boats, invented and perfected by Charley Feige in 1896. The adventurous could ride on a stagecoach over the rough back roads of the interior. William Banning was the finest amateur six-in-hand stagecoach driver in the United States and traveled Catalina's twisty roads at breakneck speed, even by today's standards. (His father, Phineas Banning, was the builder of quality stagecoaches in Wilmington, California, and a pioneer who ran a stage line along the Southern California coast.) The Bannings built a dance pavilion, a public golf course, and a steep incline railway to provide a stunning view of the town and bay from atop Buena Vista Park. All of these attractions, along with the glass-bottom boats, were included in the price of the boat ticket to Avalon, or offered for very little extra.

Tent City
In 1887 Avalon was a lovely little tent city, where residential lots were auctioned off for as little as $150; today you're lucky to buy one for $100,000 (and at that price you won't see the ocean). In the early days, water was at a premium, sold on street corners by the gallon after being hauled to the Island in barges from the Mainland. The visitors didn't seem to mind; they were on a holiday!

The Tuna Club was spawned in 1898 by eight fishermen who gathered on the Metropole Hotel's large porch for long nights of endless fish stories. Along with Charles Fredric Holder, noted fisherman and writer, these sportsmen set down gentlemen's rules for fishing. To belong you had to be one of the few who had taken "a tuna weighing 100 pounds or over or a swordfish or marlin swordfish weighing 200 pounds or

over on regulation heavy tackle; or a tuna weighing 60 pounds or over or a marlin swordfish or broadbill weighing 100 pounds or over on regulation light tackle." This still-active club's first building, constructed at the turn of the century, was destroyed in the 1915 fire. The present structure was built in 1916 at the same location on the edge of the bay. The original club goals still apply, and the Tuna Club carries on as a

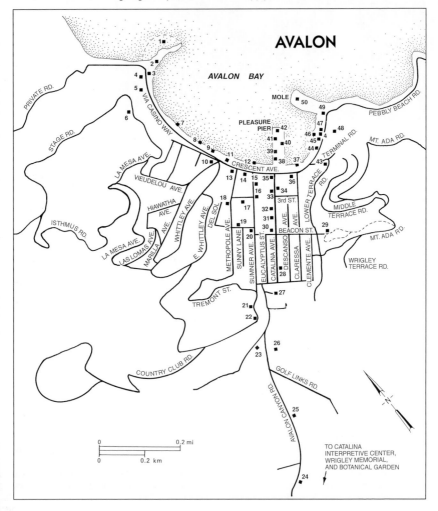

place where gentlemen anglers mingle, honor, and protect the sports-fishing waters of Catalina.

A Growing Town
As more people visited Catalina, the permanent

AVALON

1. ..Underwater Park	27. .Day Care Center,
2. Casino theater, museum, ballroom, Art Gallery	roller skate rink
	28. ....Catalina Bible Church
3. ..Shipwreck Joey's Cafe	29. ...St. Catherine's Church
4. ......doggie park	30. ....Miniature Golf
5. ....Chimes Tower	31. ..shuttle bus stop
6. ..Zane Grey Hotel	32. ....County Parks Office
7. ....Yacht Club	
8. ....Tuna Club	33. ....grocery store
9. ......north beach	34. ..Scuba Luv Dive Shop
10. ......El Encanto	
11. ...Antonio's Pizza and Catalina Cabaret	35. ..Catalina Vistor's Center
12. ....middle beach	36. ..C.C. Gallaghers Gift Shop
13. .Metropole Marketplace and Hotel Metropole	37. .....south beach
	38. ....Pleasure Pier
14. ....bank	39. ......Chamber of Commerce Office
15. ...Antonio's Pizza	
16. .....Island Plaza	40. ......boat rentals
17. Post Office Arcade	41. ....dive shop
18. ....grocery store	42. ......fish market
19. ......Community Church	43. ..playground/park
	44. ..basketball court
20 ....library	45. ...volleyball court
21. Country Club Tennis and Golf Club	46. ......playground
	47. ......doggie park
22. Municipal Hospital	48. ......picnic area
23. ..Sand Trap Cafe	49. ..Holly Hill House
24. ....Hermit Gulch Campground	50. ......boat tickets (mainland boats)
25. ..Catalina Stables	51. ....Cabrillo Mole/boat docks
26. ....golf links	

---

population increased, though the winter population leveled out at 300-400. Entrepreneurs could see the money to be made, and competition developed over transportation to Avalon. This was the beginning of a nine-year waterfront war, during which barbed-wire fences were raised, torn down, and raised again to keep passengers brought by non-SCI Company transport away from Avalon. Beachfront fisticuffs were a common occurrence each summer. The Avalon Freeholders Improvement Association was formed in 1909 to bring peace to the Island community.

In 1913, after a hard-fought election--backed by proof that it had 500 residents--Avalon was incorporated as a sixth-class city, the 30th city in Los Angeles County.

The Banning Shipping Company, however, was still responsible for providing water for the town. Many townspeople thought that the Bannings were not exerting their best efforts to establish a good water system. Much of the water was hauled in on steamers from the Mainland and locally on small boats from Torqua Springs, an expensive proposition. Though the Bannings' dream was coming to life, profits were slim and the strings of control were inexorably slipping from their hands.

The Fire of 1915
A devastating fire on Nov. 29, 1915, leveled one-third of Avalon, horrifically demonstrating the need for a viable water system. For years an aura of suspicion surrounded the mysterious start of the conflagration. Was this someone's way to get rid of the Bannings and perhaps put an end to the ongoing problems of the new city of Avalon? No one knows. After this catastrophe the Bannings built an electric plant and saltwater mains for fire protection and sanitation. Drinking water was still hauled in. To replace the fire-gutted Metropole, the SCI Company completed the St. Catherine Hotel in Descanso Bay by the summer season of 1918. But the financial blow was more than the company could absorb. So after 27 years of Banning management, William Wrigley Jr. bought the Santa Catalina Island Company in 1919. Wrigley proceeded to build and broaden Catalina beyond the wildest dreams of either George Shatto or the Banning family.

WRIGLEY'S ISLAND

Tourism

If Avalon were to become a resort, the first order of business was to improve the water situation. William Wrigley Jr. built Thompson Reservoir; pipes were connected, electric cables were laid. Water was pumped over the mountains into Avalon, a veritable miracle of the time! (Today, the Southern California Edison Company provides electricity and water.)

From 1919 until the beginning of WW II, Avalon's facilities and popularity did nothing but grow. It was the "in" place for Southern Californians to visit. Wrigley was a wise and daring businessman, not afraid to spend money advertising the Island. The Wrigley $10 package deal included roundtrip transportation from Los Angeles, a night at the luxurious St. Catherine Hotel, four meals, and an excursion in a glass-bottom boat. He built the Island Villas to replace the tent city that had grown larger every summer during the Bannings' ownership. The lines of tents for rent were replaced with close rows of "villas," small canvas-topped bungalows with double beds, rugs, dressers, chairs, electricity, daily maid service, and clean daily linens where families could stay inexpensively.

The Economy

As interest in the Island grew, and the Wrigleys continued to build, it was obvious that the year-round population was going to continue to grow. In the beginning most of the business was "summer only," but the Island needed a year-round economy. William Wrigley was always concerned about the average *Joe-citizen,* and so tried several industries that might solve the problem. Most of the new enterprises were closely linked with Wrigley's building phase, which he seemed to believe would go on forever.

Furniture Factory

With the addition of the villas, and then the Atwater Hotel, furniture was in demand. Wrigley started a furniture factory, which at first stood near today's Avalon Schools; later it was moved to Pebbly Beach.

Catalina Tile

Quite by accident one wet, rainy day, William Wrigley was driving around on the golf course with Catalina pioneer David Renton when their car got stuck in the mud. Trying to extricate the car they both sank into the mud up to their elbows. Renton recognized the mud as clay. From this spot, the first mud bricks were made for Catalina construction projects, probably in 1923. The clay was subsequently found in several locales: Echo Lake near the junction of Black Jack Mountain, Little Harbor, and the west end of the Island.

Wrigley built a tile plant to produce bricks and decorative clay building tiles in Pebbly Beach, complete with a dock for shipping the clay tiles to the Mainland. The factory later produced colorful glazed tiles in designs that included a variety of birds you could see at the bird park, sea life, and clever floral designs.

Wrigley had a master plan for the Island; he designed all his new buildings to be reminiscent of early California's Mexican flavor. The tiles fit right in and were beautifully used on buildings, fountains, the downtown "wall," and in unexpected nooks and corners. One of the finest examples of Catalina tile is at the Wrigley Memorial; it's worth the trip just to examine the fine ceramics.

The roof of the Casino building was covered with 105,000 roofing tiles in 1929. Decorative glazed tiles were joined to wrought-iron bases to create lovely small tables. By 1930, the factory produced Catalina Pottery, brightly colored dinnerware and decorative pieces that included vases, ashtrays, salt and pepper shakers, candleholders, pitchers, and items that the tourists loved.

Because of problems with the clay, in 1937 the Wrigleys sold the molds and the name Catalina Pottery to Gladding, McBean. It eliminated the glazed tiles but continued to make the art pottery and dinnerware for several years. The war brought many changes, and interest in Catalina art pottery dwindled. Today, Catalina pottery has become a valuable collectible. The resurrection of interest in American art tile has certainly brought Catalina tile and pottery back into the limelight. Collectors can find pieces in a number of shops on the Island; what may have sold for 50 cents in the '30s now sells for hundreds of dollars. You can't help but notice many buildings with the old tile. Interestingly, newly

KATHY ESCOVEDO-SANDERS

made tiles resembling the old Catalina tile have become a popular item in the gift shops around Avalon.

Wrigley-Inspired Events

Wrigley sponsored the Wrigley Ocean Marathon in January 1927, awarding $25,000 to the winner of a swimming race from Two Harbors to the San Pedro shore (22 miles). A 17-year-old Canadian, George Young, had motorcycled from Toronto, Canada, to take part, and of 103 contestants only he completed the swim. His official time of 15 hours, 46 minutes, was swum in 56-62° F waters. Over and above the $25,000, Wrigley had offered a special prize of $15,000 to any woman who finished. Hours after Young had landed, two determined women were forcibly removed from the water and awarded $2,500 each for their efforts. Since then, many swimmers have succeeded and failed. On September 21, 1952, Florence Chadwick swam the channel in 13 hours, 42 minutes. In 1958, Greta Anderson swam to and from the Mainland within 26 hours.

To Philip K. Wrigley

After the death of William Wrigley Jr. in 1932, his son Philip K. Wrigley assumed the leadership of the family-owned SCI Company, carrying on the Wrigley tradition of making Avalon an ex-

citing place to visit and an ideal place to live. Everyday utilities taken for granted on the Mainland improved on the Island.

The first of the big bands came to play in the Casino in 1933; Kay Kaiser, Benny Goodman, Freddy Martin, and Dick Jurgens were but a few.

antique matchbook covers

A LIFESTYLE DEVELOPS

COMMUNICATIONS

Early Methods
The Indians' signal fires between the Island and Mainland were the first means of communication across the channel. Later, it became common to send messages on infrequently passing boats. By the 1850s, letters arrived by boat once or twice a month. Later, the miners kept homing pigeons; records show that as late as 1899, carrier pigeons were sent to Los Angeles in as little as 45 minutes! In contrast, a letter sent in 1864 from Two Harbors took 10 days to reach Wilmington, then a stagecoach stop on the Southern California coast. Today, Avalon's post office still cannot match the speed of feathered "air mail."

Newspapers
The first newspaper printed in Avalon was *The Jew Fish,* published in 1889. In 1894-1897 the carrier pigeon was used to send local news to the Mainland. The next was the *Catalina Wireless,* a small daily published in 1903 by the *Los Angeles Times,* which used the wireless telegraph to communicate news between Avalon and the Mainland. This proved unprofitable and lasted only a short time. Another short-lived paper was a summer tabloid published in the early 1900s by Ernest Windle and George Channing. In 1912, a new *Catalina Wireless* appeared, surviving as a weekly until the big fire of 1915. In 1913, Ernest Windle founded the *Catalina Islander,* which is now produced weekly using the most modern technology. The newest weekly paper, begun in 1990, is the *Avalon Bay News.*

Telephones
In 1902, the world's first commercial wireless radio station was opened in Avalon. In 1903, the Banning Company built a telephone line from Avalon to Two Harbors via Middle Ranch and Little Harbor. Pacific Telephone and Telegraph installed the first commercial telephone system in 1919 at Pebbly Beach, with a sister station at San Pedro. In 1923, Pacific T&T laid two 23-mile-long, 300-ton submarine cables to the Mainland. The Avalon telephone system, one of the longest-lived "number please" systems in operation in the country, wasn't replaced by direct dialing until 1978.

Retired Avalon operators still tell stories about the personal-style communication that lasted for so long. If, for instance, an Islander were spending the evening at a friend's but expected an important phone call, he'd just lift the receiver and ask the operator to transfer it; today you pay for that same service, called "call forwarding." The operator knew which numbers were those of the elderly and infirm. She averted would-be catastrophes by quickly sending a police car to check out any irregularity of a light on her switchboard. One little old lady patient at the hospital, in spite of repeated instructions on how to use the buzzer to get a nurse, knew only that if she lifted the phone, a person would be there waiting. She'd tell the telephone operator to "get that nurse in here right now!" With small-town care and concern the operator would then telephone the hospital main office to pass on the request.

Today, Catalina has direct dialing like everywhere else in the United States.

Broadcasting
Catalina's first radio broadcasting station, little more than a crystal set, was built in 1921 by Lawrence Gordon Mott at his residence on Clarissa Avenue. During the winter of 1922-23, he maintained contact with the McMillan Expedition at the North Pole--for three weeks, he was the only contact the expedition had with the outside world. In the late '20s and '30s, radio shows were common on the Island. Strolling

"WHERE IS VINEGAR HILL?" A TOURIST ASKED

The oldtime locals know of the area called Vinegar Hill. Up Marilla Street at Vieudelou sits the oldest house in Avalon. It was in this general area back in the 1920s that some locals indulged in the manufacture of moonshine. The "revenooers" would come from overtown (islander talk for the Mainland), break up the stills with axes and clubs, and dump the whole mess down Marilla Street. The smell after a few days of fermenting on the street caused the area to become known as (right!) Vinegar Hill.

Television

The town has cable TV, offering the latest movies, concerts, and soaps, as well as the even more dramatic weekly meetings of the Avalon City Council. Surprisingly, many channels come in loud and clear across the ocean without cable; it all depends on the location of the TV receiver.

EDUCATION

From two students in 1888, the Avalon school system has grown to 370-400 children in grades kindergarten through 12, with 20 teachers. Over the years the "schoolhouse" has been located in a variety of buildings, including the Congregational Church, the Whittley St. School House, the old Sugarloaf Casino, and the present Casino. The 1902 election approved funds to buy property for a schoolhouse. Fourteen votes were cast, all in favor. In 1923, Avalon Schools became affiliated with the Long Beach School System. William Wrigley Jr. donated a six-acre lot in Falls Canyon, the current site of the elementary and high schools. A handful of students are bused from the Two Harbors coastal area of the interior, a 45-minute trip each way. A new,

announcer Gary Breckner was a familiar sight in Avalon, especially when the SS *Catalina* was about to dock. Radio shows consisted of random street interviews with vacationers or regular broadcasts of big-band music from the Casino. One of the world's first civilian microwave radio systems was installed in 1946, and in 1952 a 10,000-watt radio station, KBIG, was built in the interior of the Island.

CATALINA ISLANDER

Avalon's "number please" operators shortly before the system was abandoned for a high-tech system

red, one-room schoolhouse at Two Harbors run by the Long Beach School System makes it possible for kindergartners through fourth-graders (about 14 students) to be instructed close to home.

Reunions
Graduates have always considered themselves a special group of people, fortunate to have grown up in the homey, small-town atmosphere of Catalina Island. Class reunions are held regularly. The largest was held in 1982, open to all students who had ever attended Avalon schools. It was a tremendous turnout; 1,500 people of all ages came from around the world for a weekend of street parties, barbecues, picnics, and informal get-togethers. It culminated in a grand dinner dance at the Casino Ballroom. The proceeds were donated to the Avalon School to buy modern computer equipment. Businesses such as Eric's Hamburger Stand, an institution and student hangout on Pleasure

MUSIC AND STORIES

Many people impressed by Catalina's natural beauty have communicated this awareness in songs and stories. Al Jolson's "Avalon" continues to perpetuate the town's popularity, and in the '50s the Four Preps' popular "26 Miles Across the Sea" was heard repeatedly on pop radio stations. Catalina has inspired fictitious legends about Indians as well as contemporary stories. Even Leroi, the well-fed and much-loved town cat usually found napping in the sun on the Pleasure Pier, had his story written and published by Avalon author Elizabeth Grieson.

When determining the design of the Casino, William Wrigley Jr. imposed several restrictions before construction began: that Sugarloaf Rock on the point and Mrs. Wrigley's flower garden at the base of the cliff be preserved. The spit of land, being triangular in shape, dictated a circular building as the most logical. Wrigley envisioned a Moorish-style structure with a theater on the bottom level and a large ballroom above. Today the Casino stands alone. Sugarloaf Rock was ultimately removed during the construction.

Pier, dropped prices to the "old days" level. Treasured mementos such as old photos, school sweaters, yearbooks, athletic awards, and trophies were displayed in shop windows.

ISLAND LIVING TODAY

Life has its trade-offs, and the pleasant things about living on Catalina Island (besides its great beauty) may not all be measurable in the usual terms. Perhaps the nicest thing about Avalon is its small-town warmth combined with the bonus of the Island's natural beauty. Everyone knows everyone else. Some of the families on the Island trace their roots to the early settlers, and the Catalina Island Museum presents special certificates to longtime Island residents. Islanders value their history, and old-timers' memories are guarded carefully in taped interviews. In Avalon, social activities abound. Island moms don't become a taxi service (as on the Mainland) since the kids can walk everywhere they want to go. Crime is rare. When tragedy hits, the whole town rallies. And the most amazing thing is that all this is less than an hour from Los Angeles.

Of the one million people who travel to Santa Catalina Island every year, there are always a few who decide that this is the way of life they would like to pursue permanently. So the year-round population (about 2,500) of Avalon grows --but not rapidly. Housing is a major problem. Because the town is small, the number of dwellings is restricted, and the cost of housing is very high.

Only the Hardy Need Apply
The hardier pioneer types adapt to Island living, and it's a joy, but those people who aren't flexible should dismiss the thought. What one person considers an adventure could turn into a nightmare for another. Everything that is eaten, drunk, worn, built, or driven must be brought from the Mainland by barge. And though freight service is excellent 90% of the year, the barge is occasionally halted by a raging wind or an irate sea. Rarely do two days in a row go by, however, that the barge or boat can't make it. But when this does happen, grocery store shelves start to empty and the fresh milk and bread supply gets very low. There's no outgoing or incoming

mail, no Mainland newspapers, and of course if you happen to be on the Mainland, you're stuck there until the storm subsides. Sometimes the sea crashes over the beaches and rushes across the road and sidewalk on Crescent Avenue. In 1982, the ocean really flexed its muscles, tearing out part of the seawall around the Casino and almost destroying the road and boardwalk to Pebbly Beach.

Water: Troubles

Other times it's the rain that affects the Islanders --or the lack of it. Avalon depends *almost* entirely on rainfall for fresh water--75% is captured in dams and reservoirs before it runs into the sea. Another 25% comes from the ocean, converted by a high-tech desalination plant implemented in 1991. Thompson Reservoir holds 326 million gallons. Two pumping stations and eight miles of pipeline convey the water 800 feet up over "The Summit" and back down to Avalon town, where it is mixed with the desalinated water before delivery to consumers. During the drought years of 1977-78 and again in 1991-92, Islanders were forced to learn a new way of life. Each family was allowed to use only a given amount of water each month; after two warnings the Edison Company turned the family's water down to a dribble. This didn't happen to many, for most dealt with the water shortage effectively.

Five-minute Navy showers became the norm and faucets were never left to run for any chore.

Households learned the easiest ways to recycle their washing machine water--pumping or hand-dipping it into the garden. If toilets weren't already hooked up to a saltwater line, they were converted. All fire hoses use salt water, and during the drought the streets were hosed down with salt water. If one had a swimming pool and wanted to keep it filled, water was brought from the Mainland in huge tanks on a barge at the pool-owner's expense. These measures proved effective, and many Islanders have continued this frugality with water as a way of life.

Some years the skies open and water comes in a nonstop deluge. The streams get high, all the reservoirs fill to capacity, and overflow plays havoc with the interior roads. Children who live in any one of the many coves around the Island have to travel to and from school in Avalon by boat when interior roads wash out. Surprisingly, though houses in Avalon are built up the sides of the hills, not one has ever slid down, as in some Mainland areas.

Today, the Edison Company and modern technology have made water a little easier to come by with reservoirs and pumping stations, though water will always be a problem since its source is unpredictable Mother Nature.

Progress

New hotels and homes continue to spring up in the one-square-mile town. Vacationers now have the choice of newly built resorts or histori-

Bikes are a favorite way to get around.

OZ MALLAN

cal "quaint" and "charming" old inns--Avalon even offers a campground.

Most residents and visitors agree that the changes have greatly improved Avalon. But they have taken great care not to destroy the natural beauty of the bay, even though it's crowded most weekends with small and large boats. The harbor is kept clean, a project in which most boaters are happy to participate. The mountains surrounding the town are as beautiful as ever. Not now nor ever will there be buildings marring the natural rhythm of the rolling hills.

Transportation

In the past, few cars were kept on the Island. Most Islanders enjoyed the fact that they didn't need the extra expense. Instead they might keep a car parked on the Mainland for trips overtown.

As California has increased its love affair with the auto, more and more have been brought to the Island. The small town of Avalon can handle only so much traffic on its narrow streets, and parking is almost impossible. Finally, enough was enough. The city leaders decided that there must be a limit to the number of cars brought over (certainly some businesses *do* need vehicles). They developed a permit system and established a maximum number of cars allowed on the Island. The cars already on the Island were grandfathered into the system and given a permit. Then a list was begun, and anyone else who wished to bring a car had to wait until there was an opening in the numbers. Some folks have had to wait for years.

A Cart Cult

If you've been to the Island lately, you'll notice a more diminutive form of vehicle all over the town, the golf cart. Golf carts don't fall under the permit system, and as a result they have proliferated on the Island. They are not permitted on the roads out of town (which are all privately owned and maintained by the Catalina Conservancy). But for carrying the groceries home, and running around within the town limits they are great (cheap) transport--especially if you live on the top of East Whittley. Yes, parking is sometimes a problem, and a parking ticket will cost you about $30, so drivers beware.

Shopping

Avalon has a great selection of small shops that carry almost everything needed for day-to-day living. For TVs, refrigerators, large appliances, and furniture, buyers must go to the Mainland or order from a catalog such as J.C.Penney's. Goods cost more on the Island since everything must come over on the barge and freight costs are steep. Most Islanders believe, though, that the slight increase in price balances their diminished auto expenses. A few people *(very few)* go to the Mainland for groceries and haul them back to Catalina on the boat. (Some even refuse to pay freight charges. One man carried most of an automobile to the Island on the boat every week, piece by piece, hidden in boxes and suitcases. Eventually he did have to ship the motor and a few large parts, but he put his car together, content to have saved a lot of money.)

OZ MALLAN

Carts are used for everything.
Congratulations!

KATHY ESCOVEDO-SANDERS

EXPLORING AVALON

GETTING AROUND

Avalon town is small, just one square mile. It boasts clean, fresh air, broad walkways along the ocean with spectacular coastal views, and narrow, scenic streets up Mediterranean-like hillsides. Visitors often ask if they can bring their cars to the Island, and of course the answer is no. Islanders (with permits) ship them over on a barge. But there's plenty of public and private transportation, cart and bike rentals, and--always the best--your own two feet.

Walking
By far the most popular way to get around this small town is by foot. Many Islanders remember when autos were used only for business and deliveries. In those days the town guardians didn't think twice about barricading a street for a roller-skating party, since there wasn't enough traffic to hinder and no one ever complained.

During WW II part of Crescent Ave. was routinely closed off for Saturday night street dances for the servicemen stationed on the Island.

Most Avalon streets were built before cars were common transportation, so streets and sidewalks are narrow. Walking these delightful winding streets or alongside the clear blue water surrounding this smog-free island community remains a favorite pastime of visitors and residents alike.

Foot Traffic
A section of Crescent Ave., the main street that fronts the bay, is reserved for foot traffic (even dogs on leashes are not allowed). One side of the street is lined with shops, restaurants, sidewalk cafes, and small hotels, while the other parallels the beach and Pleasure Pier. Bikes also are not allowed.

Look out for cart traffic.

OZ MALLAN

Taxi

One taxi company operates within Avalon city limits: **Catalina Cab Company.** It runs year-round, with a stand on Crescent Ave. across from the Metropole Marketplace, and is easy to find. Several taxis meet each boat; rates run about $5 per couple and 50 cents for each additional member of your party. Many of the hotels offer free transport on the cabs, so check with your hotel when you make reservations; $5-7 will get you up most of the Avalon hills.

Bike Rentals

Brown's Bikes, at 107 Pebbly Beach Rd., tel. (310) 510-0986, charges $5 per hour, $12/full day for a single-speed bike, with five- and 18-speed bikes and tandems available. Ask about special group rentals, strollers, wheelchairs, and baby seats for the bikes. These bikes may not be taken out of the city limits.

Bring Your Own Bike

Each boat company handles bicycle portage in its own way. (See "Getting There.") Bikes are allowed on the roads of the interior but you must buy a bike permit for Conservancy insurance purposes. The $50 permit is valid for one year and available from the Catalina Conservancy at 125 Claressa Ave., tel. (310) 510-2595. Don't bother chancing it as Conservancy rangers and patrolling sheriff's deputies always check for permits.

If you go, be in shape, bring water, energy snacks or a picnic, and be ready for a wonderful biking experience. Trips to the Botanical Garden, Pebbly Beach, and the Casino make good rides for youngsters and adults.

Cart Rentals

Catalina Auto and Bike Rentals is on the corner of Metropole and Crescent, tel. (310) 510-0111. You can drive within the city limits only; Botanical Garden and Pebbly Beach are within the city limits. Others are **Island Rentals,** 125 Pebbly Beach Rd., tel. (310) 510-1456, or **Cartopia Car Rental,** 615 Crescent Ave., which rents electric golf-type carts for about $30 per hour with a $30 deposit.

KATHY ESCOVEDO-SANDERS

WALKING TOURS OF AVALON

SHORT WALKS

In Avalon strike out on foot. Avalon is a small town with attractive narrow streets to explore and many architecturally unusual houses to view. Some stand on the original 20-foot-wide lots laid out by George Shatto in the late 1800s. Land is scarce in Avalon and property values have skyrocketed over the years, so landowners have remodeled to garner every possible inch of living space. About half the homes are built on the level streets just up from the Pleasure Pier, called the "flats" by the Islanders, while the other half climb the hills, giving Avalon a sunny Mediterranean-island appearance. On these walking tours you'll discover homes built before there were many roads in Avalon; a few streets become flights of stairs straight uphill to the front door.

Take your camera, your *Guide To Catalina Island,* water, a hat, and sunscreen. Wear your walking shoes and be prepared for a few steep climbs.

Golf Course/Catalina Stable/Botanical Garden

From downtown, walk up Sumner Ave. and follow it to the left of Country Club Road. Pass the golf course on the left, and take the left "V" when you come to the Sand Trap Restaurant. Continue past the Catalina Stables and you see what used to be the old Bird Park. Just beyond the picnic grounds lies the graded dirt road to the Botanical Garden. This easy hike takes about an hour each way, depending on how many times you stop to smell the roses, or in this case, admire the many species of cactus.

Whittley Walk

From Crescent Ave. on the shoreline start up Whittley. Turn left at East Whittley, the first street you come to, and follow its steep curve up around to the right. As you walk up East Whittley you pass several small houses; the second from the corner on the right was built in 1903 for $500 and is still occupied by the Trout family, descendants of the 1911 owners. Originally the

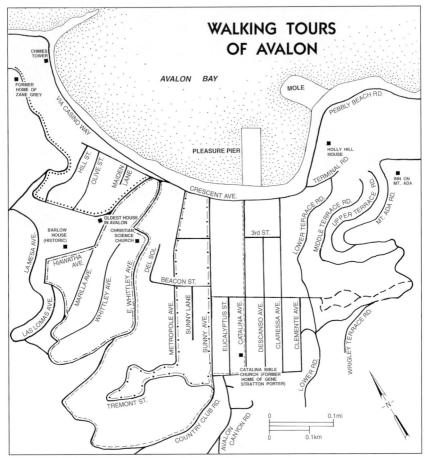

WALKING TOURS OF AVALON

AVALON BAY

CHIMES TOWER

FORMER HOME OF ZANE GREY

VIA CASINO WAY

MOLE

PEBBLY BEACH RD.

PLEASURE PIER

HOLLY HILL HOUSE

TERMINAL RD.

INN ON MT. ADA

HILL ST.

OLIVE ST.

MAIDEN LANE

CRESCENT AVE.

OLDEST HOUSE IN AVALON

CHRISTIAN SCIENCE CHURCH

BARLOW HOUSE (HISTORIC)

LA MESA AVE.

HIAWATHA AVE.

MARILLA AVE.

WHITTLEY AVE.

E. WHITTLEY AVE.

DEL SOL

3rd ST.

LOWER TERRACE RD.

MIDDLE TERRACE RD.

UPPER TERRACE RD.

MT. ADA RD.

LAS LOMAS AVE.

BEACON ST.

METROPOLE AVE.

SUNNY LANE

SUNNY AVE.

EUCALYPTUS ST.

CATALINA AVE.

DESCANSO AVE.

CLARESSA AVE.

CLEMENTE AVE.

LOWER RD.

WRIGLEY TERRACE RD.

TREMONT ST.

CATALINA BIBLE CHURCH (FORMER HOME OF GENE STRATTON PORTER)

COUNTRY CLUB RD.

AVALON CANYON RD.

0   0.1mi
0   0.1km

-N-

little house was built on one of the small lots leased from Banning's SCI Company. When Whittley St. was widened, the house next door on the corner of Whittley and East Whittley was moved eight feet and pushed right up under the eaves of the Trout house. After Wrigley bought the Island, the Trouts were able to buy the land beneath their house.

Farther on your right you come to the Christian Science church and a Spanish-style house with a red-tile roof. Both were built by a devout Christian Scientist, Count Mankowski, an avid fisherman who loved Catalina. The count was married to an American woman named Morris; though of Polish descent the count was a British citizen who enjoyed summers on Catalina. The church next door was built at the same time and in the same Spanish style as his classic home; he kept his horses across the street in a stable that overlooked the bay. The stable has been replaced by a modern apartment building.

Continue to the top of the hill, from where East Whittley curves to your right and then turn left over to Marilla Ave. downhill. Follow Marilla a short distance to Hiawatha Ave. on the left

top: Cherry Cove, Catalina's west end, bottom: Wrigley's Rancho Escondido

top left: cruising to Avalon, top right: Little Harbor, Catalina
bottom: Avalon Bay

ready to explore Catalina

OZ MALLAN

and up another short street, where you'll come to the Barlow House with its wide circular porch. From Hiawatha Ave., look back toward the hills to see Camino Del Monte, built by Philip Wrigley and still the family home.

Barlow House

In the early 1900s a circus act called the Travillo Brothers came to Catalina Island on a talent hunt for a new team member. The search took them to Seal Rocks off the east end of the Island, where the California sea lion hauling ground was mobbed with potential ball-bouncing circus stars. While on the Island the family quickly decided to settle in Catalina. The Travillos built the charming circular house in 1906. Their sea lions trained in the yard overlooking Avalon town. Mrs. Travillo started a gift shop on Crescent Ave. and sold abalone shells provided by her diver sons, Ford, Jack, and Guy. They were also among the avid coin divers who would meet the boat and shout, "Throw a coin!" These divers could hold a mouthful, and actually had a lucrative business going.

The family sold the house to an opera singer who spent her summers on the Island, and she in turn sold it to Mr. Feek, principal of the local school. In 1923, Sarah C. Smith bought the house. It has remained in her family ever since. The family used it as a summer home until 1973, when Sarah's daughter, Liz Barlow, retired from her teaching career and moved to Catalina. This elegant home, designated as a Historical House, will be preserved in its gracious turn-of-the-century style for future generations to appreciate. From here Hiawatha soon completes its angular half circle to meet Marilla Ave., from where you return to Crescent Ave., your starting point.

Casino/Descanso Beach

Walking to the Casino is a pleasant, easy walk on flat ground, with just a slight rise as you approach the Casino. The walkway passes through the Via Casino Way, winds its way just above the rocks and water past the boats in the harbor just a stone's throw away, past the Tuna Club and the Yacht Club. An occasional bench scattered along the walkway offers a great location to enjoy a morning sunrise over the bay. This is also a good place for tidepooling at really low tide. Climb over the fence and onto the rocks, study the tidy, almost empty pools, and you'll see tiny bits of marine life. These are very fragile organisms and it's best to just look.

Once at the Casino, enjoy the dynamic architecture and artwork. Walk around the building and past the fuel dock and Shipwreck Joey's (a great little open air cafe); note the divers. Just over the wall, down the rocks, and into the water, you'll find the Catalina Underwater Park, where thousands of people learn to dive each year. (For more details about the Casino structure and its history, see "Casino Point" under "Avalon Sights.")

To Descanso Canyon

From the entrance of the Casino, continue walking toward Descanso Bay, another beautiful cove where you'll find an outdoor cafe and bar. This bay has a colorful history: it's the site of Hancock Banning's family home built in 1896, and then the site of the St. Catherine Hotel from 1917-1966. Feel free to use the beach, swim, stop for lunch, and explore the few remaining bits of the old hotel. If you hike up the canyon on the north side, you'll eventually come to a lookout from where you can see into the next cove, Hamilton Cove, and its dozens of condos. Hamilton was at one time the site of the original seaplane terminal.

Zane Grey Home

This walk takes you above the Casino building for another spectacular view of Avalon and the bay. From Crescent Ave. head up Marilla Avenue. Turn right on Vieudelou and follow the curve to Chimes Tower Road. Before you arrive at the Chimes you pass on your left the Zane Grey Hotel, built in 1926 by Zane Grey, big-game fisherman and famed Western novelist. This Hopi Indian pueblo-style home fit the rough-and-ready lifestyle of its remarkable owner. The living and dining room, graced by a fireplace with a log mantel, has open-beam ceilings shaped from teak brought from Tahiti aboard Grey's yacht, *The Fisherman*. An oak dining table with heavy benches, a grand piano,

and other massive furnishings still grace the home. Zane Grey spent most of his later life in Avalon writing and fishing. As he said about Catalina in *What the Open Means to Me*:

> *"I used to climb the mountain trail that overlooked the Pacific and here a thousand times I shut my eyes and gave myself over to sensorial perceptions. . . . It is an environment that means enchantment to me. Sea and mountain! Breeze and roar of surf! . . I could write here and be at peace."*

Born Pearl Zane Grey in Zanesville, Ohio, in 1872, Zane Grey wrote 89 books before he died in 1939 at age 67.

Chimes Tower/Hogsback/Gate

This walk is more strenuous and steeper than many of the walks described in this section and will take several hours. Head up Marilla Ave. between the El Encanto and Ristorante Villa Portofino on Crescent. Turn up Vieudelou (to the right) and as you do, look at the house on the corner to your left; it's the oldest house on Catalina, surviving the fire of 1915 that destroyed almost everything else along the front edge of town. As you wind around, you'll pass Zane Grey Pueblo, now a great little bed and breakfast. Farther up and across Zane Grey Rd. stands the Chimes Tower. Manufactured by the

Catalina stable

OZ MALLAN

Deagan Company in Chicago at a cost of $25,000, these chimes have been tolling the time every 15 minutes since 1925, when they were presented as a gift to the town of Avalon by Mrs. Ada Wrigley. On holidays and special occasions the electric console is played manually, the resonance blending with the surrounding harbor-sounds to create a cadence unique to Catalina. From this spot, looking across the bay you'll have a good view of the Holly Hill House on the southeast tip of Avalon Bay. You can't miss its conical roof.

Be careful on this road; it's narrow and becomes one way here, with buses coming down hill from the interior as you proceed uphill. You'll come to a good viewing area from where you can see Descanso Beach, surrounded by the countryside of Catalina. The road meanders and winds and ultimately you'll come to to a stucco wall, dotted with colorful tiles. This is an electronic gate, and only drivers with plastic gate passes can proceed farther. Hikers are welcome to pass through and to hike into the interior, but they must first obtain hiking permits from the Conservancy Office (permits are free), 125 Claressa. This road continues to the summit and has been used for decades, beginning with the original tour groups--in stagecoaches. You return the same way. The views from along here are lovely and include the first green of the golf course.

Pebbly Beach/Mt. Ada Walk

This is a good early-morning stroll. Walk to and past the mole where the passenger boats dock, and continue on Pebbly Beach Rd. along the ocean, where you'll meet other early risers--fishermen, walkers, and joggers. The sun rises here and it's a sparkling, invigorating walk past Abalone Point with its cluster of tall pointy rocks and on past Lovers Cove Beach, a nice place to stop and watch the fish splashing out of the water looking for breakfast. Lovers Cove is a fish preserve, and snorkeling and swimming only are allowed. No scuba diving or fishing, thank you.

Continue past Pebbly Beach, where you'll see a small heliport and the Island Express Helicopter office, plus a cement ramp for landing amphibious planes. Lots of traffic flies in and out of this little airport. A special amphibian

oldest house in Avalon

brings in freight, and passenger-carrying helicopters land here throughout the day. Stop for breakfast (or lunch or dinner) at the Buffalo Nickel Restaurant. If you're a plane buff, the rooftop patio offers a great vantage point from which to watch the helicopters come and go. Meals are served inside or on the outside patio (you can get buffalo burgers here). You'll find public restrooms on the other side of the patio.

The Southern California Edison Company maintains its desalination and utility plant in Pebbly Beach, and about a dozen families live across the road. The freight office is out here, as are the docks where the barges bring in most everything to the Island.

Past the houses the road turns up the hill and eventually meanders by the former home of William Wrigley Jr. In 1919, after the Wrigleys bought the Island, they chose Mt. Ada, 350 feet above the bay, for their future home. The story goes that Mrs. Wrigley (Ada) determined that from here she could see the sun rise and set with the purple hills of Avalon as a backdrop. The house was built in 1921, with only the immediate area around the structure landscaped. (At night well-positioned floodlights turn the building into a floating white mansion against the black hillside.)

In 1978, the family donated the estate to the University of Southern California for use as an academic and cultural center. Managed by the university's Institute for Marine and Coastal Studies, seminars and workshops were held here year-round for such groups as the U.S. Geological Survey, the U.S. Office of Naval Research, and other organizations from many parts of the world. Everyone who stayed fell in love with it. Why not? Today, Wrigley's home is a fabulous bed and breakfast called **The Inn on Mt. Ada.** For the lazies who don't hike, the Avalon Scenic Tour passes Mt. Ada (see "Guided Tours," below).

Mount Buena Vista

While walking, look across the street and below the front entrance steps to Mt. Ada. A large white cross stands on the side of the hill. At one time Mt. Buena Vista was the location of a park and terminus of an old incline railway, called Island Mountain Railway. The little railroad operated two cars: one going from the amphitheater (today the city park at the end of Crescent Ave.) to the summit at Buena Vista, and one descending from the summit to Lovers Cove. It

small houses of Catalina

was built in 1904 and dismantled in 1920.

For more than 60 consecutive years the Islanders have presented the colorful costumed

Hogsback gate to the interior

OZ MALLAN

Easter sunrise pageant on Buena Vista. If you happen to be in Avalon on Easter, the city provides free bus service to the hill site from downtown on Easter morning (ask the chamber of commerce for time and details). To return to Crescent Ave. from Buena Vista, continue walking down the hill as it winds around and you'll end up on lower Clemente St. a half block from Crescent Avenue. You'll pass some of the original condos built in Avalon. The views from Buena Vista and Mt. Ada of the bay, the town, the harbor, and the purple mountains are breathtaking.

Tremont Street
From Crescent Ave. turn up Sumner Ave., continue to the end, and turn right onto Tremont Street. On your left you pass newly built rental condos and a few of the original stucco "ranchitos" built by William Wrigley Jr. for the many

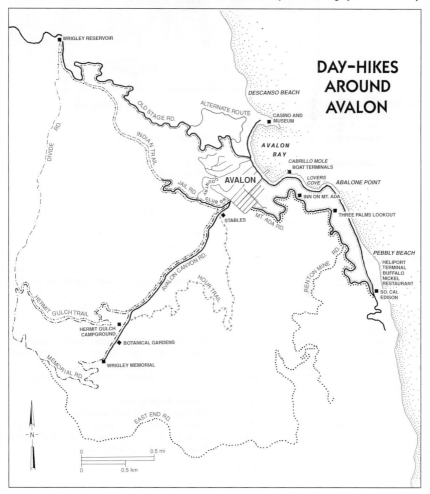

DAY-HIKES
AROUND
AVALON

WRIGLEY RESERVOIR

OLD STAGE RD.

DESCANSO BEACH

ALTERNATE ROUTE

CASINO AND
MUSEUM

INDIAN TRAIL

DIVIDE RD.

AVALON
BAY

CABRILLO MOLE
BOAT TERMINALS

JAIL RD.

CLUB DR.

AVALON

LOVERS
COVE

ABALONE POINT

INN ON MT. ADA

STABLES

MT. ADA RD.

THREE PALMS LOOKOUT

AVALON CANYON RD.

HOUR TRAIL

RENTON MINE RD.

PEBBLY BEACH

HELIPORT
TERMINAL
BUFFALO
NICKEL
RESTAURANT

SO. CAL
EDISON

HERMIT GULCH TRAIL

HERMIT GULCH
CAMPGROUND

BOTANICAL GARDENS

MEMORIAL RD.

WRIGLEY MEMORIAL

EAST END RD.

-N-

0   0.5 mi
0   0.5 km

seeing the interior of Catalina

SCI CO.

Mexican families that he hired to help with the development of the Island. Turn left on Metropole (another steep incline), following the hill down to Crescent Avenue.

Country Club Road Walk

From Crescent Ave. walk up Catalina Street. In the second block on the left you pass the Catalina Bible Church. This building was the home of author Gene Stratton Porter, born in 1868 in Indiana. Two of her national best-sellers were *Freckles* and *Laddie*. Ms. Porter spent several summers in her home, called Singing Waters, before she died in a traffic accident in 1924.

At the end of Catalina St. turn right past Avalon Canyon Rd. and go left up Country Club Road. Continue on this road, which wanders past the Country Club (once the social hub of the Island), putting green, golf pro shop, tennis courts, tee-off area for the first golf green across the road below. This is a good place to stop for a cool drink from the Pro Shop.

Farther on is the turnoff for the cemetery on the left. Country Club Rd., bordered by dozens of eucalyptus trees, takes you past the large, pleasant Catalina Canyon Hotel. Turn left on East Whittley, continue down, and veer to the right on Whittley, which ends at Crescent Avenue.

DAY HIKES

In most cases these are a little more strenuous and longer. Trails take you short distances out of town, and some backtrack on the same trails; others meander a circular route. Hike with a companion and bring water since it's not available on the trail. Note that the trails are marked on the **Day-Hikes Around Avalon** map.

Jail Road/Indian Trail to Stage Road

This walk runs along fire roads, most involving steep slopes. It climbs to 1,460 feet and a spectacular vantage point. From here you can see the Island's rugged coastline and, when Mainland smog doesn't interfere, the San Gabriel Mountains across the channel. It's a strenuous hike.

Hermit Gulch Trail/Canyon Road/Divide Road

These steep slopes on undeveloped pathways combine for a strenuous hike: five hours for a good hiker, with little shade along the way.

Renton Mine Road/
Mt. Ada Road to East Mountain

Expect moderate to steep slopes along a graded dirt road for a strenuous hike; plan about three hours for the hardy hiker.

AVALON SIGHTS

CASINO POINT

History

Since prehistory, a large, loaf-shaped rock has jutted into the sea, the Bay of the Seven Moons curving around it in a gentle crescent. Though the profile and name have changed, from this spot once known as Sugarloaf Point you can clearly see the hills of the Mainland on a crystalline day.

A Second Sugarloaf

In the 1890s, the Banning brothers tried to blast a tunnel between Avalon Bay and Descanso Bay (at that time known as Banning Cove). The cove was to be the site of the Bannings' home and the tunnel through Sugarloaf Point would provide easy access. The Banning house was built in the cove in 1895; the tunnel collapsed in 1906. What appeared to be a setback provided a firm foundation for a new road that followed the coastline from Casino Point to Descanso Bay. The collapse of the tunnel, the first of several changes to the skyline at the Point, left two distinct rock formations instead of one: Big Sugarloaf and Little Sugarloaf.

Big Sugarloaf Bites the Dust

In the devastating fire of 1915, many of Avalon's premier buildings were destroyed. One of the victims was the large, gracious Hotel Metropole on Crescent Avenue, then considered one of the finest hotels in Southern California. By 1917, the Metropole had yet to be rebuilt. The Bannings decided to level Big Sugarloaf and build the new hotel in its place. They blasted the rock completely away with black powder--a tricky demolition job in those times. After removing the last of the rock in 1918, they finally built the long-awaited hotel, called the St. Catherine--not on Sugarloaf Point but in Banning Cove (renamed Descanso Bay). At that time, Little Sugarloaf was still a landmark for sailors because they could see it from great distances. It had a

treacherously steep stairway, built in 1896, where enterprising Island boys offered a steady arm (for 25 cents) to the less hardy who wished to climb to the peak. And it was the favored place to shoot off fireworks on the Fourth of July.

More Construction

Builders next altered the Point in 1920 with the addition of the "Sugarloaf Casino" (not to be confused with the present-day Casino). The Sugarloaf was an octagonal, steel-framed stucco building surrounded by a large wood-planked deck. The dance floor, large enough for 250 couples, was also used as a roller-skating rink. One of its two wings once housed a Chinese Tea Room, and it housed an elementary school until the Falls Canyon School was completed in 1925.

Ocean Access

In 1921, a freight wharf was added on the Avalon side of the Point. Shortly after, a ramp and float were installed to receive passengers flying into Avalon from Wilmington on Curtiss Flying Boats and bimotored Sikorskys. The landings continued until 1931, when the Hamilton Beach Amphibian Airport was completed.

The "New" Casino

The destiny of Sugarloaf Point was decided in 1928, when William Wrigley Jr. chose it as the location for a mammoth new casino. The smaller Sugarloaf Casino was dismantled and its octagonal steel frame was placed well up into Avalon Canyon to become the world's largest birdcage, subsequently expanding into the Catalina Bird Park. In March 1929, builders blasted away the last of Little Sugarloaf, and the spectacular new Casino began to take shape. The years have brought other changes. Landfill provided a parking lot. During WW II a battery of antiaircraft guns was mounted there and a large wooden armory was constructed. Merchant seaman trainees practiced maneuvers on a wooden ship's bow that had been built on the wharf. It was quite common to see the *gleeps* (as the Islanders called the trainees) marching in their white or navy-blue uniforms along the Casino Road. The wartime buildings have since been removed.

Note: When some people hear the word *casino,* they immediately think of gambling. That's not the case in Catalina--no gambling here!

Diving Bell
In 1951, a diving bell became the new attraction on the Point. Viewers descended in a metal tank pierced with small windows that looked out upon darting fish and undulating giant brown kelp in the clear waters. The bell was removed 10 years later, though divers continue to enjoy exploring in this underwater park.

Storms
In 1964, the seawall was reinforced and a short breakwater was built with rocks from the Pebbly Beach quarry. It protects Avalon during the northeastern storms each winter. The Catalina Channel can turn vicious on occasion. In February 1982, Casino Point bore the fury of one of the worst storms ever recorded on the Island. All through the night the ocean crashed repeatedly over the seawall and breakwater, tearing away giant chunks of concrete and hurling them as though they were toy blocks. Fortunately, outside of some water seepage in the lower-level rooms, the Casino--staid lady of Avalon--suffered no harm.

THE CASINO BUILDING

The Casino is much the same as the day it was completed in 1929. The years have proved it a sturdy monument to the builders of the past. Large enough to hold Catalina's entire year-round population, it is the city's civil-defense shelter. Stored in its many corners and caverns are enough water and emergency supplies to last two weeks.

The Casino has become a landmark. Its image *is* Catalina. It gleams white against the sea in the brilliant sunshine and at night lights create dramatic shadows on its walls.

Building the Casino was a tremendous engineering feat. Designed by Los Angeles architects Walter Webber and Sumner A. Spaulding, the Mediterranean design with Moorish Alhambra influences won a special award from the American Institute of Architects in 1930. A cantilevered structure, its two 178-foot girders weighing 50 tons each span the building at right angles. Steel and concrete columns and beams support most of the weight of the roof and all floor weight except that of the ballroom. The exterior buttresses carry a vertical load. With its 40-foot-deep foundation, 100,000 sacks of cement and 25,000 yards of concrete, it's a monolith that has already stood for more than 50 years, and it will continue its constant vigil over Avalon Bay for years to come.

Avalon Theater
The main floor of the Casino holds the Avalon Theater, the Catalina Island Museum, and the art gallery. The movie theater was designed in the late '20s, about the time "talking pictures" were introduced. Though Wrigley, along with most, didn't have much faith in the success of the talkies, he insisted on perfect acoustics for the theater's sound system. His system was so well-designed that in 1931, when the Radio City Music Hall was being built in New York City, engineers involved in that project visited the Island to study the acoustics of the Avalon Theater.

A large Page organ was installed in the theater to provide musical accompaniment to the silent movies that soon faded into the past. Still, the Page was used for several years to add drama and excitement to early talkies shown in the Casino. Organ music itself was popular entertainment in the '20s and '30s, and organists gave free concerts every day in the summer.

Today, the Page organ has great historical value. During the spring of 1979, six men from the Los Angeles Chapter of the American Theatre Organ Society performed the tedious, time-consuming task of replacing leather and felt parts that had been gnawed away by mice who lived in the vast mechanism of the organ during its many years of nonuse. They repaired electrical connections and gave the organ a general overhaul for the 50th anniversary of the Casino when, once again, the organ came to full vibrant life. This full-scale pipe organ has 16 ranks of pipes, with 73-85 pipes per rank. Manufactured in Germany, the pipes are made of lead, tin, zinc, and wood. The largest pipe measures 16 feet and the shortest is one-quarter inch long.

Today's Theater

The grand-scale art-deco murals in the auditorium have survived intact for nearly seven decades. They were designed and sketched in 1929 by John Gabriel Beckman a well-known young artist who also painted Grauman's Chinese Theater in Hollywood. He went on to become an art director for Columbia Studios. In 1986, Beckman, was commissioned to complete the tile mural along the box office wall. He had originally designed it in 1929, but it was never finished. More than 60 years later the tile was set. Today it's considered one of the finest examples of Art Deco in the world; in 1929 critics called the work "futuristic." Motifs include hooded friars, exotic birds and flowers, leaping goats, a waterfall, and elegant monkeys. These theater walls have an intrinsic history and value, which is probably why they have never been replaced or painted over.

Although the theater was primarily designed to show movies, many live stage productions have also been performed. During WW II, the theater was used as a classroom for merchant seamen and for USO shows, alive with Hollywood's finest stars: Bob Hope, Alice Faye, Kate Smith, Danny Kaye, and Spike Jones, to name a few. Boxing was a weekly event for the servicemen, along with band concerts and radio shows. Today, community groups use the theater regularly for local entertainment, as do convention groups from all over. The theater shows a first-run single feature twice nightly during the summer, at 7 p.m. and at about 9:30 p.m.; admission is adult $7, child $3.

The Catalina Island Museum

This growing museum is well worth visiting. The history of Catalina Island is its primary area of interest. Its displays of Indian artifacts from various parts of the Island chronicle the history of Catalina from the days of earliest Indian habitation. See photographs from the 1880s and watch videos of Island events. The entrance to the museum, in the Casino's bottom level, is on the south side of the building.

The Museum Society is a private, nonprofit corporation. It conducts research, offers free lectures on Island-related topics, stages slide shows with taped commentary, and organizes tours of the historical Holly Hill House. Membership is invited; donations and other financial support (tax-deductible) are welcomed. For more information write to Catalina Island Museum, Box 366, Avalon, CA 90704, tel. (310) 510-2414.

The museum is open daily 10:30 a.m.-4 p.m. year-round; admission is $1.50 adults, $1 seniors, children 6-11 50 cents, under 5 free.

Catalina Art Gallery

Next to the museum, also on the lower level, is the entrance to the Catalina Art Gallery, admission free. The exhibits, which change frequently, represent Island and visiting artists. The active Catalina Art Association initiated the Art Festival more than 20 years ago. Held in late September, this event has since become one of the most prestigious art festivals in Southern California and beyond. The association invites award-winning artists to take part in the judging, and it awards cash prizes for the best art entered. The streets of Avalon become an outdoor gallery hosting an array of international artists and art enthusiasts, and the town is proud to boast many prize-winning local artists. For more information, write to the Catalina Art Association, Box 235, Avalon, CA 90704.

Ballroom

The top floor of this Moorish-flavored structure is the world-famous Casino ballroom, scene of massive crowds during the golden era of the big bands. In those days the big white steamer SS *Catalina* carried thousands of passengers to the Island to hear such greats as Benny Goodman, Jan Garber, and Kay Kyser. Designed to give the largest unobstructed dancing area possible, the engineering allowed for 20,000 square feet of dance floor. Built to accommodate 1,500 couples, it very often did. The dance floor is surrounded by a 14-foot open balcony that provides a romantic setting from which to view the lights of town at night. In 1929, when the Casino opened, it offered only sodas and ice-cream sundaes at the bar; even after Prohibition was repealed, Wrigley's attitude that Avalon would

WRIGLEY MEMORIAL AND BOTANICAL GARDEN

The Wrigley monument sits at the head of the canyon like a crown. Walk through the entire Garden. If it is early enough, and with luck, you might be the only one there to enjoy lilting birdsong, the sonnet of the hawk, a skittering squirrel, and brilliant colors of wax-like cactus blossoms. The variety of cactus and trees within the 38 acres of garden are myriad.

Investigate the structure, climb the stairs into the monument. Within the building, designs are of the same art deco motif as that in the Casino. Look for the same sleek running deer, here, carved in stone. Ornate grid-work creates a multi-paned window peering over the grounds.

A smooth circular marble floor, rounded steps, and subtle colors blend with desert-like surroundings.

If you're a fan of cactus flowers, visit in March-April when the blossoms are vivid. Although something is in bloom year round; you'll be amazed at the variety. Still another fine Catalina hike; take a picnic, or just enjoy the tranquillity.

Hardy hikers: just behind the memorial building is a path that takes you up to the top of the divide. From here you'll have a marvelous view of the mountains falling dramatically into the ocean, with the open sea beyond.

provide wholesome entertainment for the entire family continued to prevail. It was not until immediately after WW II that the Casino ballroom began serving liquor.

In 1987, the Casino ballroom was refurbished: new paint, new carpet, new drapes, a new stage, and new kitchen. It is also run by the Santa Catalina Island Company, which encourages the public (both on the Mainland and in Avalon) to rent the ballroom for the evening or afternoon for weddings, receptions, banquets, dances, or other private events. For more information, call (310) 510-2444. Catering is available.

Building Maintenance

Maintenance of the Casino is a major expense of the Santa Catalina Island Company. During peak season, it uses about 570,000 gallons of water and as much as 66,000 kilowatts of electricity per month. A resident maintenance man lives in an apartment at the top of the east wing. Only three families have occupied this apartment since 1929. Bill Bowman was the early maintenance man from 1929 to 1947.

Next, Dale Eisenhut was hired as the electrical engineer. He and his wife, Donna, moved in with their three young daughters. The giant building--as unusual a home to grow up in as one could imagine--became the romping backdrop for the unfolding lives and energies of growing kids. These little girls tricycled around a balcony, which by night metamorphosed into a splendid promenade filled with romance-minded young couples. The girls added a bit of excitement as they grew up; they made an occasional attempt at "tightrope" walking across a 10-story-high balustrade, and with the passing years the roar of their motorcycles was frequently heard as they climbed the broad indoor ramps to the front door of the Eisenhut apartment.

Today, Billy Delbert holds the position. One important duty is the special cleaning and waxing of the decades-old dance floor. Not only has the floor been constantly maintained, but it also has been enhanced by continuous use. The late Dale Eisenhut commented that the floor was the cleanest and brightest he'd ever seen after a crowd of 4,835 people had danced on it all evening.

WRIGLEY MEMORIAL AND BOTANICAL GARDEN

A Man and His Island

William Wrigley Jr. maintained his enthusiasm for Catalina Island from his first visit in 1919 until his death in 1932. He generously spent millions for the development of the Island and put his energies into many projects many that are still an important part of the Island's culture. After his death, the Santa Catalina Island Company built an imposing memorial to honor him at the head of Avalon Canyon.

The Wrigley Memorial and Botanical Garden, including the site of the memorial, covers almost 38 acres.

Getting There

It's a 1.7-mile walk up a gentle incline from downtown Avalon to the Botanical Garden. The road leads past the golf course and the Hermit Gulch Campground. A tram operates between the Island Plaza and the Botanical Garden, $5 RT.

Admission into the Botanical Garden is free for children under 12, and for anyone who belongs to the Wrigley Memorial Foundation. For all other visitors the charge is $1. If you're interested in joining the Wrigley Memorial Foundation, write P.O. Box 88, Avalon, CA 90704, tel. (310) 510-2288.

The Monument

Wrigley's memorial was built mostly from native Catalina materials. A graceful lookout tower, it stands 232 feet wide, 180 feet deep, and 130 feet high from the bottom of its wide circular stairway to the top of its main 80-foot tower. Climb the stairs for a stunning view of the Botanical Garden that spreads across the canyon floor below. The now-defunct Catalina tile production plant initiated by Wrigley made the red roof tiles and the colorful handmade glazed tiles used for the interior. Blue flagstones from Little Harbor surface the ramp and both terraces of the tower. Pink and green marble was brought from the state of Georgia only because it had the coloration to provide the desired finishing effects. At one time Wrigley's body was entombed here, but it has since been moved.

KATHY ESCOVEDO-SANDERS

The Garden

Mrs. Wrigley began planting a garden of cactus and succulents in picturesque Avalon Canyon shortly after 1919. In 1969, the Wrigley Memorial Garden Foundation undertook to expand and revitalize the garden; it has since grown into a botanical showcase attracting visitors, researchers, students, and teachers. It's a living laboratory for the study of plants endemic to Catalina. It also provides a thriving natural habitat for study of how certain plants may be used to ecological advantage. Hundreds of plant species are available for your inspection.

Botanical Studies

All eight known plants endemic to Catalina grow in the garden's collection. In addition, a number of special plants from Santa Rosa, San Clemente, and other California Channel Islands, many of them extremely rare, have been planted in recent years. The garden includes an herbarium, an area for students to study the herbarium specimens, and an excellent research library.

Note: An herbarium is a collection of dried plant specimens usually mounted and arranged for reference.

Education and Display Center

Groups gather in this small open theater, where an informative video plays automatically throughout the day. Naturalists conduct seminars on the flora of the Island and the garden. Catalina Conservancy naturalists escort the Nature Walk, an informative stroll through the garden and Memorial. The Nature Walk is free, lasts about one-and-a-half hours, and departs from the entrance of the Wrigley Memorial Botanical Gardens Tuesday and Saturday at 10:15 a.m. If you wish to double-check the schedule, call (310) 510-2595 ext. 100 or ext. 108.

HOLLY HILL HOUSE

From almost anywhere on the bay you can see the Holly Hill House perched on the hillside above the mole; look for its conical roof. In 1888, a remarkable man named Peter Gano bought what some consider to be the choicest parcel of land in Avalon from George Shatto for $500. An engineer with extensive experience in waterworks, Gano generously offered to design Avalon's first freshwater system, laying pipe from Avalon Canyon Springs to the only large building at that time, the Metropole Hotel. He shipped building supplies from the Mainland to Avalon aboard his boat, the *Osprey*. His only helper on the project was Mercury, a former circus horse that performed the heavy labor of this monumental task. Gano designed an ingenious cable-car system to carry his equipment up the steep incline to the top of the hill. Mercury, on whistle command, walked down the hill, pulling ropes wound around pulleys to power the loaded cable car up the hill to the building site. Gano also laid water pipes directly to his home site and designed a three-cistern system to catch rainfall. He was a craftsman who took great pride in his work, building the house to last with strong, durable materials. The open-air circular cupola patio with the cone-shaped roof captures the attention of everyone who visits the Island. And living in the house must be an even greater pleasure; every window opens to beautiful vistas of the sea and Avalon town.

This remarkable man has a bittersweet legend associated with his name. Fable tells us that he labored on the house for the love of a lady. But when it was completed, she couldn't bring herself to give up Mainland society for life in a small seaside village--even in a fabulous house built for entertaining. She told Gano it was either her or the house. Convinced she would change her mind, he chose the house--naming it **Look Out Cottage.** The battle of wills ended when ultimately she married another, leaving Gano to live alone in his hand-built masterpiece until very old age. Old-timers who were children during Gano's time tell of signs posted around his house that stated bluntly, No Women Allowed.

The house has had four owners since it was completed in 1890. The Giddings family bought it from Gano in 1921, renamed it Holly Hill House for the abundant holly that grew on the hill, and for the next 40 years spent summers in Avalon. In 1971, the Smiths, along with the Richard Land Company, bought it with the intention of developing the property below the house into condominiums. Excavation began, destabilizing the foundation of the house. Extensive steel, concrete and Gunite repairs made the hill safe again, but the condos were never built. Soon after the repairs were completed a fire destroyed the cupola roof.

Victor, frequent visitor to Catalina and longtime admirer of this Victorian house on the hill, bought Holly Hill House in 1971. Victor's first project was to rebuild the cupola; since then he and his family have been involved in an energetic restoration program. In an ongoing project, they study old photos and painstakingly approach every detail with the original Gano house in mind. They have replaced modern improvements from earlier renovations with antique or old-style carpentry and appliances. They have stripped the woodwork and brought it back to its original luster; they have brought in furniture of the era--the family uses a 1907 gas stove in the 1890s kitchen. Visiting this house is a trip into the past. Contact the Catalina Museum, Box 366, Avalon, CA 90704, tel. (310) 510-2414, for information about special group tours (admission charged) that docents frequently conduct to benefit the Catalina Museum.

underway on the Blanche W

OZ MALLAN

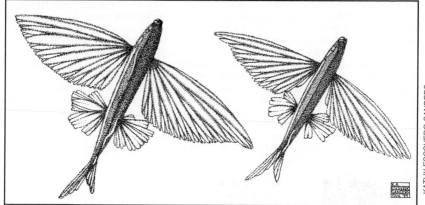

KATHY ESCOVEDO-SANDERS

GUIDED TOURS

DISCOVERY TOURS

Santa Catalina Island Company's Discovery Tours offers a variety of guided tours for the visitor who wants to see as much of the Island as possible in a short time. You can wander the hills and interior on foot, but it's a big island-- 76 square miles. For most visitors these tours are the only opportunity to see the Island's interior and its distant coves. The roomy motorstage is comfortable, the boats are fun, and the guides are witty, well-versed, and pleasant.

Many of these drivers/guides have been driving the interior roads for many years. They know every curve, and in some cases wildlife waits for them to stop and throw a doughnut or two: for a few years a wild pig waited at the same spot every day and was duly rewarded, and now a hungry raven soars over a wide spot in the road until the bus and its treat come around the bend. The SCI Company started these trips in 1894--in stage coaches; it must have been quite a thrill to career down these curvy roads pulled by horses. Some years later, visitors toured in "rag top" buses (canvas-tops) painted with Catalina scenes and wildlife. Today, the buses are high-tech, "hinged" tractor-pulled buses.

Island Plaza
Most of the buses and trams leave from the Island Plaza. You can buy tickets here from several companies, and you'll find public restrooms, a great little outdoor cafe (Pete's), and several giftshops. The Plaza is between Catalina St. and Sumner, about a half block inland from Middle Beach.

Visitor's Information Center
Ask about money-saving combinations of two of the described trips (below) at the Visitor's Information Center on Crescent Ave. across from the green Pleasure Pier, tel. (310) 510-2500, Box 737, Avalon, CA 90704. Here you'll find a preview of sights available, with backlighted photos, historical exhibits, a topographic display, and videos of the Island. Visitors are invited to browse the literature racks for a wealth of information and will find enthusiastic, friendly people to answer questions and make reservations. Prices below are discounted approximately 50% for children, and 10% for seniors.

Avalon Scenic Tour
This 50-minute trip is especially gratifying for the one-day visitor. The bus leaves from the Sumner Ave. side of Island Plaza and passes Avalon's major points of interest. You first trav-

EL RANCHO ESCONDIDO

Within 10 years after William Wrigley Jr. had acquired Catalina and the Santa Catalina Island Co., his son Philip began making plans for the development of the interior. After many months of traveling through the beautiful countryside, he came upon a setting called Cottonwood Canyon that he thought would make an ideal site for a horse ranch. He and the rest of his scouting group set up camp to get acquainted with the area. It was a good move; the wind howled through the canyon, and it turned out to be a cold place. As Wrigley put it, "We quickly found out from bitter experience that it was the wrong spot except during the middle of the day."

As it turned out, Cottonwood led them to the location that would prove to be just right, only a short distance away. The setting was lovely, but as they discovered, it was not easy to locate the second time. Undoubtedly that's why the ranch was ultimately called El Rancho Escondido ("The Hidden Ranch"). Even now, surrounded with tall eucalyptus, the ranch remains hidden from sight until you're just a few hundred yards away.

As the first set of buildings was begun, plans were in the making to breed a Catalina Arabian horse. Helen and Philip Wrigley were the owners of two Arabians and were much impressed by their beauty and stamina. They then found Jack White, a longtime cattleman, to take charge of this frontier location and develop it into a ranch. In 1931, this lanky, leathery-faced Westerner, who felt more at home on a horse than anyplace else, tackled the job. It was at about this time that the first gray stallion, called Kaaba, was transported to the Island. The horse and White did a good job; Jack didn't even mind sleeping in a tent for the first months while the ranch took shape.

The breeding program was initiated under the experienced eye of Millard Johnson, who said he'd try it out for a "few months." Jack White eventually took over the SCI Co. cattle ranch, and Johnson ended up running the ranch for the next 16 years. During WW II the breeding program was put on hold, but by 1949 Escondido had grown to include over 75 horses and was the largest purebred Arabian breeding ranch in Southern California.

Millard Johnson's young assistant, Joe Dawkins, took over in 1951. He knew horses and he liked people. Tourists who took the new "Inland Motor Tour" of the interior, enjoyed the donut-and-rodeo stop at Rancho Escondido. It continues to be a favorite attraction on Catalina. Escondido's Arabians have garnered hundreds of awards over the years and have started a dynasty of Catalina Arabians. The number of Arabians on the ranch varies between 16 and 20. The Wrigley family visits the ranch several times a year, and needless to say they are all avid riders.

Since Dawkins retired in 1972, several ranchers have managed El Rancho Escondido. The Spanish-style ranch buildings are graceful and built mostly from Catalina materials, right up to the red tiles on the roof (from Catalina's old tile factory). Shaggy eucalyptus trees surround the buildings, giving welcome shade on hot, sunny days. Visit the tack room, with its hundreds of ribbons, awards, interesting saddles, and pictures of the Wrigley family and their horses. A video of the Wrigleys and their horses is shown during the stopover.

The most exciting part of the visit is the show put on each day (twice daily during summer months) for visitors. The ranch manager explains the history of the Arabian horse. In an arena with bleacher seats for guests, ranch-hands, in western dress as well as Arabian garb, put the horses through exercises that show what the breed is capable of doing as a working ranch animal. Don't miss this great show, even if you aren't a horse person.

el along some of Avalon's beaches and into the hills that surround its sparkling bay. The bus takes you by the **Inn on Mt. Ada** (today a bed and breakfast but originally the residence of Mr. and Mrs. William Wrigley Jr.), along the waterfront, through the residential section of Avalon, and to vistas that are perfect for picture-taking --the views are fabulous; $8.

Skyline Drive

This two-hour tour is a good way to see part of the interior if you have only a day. It takes you 10 miles inside the Santa Catalina Island Conservancy's nature preserve to the Airport-in-the-Sky. Along Catalina's skyline you see mountain scenery on one side and deep canyons and hidden coves notching the coastline on the other. Flora here, such as the Catalina ironwood tree, grows only on Catalina. Ironwood trees, once common in the western United States, have been extinct on the Mainland for more than 20,000 years. This rugged country is also the home to Catalina's wild animals: buffalo, deer, boar, and fox. The tour departs from the bus terminal in the Island Plaza; reservations required. Part of the fare goes to the Santa Catalina Island Conservancy and is a tax-deductible contribution; $16.50.

Inland Motor Tour

If you plan to spend several days in Catalina, take the four-hour Inland Tour. Though more expensive than some of the other trips, this half-day trip is well worth your time and money.

The tour goes to the heart of the rugged wildlands owned by the Catalina Conservancy. You travel along a high ridge, with vistas of rolling hills on one side and the vast Pacific on the other. You'll see Middle Ranch nestled in a valley among crops and farmhouses. (Heavy storm damage in 1995 closed the road into Middle Ranch.)

At **Rancho Escondido,** you're a guest at a demonstration in which two riders (one Western, one English) put the purebred Arabian horses through their paces. Wander the grounds of the ranch and visit the tack room that stores the Wrigley family stable gear, including remarkable silver riding equipment, ornate bridles, carved saddles, and old and new photos of the family in equestrian gear. In the trophy room

watch a video that shows the Arabians and tells the history of the Wrigleys, their horses, and Rancho Escondido. In another part of the ranch sit old stagecoaches that at one time carried tourists along Catalina's dirt roads. Today's modern buses were designed to somewhat resemble the old stages of yesteryear. Coffee and snacks are served at the ranch before you return to Avalon. The bus circles back by way of the Airport-in-the-Sky and along the high ridge overlooking hidden coves along the Catalina coast. The bus leaves from the Island Plaza daily at 9 a.m. and 3 p.m.; reservations are required; $29.

Casino Tour

Take this 45-minute walking tour, $8, for a complete circuit of the Casino. Either a walk or a tram ride from the Island Plaza brings you to Casino Point, and from there a guide escorts the group through the landmark building. You're taken into the theater on the bottom floor to view the heroic-sized murals, intricate architecture, and the colossal Page pipe organ (though not advertised, once in a while an organist will demonstrate its many sound effects). From here you'll walk the ramp to the mezzanine and the large ballroom. The balcony surrounding the dance floor is a perfect vantage point from which to photograph Avalon Bay--and to imagine the romance of an evening, of music, and a moon lighting the sea. Don't miss this trip; this is probably the only way you'll get to see the inside of the theater, ballroom, and everything else in one visit.

Coastal Seal Rock Cruise

The 55-minute cruise goes to the eastern tip of Catalina--past the "working" side of the Island. Here's where boaters find the boat yard, where the Edison Company runs its desalination and electric plants, and from where the barge hauls freight back and forth to the Mainland. The cruise boat passes the small seaplane airport and helipad, and farther down, the rock quarry where millions of tons of rocks and boulders have been removed from the Island to build the seawalls and breakwaters around Los Angeles Harbor and Southern California's coast.

When the sea lions are "at home," the cruise is a wonderful opportunity to see them in their natural habitat. This haul out area is also a birthing spot for more than 100 sea lions a year. They're a noisy, clownish group to watch. One Catalina seal, Old Ben, has become "famous," there's even a statue of him on the mole. He seemed to like humans more than his pinniped family, and was constantly begging for food, sometimes up close and personal; $8.

GLASS-BOTTOM BOATS

History
In addition to its many other unusual "firsts," Catalina holds the distinction of being the place where a glass-bottom boat was first used. Inspired by the glass-bottom box that fishermen used for a better view under the water when untangling lines or spotting abalone on the rocks below, Charles Feige created the first practical glass-bottom rowboat in 1896. In 1897, P.J. Waller built a glass-bottom sternwheeler of boiler iron; it was operated with wheels, bicycle fashion. Then studies found that power-driven boats didn't disturb the water and its inhabitants as originally believed.

If you've been coming to Catalina for years, you'll notice the absence of the lovely old glass-bottom boat the MV ***Phoenix.*** The grand lady was built in Wilmington, California, in 1931, and operated daily by the Santa Catalina Island Company. The *Phoenix* leisurely cruised Catalina's marine gardens in Lovers Cove and in the evening carried guests toward the west end of the Island, playing live music and serving a great buffet. The old ship was retired to the Mainland in 1994 and replaced by high-tech semi-submersibles.

Semi-Submersibles
A rather unusual looking vessel, the semi-submersible features a bottom passenger section that rides underwater and that is surrounded by glass. Passengers take a few steps down and suddenly they're in the marine world. Schools of fish zoom past the windows, especially when the captain "chums" the water with gastronomical delights (from a fish's perspective, of course).

The semi-submersible floats around Lovers Cove, where radiantly colored fish thrive. The most vivid resident is the golden garibaldi, a species of perch. Others you may see are the silver perch, button perch, and the toothy sheepshead. Occasionally, a transparent jellyfish will float by. Adding grandeur to the scene is the iodine kelp forest; its amber tendrils and leaves, supported by air bulbs, reach up 100 feet and more to the surface. Daylight trips aboard submersibles *Starlight* and *Emerald* depart from the Pleasure Pier frequently during the summer and take 40 minutes. The *Night Undersea* is a great trip into the night-world of fish aboard the same boats with a brilliant light spotlighting the denizens of the water world. Daytime trips are $19.50, at night $21.

OZ MALLAN

Starlight
semi-submersible

OTHER DISCOVERY TOURS

More Glass Bottoms
The *Moonstone* and *Nautilus* glass-bottom boats continue to run daily and leave from the Pleasure Pier; fares are $8.

Flying Fish Trip
The ***Blanche W*** cruises along Catalina's stunning coastline for an hour. The comfortable 90-passenger motor vessel makes this trip during the summer only; that's when the flying fish come to Catalina waters. This is a special evening of romantic cruising under the stars, and scanning the seas for flying fish, aided by the *Blanche W*'s 40-million-candlepower searchlight. It's great fun to watch the silvery-finned fish skim along the wave tops. Often the light pinpoints Catalina wildlife wandering the shoreline or the cliffs--you might see seals, goats, or a fox. Be sure to bring a jacket for the return trip. If can get chilly on the ocean at night; $9.

ADVENTURE TOURS

This tour company offers a variety of tours and will give information at one of its six ticket offices. Adventure Tours sell tickets on the Mainland at the San Pedro Boat Terminal, aboard the Newport Flyer, and at the Long Beach Catalina Landing Boat Terminal, as well as on the Island on the Pleasure Pier, Shore Boat Float, and at the Cabrillo Mole.

Glass-Bottom Boat
The company's glass-bottom boat, the *Ocean View,* looks at fish the old-fashioned way, through the bottom of the vessel. Day and night trips take visitors across the bay and to Lovers Cove. Catalina's undersea world at night can be spectacular: the 3000 watts of Quartz highlights many creatures that hide by day, including the shy spiny lobster slowly migrating across the bay floor.

City Tour takes passengers around the heart of Avalon and tells them Catalina stories and history. **Inside Adventure Tour** travels to the hills and beyond on comfortable coaches. Visit the Island's magnificent interior and enjoy peaceful coves, with breathtaking views, fascinating landmarks, and unique wildlife. A combination

City and Botanical Garden Tour delivers you to the garden for a self-guided tour; admission included. Call (310) 510-2888.

CONSERVANCY TOURS

Jeep Eco-Tour Program
The Conservancy offers several exciting tours. These very popular trips into the interior and seaward side take you into rugged areas of the Island that up until now only hardy hikers could explore. These jeep trips are private tours and include half day and full-day trips; the newest is a two-hour East End Tour. Think of these as mini-safaris. For prices and reservation information call Tina or Erica, tel. (310) 510-2595, ext. 100, or talk to any Conservancy person.

Summer Naturalist Program
The Conservancy offers nature walks, hikes, multimedia presentations and campfire talks in and around Avalon. For more information call (310) 510-2595 or drop by Conservancy House at 125 Claressa.

OCEAN TOURS

Catalina Ocean Rafting
Something new on the tour scene, **Catalina Ocean Rafting** is an exciting way to experience miles of beautiful Catalina coastline. The 24-foot hard-bottom inflatable carries up to 12 people, cruises at speeds of up to 25 knots, and is capable of turning so sharply that one side of the boat rides at water level while one side lifts into the air. The boat was designed to do this and thus the "rafting" in the name.

The company offers several options, among them trips that take you very close to such sites as the Blue Caverns sea caves, Eagle Rock, Ribbon Rock, or Two Harbors. The raft stops at many scenic points, and your captain shares local history and geological lore. Sometimes you cruise a couple of miles offshore to look for dolphins; other times you'll hug the coastline, looking for the American bald eagle, sea lions, and whatever else might be in the neighborhood. Ask which trips are suitable for children under 12.

A typical **half-day trip** begins in Avalon and heads toward the west end of the Island. A 45-

OZ MALLAN

seeing Avalon by tram

minute stop at Two Harbors gives you enough time to peek at the small village, and then a short jaunt to a secluded cove gives you an hour of snorkeling. The company provides gear (when the water is cool, you might want to rent a wetsuit from one of the many dive shops in town). After snorkeling, snacks and drinks are available while you warm up in the sun. The raft cruises offshore for the entire trip back to Avalon. **Full day trips** circumnavigate the entire island. Lunch is included. The two-day, one-night **overnight campouts** are really special. After a coastal cruise, the boat drops anchor at one of the coves. When you swim ashore, you'll find tents and all your personal gear ready for you. Kayaks and other water toys have been brought in from Avalon, and your guides cook steaks and chicken and other good eats while you swim, read, kayak, snorkel, hike, or veg out on the beach. For reservations and prices, call (310) 510-0211, 800-990-RAFT, 103 Pebbly Beach Road.

Kayaking

A guided tour with Descano Beach Ocean Sports by kayak down the coastline, especially with snorkel gear, provides fun for the whole family. The company offers several guided tours, including Kayak Kids morning special, Paddling for Fitness, Willow Cove Expedition, Journey to Frog Rock, Full Moon Paddle (once a month, of course). You guessed it--the moonlight paddle is the most popular. Departure times vary with the season but expect to paddle about 1.25 miles down the coast and back. Return and relax on the beach with a free cocktail or soda. For more information, call (310) 510-1226. The outfitter is about a three-minute walk from the Casino at Descanso Beach.

Note: Kayaking from Descanso Beach saves you about 20 minutes getting out of the harbor.

SEEING AVALON BY TRAM

Island Tram Tours

An open-air tram takes you all around town on the Avalon City Tour (50 minutes, narrated), or on the Botanical Garden Scenic Tour, (90 minutes, admission included). The tram also operates a shuttle to the Botanical Garden; stay as long as you wish. Check the schedule and prices in the Island Plaza. The fare includes admission into the Garden; call (310) 510-1600 or write Box 1919, Avalon, CA 90704.

KATHY ESCOVEDO-SANDERS

A KID'S ADVENTURE

Catalina is a family kind of place where parents bring their young children year after year, generation after generation. This is an island of adventure and learning for kids, who often return with their own children. This chapter deals with what to bring and suggests many things you can show and do with the kids, as well as many activities they can do on their own. Actually, this information is pertinent to "kids-at-heart" of any age, who are certain to get a childlike thrill on a trip to Catalina.

THE TRIP

What to Take
For summer travel, bring beach towels and a couple of changes of swimwear. Small children should have hats to protect their heads from the sun, along with sunscreen. Even when the sky is overcast the sun's rays will burn; the reflection from water and the white sand increases the risk. If you forget to bring these necessities from home, drugstores and gift shops carry lotions and sun hats. Pack 10 or 20 small plastic sandwich bags and 20 small plastic garbage bags; these come in handy for stashing wet bathing suits and dirty clothes, and for toting and saving a variety of things during your vacation.

Flying
Getting to your destination is a large part--if not the largest part--of a child's visit to Catalina. If your youngster hasn't had the opportunity to travel on a helicopter, you might choose to fly to Catalina. This adds to the thrill of the trip and is a quick way to get there--it's only about a 20-minute flight from San Pedro Harbor to the Island. However, if the budget squeaks at airfare (see "Getting There"), boats are an enjoyable, economical way to go.

Boat Travel
Depending on which boat you choose to cross the channel to Catalina, the trip can take anywhere from 55 minutes to two hours. Do your children get carsick? If so, you may presume your child will get an upset stomach at sea. And if not, it's still wise to be prepared. Many over-the-counter remedies are available for motion sickness. Ask the druggist to give you one that doesn't cause drowsiness (unless you *want* your child to sleep crossing the channel). To be effective the medication should be taken at least an hour before departure. Seasick pills are sold onboard, but by the time you decide you need it (usually outside of the breakwater) it's too late to do any good.

The best place to sit during a rough crossing is in the center of the lower deck. However, fresh breezes will often help allay queasiness; outside seating is available. On a clear summer day, sitting on the open deck, it's easy to get sunburned, so use protective lotions freely and sunblock for sensitive skin. Sunburn can really take the zest out of a vacation. You should also avoid windburn. A good coating of lotion prevents chapping. When you travel in the winter, remember to wear warm jackets and hats, even though the sun may be shining in the harbor; the winter wind off the ocean can get very chilly in mid-channel. On cross-channel boats, enclosed decks offer either tables and chairs or airline-type seats with trays; bring a deck of cards or other amusements in case it's the kind of day you want to spend inside.

SIGHTS

The Harbor
The first part of the trip from the Mainland takes you through the harbor full of ships and fascinating landmarks.

Departing from Long Beach Harbor, you'll pass the permanently docked **Queen Mary,** which is one of the largest of the old passenger ships that regularly crossed the Atlantic Ocean between New York and Great Britain. She not only carried passengers paying for luxury service but also brought thousands of immigrants from Europe to this country. Their quarters were on the lower decks deep within the ship below the waterline.

Today, the *Queen Mary* is a fantastic tourist complex with a hotel on board in the original staterooms and a variety of trendy shops. Nonguests can pay admission for a tour of the large ship. Its many cafes are open to the public for breakfast, lunch, and dinner onboard. The colorful ceremony of the changing of the guard, with their bright red British uniforms and tall fur hats, takes place several times a day in front of the ship, just as it's done in London. For hotel reservations call (310) 432-6964.

Ships
As you pass through either the Long Beach or San Pedro harbors, you'll see many large ships from all over the world. Some are giant tankers bringing oil to be refined from as far away as the Middle East and North Atlantic. Other ships are enormous "container craft" carrying goods in giant boxes as big as freight cars, and flying

DENISE BICKNELL

Buckle up and have fun!

flags from the farthest parts of the globe. Giant cranes handle these containers quickly and efficiently.

The Breakwater

Looking much like a stone wall, this breakwater for many miles parallels the Long Beach and San Pedro coastline, shielding the working part of these harbors from heavy winter storms. Powerful winds can turn the Pacific Ocean into a churning, heaving body of water. The breakwater is a deeply planted barrier. Thousands of huge rocks were hauled on flat barges by tugboats (from Catalina's quarries) and piled on the bottom of the ocean, building a wall high and wide enough to make the harbors safe and calm. Because of the ongoing action of the waves upon the breakwater, it needs constant repair, and more rocks.

limpet

The boat to Catalina frequently passes rock-laden barges pulled by tugboats from Catalina's two rock quarries. One is very close to Avalon, just beyond Pebbly Beach, and the other lies at Empire Landing toward the west end of the Island near Two Harbors. The rock quarries are built on mountains of stone. With dynamite and mechanical equipment, the mountains are broken up into smaller chunks of rock (some weighing as much as a couple of tons), which are then loaded onto barges with giant cranes, taken across the channel, and dumped at the spot where the breakwater is being built or repaired. Projects such as this take years to complete.

On the Boat

While you motor through the breakwater, the boat travels within the speed limit of the harbor. Fast-moving boats leave a wake behind, and a small boat caught in that wake could flip over. When passing through the entrance to the breakwater, you'll see a large flashing light that warns ships traveling at night or in fog that they're near the harbor. Once the Catalina boat leaves the harbor and the seawall, it picks up speed. Sometimes it's difficult to get your "sea legs" if the deck is pitching back and forth. If it's a calm sea the deck won't move much, but don't be surprised if it's still hard to stand.

Sealife

Watch the water for fish. Different sealife swims the channel, depending on the time of year and the currents. In the winter you'll see

shore crab

mammoth gray whales traveling south to Mexican waters to bear their young in Scammon's Bay of Baja California. Every year they travel 6,000 miles from their summer feeding grounds in the Bering Sea to Mexico and then back. When a whale blows a tall stream of water straight into the air and then dives to the sea floor with a flap of its giant tail, it's called "sounding." Often several of the huge mammals travel together--this group is called a "pod."

In the summer, passengers often see porpoises playing in the wake of the boat. They leap out of the water, jump the waves, and dive back into the wake as they follow along. These popular mammals seem to enjoy showing off. Toward the end of the summer, look for flying fish skimming over the tops of the waves. A colorful, translucent, bubble-like tube or balloon floating in the water is a jellyfish. If you encounter one while swimming, don't touch it and don't stick around; it can give you a painful sting. As the boat gets closer to the Island, sea-gazers might see a seal that has strayed from the hauling ground near the east end of the Island. Most of the pinnipeds that live on Catalina are California sea lions; intelligent and playful, they're the variety that's trained for circus acts. Sometimes the brown pelicans put on a show if they find a school of fish. Attacking the sea like dive-bombers, they fill their pouchlike bills with as many small shiny fish as possible. A flock of squawking seagulls meets the arriving passenger boats in the harbor.

Docking in Avalon

Depending on the weather, the mountains of the Island will be visible rising out of the sea during most of the trip. From several miles away the white Casino is apparent. As the ship approaches the harbor, the captain reduces speed and carefully negotiates the large boat snugly against the dock. Deck hands throw the lines ashore as departing passengers wait and watch. The gangplanks are put into position and you've arrived at Catalina's **Cabrillo Mole.** Follow the Mainland ticket seller's instructions, and make return reservations as soon as you arrive; the ticket offices for all ships are conveniently located on the mole.

IN AVALON

Hotels

If you have kids, keep several things in mind when choosing a hotel. Some have outside areas where you can wash the sand off before entering. Some also have lockers where you can store beach toys so you won't have to lug them to your room; others have outside clotheslines for hanging up wet suits and towels. If all these things are important to you, ask about them when you make reservations. Be sure to find out if there's a hotel courtesy car waiting at the mole. With children and luggage it can be a big help, especially if your hotel sits at the top of one of the many hills. If the service is not provided, taxis (white vans) also meet the boat.

Ask about their family fares; $6-7 will usually get you and your luggage to the hotel.

Beaches/Swimming

Avalon is small, a one-square-mile community, and children quickly learn the lay of the land. The biggest attractions for kids are the beaches and the ocean. Avalon is on the lee (protected) side of the Island, so the surf is calm. Although it's a very safe area for children to swim and play in, a Los Angeles County lifeguard is on duty (at all three beaches) every day until dusk. Small children should be supervised at all times. The beaches in the center of town are sandy and drop off to deep water fairly quickly--sooner than most Mainland beaches. **South Beach** and **Middle Beach** have floats anchored some 50 feet offshore during the summer.

North Beach (a very small sandy area) has a retaining wall with steps down to the water's rocky beach. When the tide is in there's no rocky beach and the water can be quite surgy. This beach is not recommended for small children or for any child who cannot swim. A walk along the shoreline from the mole past Abalone Point will bring you to Lovers Cove. This rocky beach

kids' fishing tournament

BILL MEISTER

meeting the
young horses at
Rancho Escondido

OZ MALLAN

(without lifeguard) becomes very deep very quickly, so it's not a good play area for toddlers or young children who can't swim. However, because it's a fish preserve, it's a good place to introduce the older *swimming* child to snorkeling.

AVALON RECREATION DEPARTMENT

Avalon offers a great summer program for kids. The following is the Avalon Recreation Department's typical summer schedule (from June through Labor Day) of supervised activities for kids. Unless otherwise noted, the number to call for information and schedules is (310) 510-1987.

Day Camp
Monday through Friday from 9 a.m. to 2 p.m., children (4-12 years) can attend a day camp at the City Park. Each child must bring a bag lunch and a drink that will not spoil (no refrigeration). A fun-filled half day of various activities includes field trips, games, supervised beach games, and arts and crafts. Shoes are necessary. For reservations call (310) 510-0928/1987.

Beach Games
During the summer, the department supervises a variety of beach games for kids of all ages. Three days a week sandcastle building contests offer prizes. Beach activities, swimming

races, balloon tosses, and active games keep the kids happily occupied for part of the day, free. Call for scheduled events.

The City Park
Up the steps at the end of Crescent Ave., this small park is a good place for your little ones to get acquainted with other children; it's the hub of the recreation program. Arts and crafts occur weekly. The small playground has swings, and activities go on from 9 a.m. to 3 p.m., tel. (310) 510-0928. You'll find another playground next to the volleyball courts, on the left side when walking to town from the mole.

Fishing
A favorite pastime for little kids is fishing off the Pleasure Pier. Mornings, twice a week, the city organizes fishing derbies for the kids (four years and up), with a ribbon and prize to the fisherman who brings in the biggest and the most. To participate the children need minimal fishing equipment: bait and a fishing pole (a dropline with a hook works fine). If you've forgotten to bring yours, they're for sale at Joe's Rent-A-Boat on the Pleasure Pier. Rosie at the fish market on the end of the Pleasure Pier sells frozen squid and anchovies by the small bag for bait; balls of cheese, peas, and wads of bread work, too.

Note: Your fishermen can use an outside salt-water shower near the Pleasure Pier after this activity.

Los Angeles County Library

Once a week from July 1 until Labor Day the library, 215 Sumner Avenue, tel. (310) 510-1050, offers a special story time for children preschool and up. The librarian welcomes children with an up-to-date selection of children's books.

Beach Bingo

All ages meet at South Beach Monday and Wednesday at 6 p.m. for beach bingo; 50 cents per card and lots of great prizes.

Mini-Golf Tournament

Kids enrolled in day camp can putt around Golf Gardens on Thursday for the weekly tournament.

Volleyball/Basketball

Bring a group or come to make friends at the volleyball/basketball court parallel to South Beach. Basketballs and volleyballs are available Monday through Friday; a small fee and deposit are required.

EXPLORING THE SHORELINE ON YOUR OWN

Rock Crabs and Tidepools

Little children seem to wake up at dawn, vacation or not, so it's wise to have a couple of surprises ready to keep them occupied. One morning, surprise them by taking them crab hunting.

sea star

Six- to nine-year-olds seem to enjoy this the most; younger kids might not be surefooted enough. You'll be clambering around some big rocks by the ocean, and all involved will probably get wet, so dress for the beach--swimsuits and tennis shoes.

Low tide is the best time for pursuing crabs; on the night before, check the tide timetable on the end of the pier at the harbormaster's office.

Crabs love raw hamburger or bits of ham. If you're out before the grocery stores are open (Fred and Sally's Market opens at 7 a.m.), most restaurants will sell you a raw hamburger patty. Give each child a small plastic bag of meat (it doesn't take much) and one with cracker crumbs for the tidepools if the tide is really low. One burger patty should do for two children for about half an hour.

Walk along the boardwalk toward Casino Point past the Tuna Club. Below the rails, large rocks lie along the edge of the water. Look to see if you spot any of these small crabs out scavenging a meal. If you have a sharp eye, you'll see lots of them about one to three inches in size, even though they're almost the color of the rocks. Put the tiniest pinch of raw meat on the top of a rock (not in the water), and these awkward little creatures will rush sidelong to grab the meat in their great claws.

If you have very curious children who want to

PATTI LANGE

kids on a (successful) night dive for lobster

examine the crabs up close, have them pick the creatures up carefully from behind; they will pinch if given a chance. Treat them kindly and return them gently to the rocks. Meander toward the Casino along the rocks. If it's really low tide, investigate the small tidepools; the sea is alive with little creatures, wispy grasses, kelp, and sea urchins. The water is clear enough that you can watch the fish scrambling for the cracker crumbs (crunched up very fine). Tiny, tiny crabs will dive into the sand. The tidepools are really just for looking; don't touch these little critters.

You'll find another place to investigate at low tide at Descanso Beach. You'll notice what was probably an old dock. Part of the structure remains, creating fine little pools at very low tide. This is a pleasant, relaxing way to share with your children some of the wonders of sealife and to work up an appetite for breakfast.

Bird and Fish Feeding
All small children love to feed animals, and Avalon has a large resident family of pigeons that strut around town, especially near the Busy Bee Cafe. The pigeons love cracker or bread crumbs and they'll practically do a jig for stale popcorn. The end of the Pleasure Pier is a good place to feed the fish. They'll gather in groups close to the surface for cracker crumbs; however, sometimes a clownish seagull will get there before the fish do. The seagull is such a glutton that it'll try eating just about anything, even if it's not edible. Most animals, fish and gulls included, are just like us: they seem the hungriest early in the morning and at dusk.

Boating for Kids
If your kids are 11 or older, renting a rowboat is always an adventure. Rowing around the harbor gives them plenty of exercise and they can even fish if they like.

Check at Joe's Rent-A-Boat on the Pleasure Pier; the children must know how to swim. Joe also rents paddleboards and other fun toys.

Beachcombing
Try beachcombing on another early morning. You just *might* find small treasures on any of the beaches on Catalina before the crowds arrive. Most children enjoy searching for shells along the waterline. Be sure to bring a plastic bag to hold them. One of the favorites is a small purple shell called the purple olive shell. At one time the Catalina Indians used them for money (called *wampum*) and for making necklaces and ornaments. Other Indians on the Mainland who didn't live close to the ocean would trade precious goods to the Catalina Indians for these shells. Look for tiny mussel shells and baby clamshells. Perhaps you'll be lucky enough to find a rare, delicate chambered nautilus, but don't hold your breath.

Another bit of booty found on the beaches are tiny bits of colored glass, "ocean jewels" that have been smoothed and polished by the constant movement of the surf and friction with the sand and rocks. Collect these to sparkle in a pretty glass jar full of water set on a sunny windowsill. Sea-hewn driftwood in intriguing shapes washes up on the back side of the Island where there's more surf, and who knows what else you'll find among the fascinating bits of flotsam and jetsam the sea has carried in on the last tide. Older (and richer) beachcombers use metal detectors on the sand to find loose change that inevitably gets lost each day.

Biking
Biking on the Island is great fun for the whole family. Pack a picnic and bike up to the Wrigley Memorial and Botanical Garden, out to Pebbly Beach, or along the road leading to the Casino. See "Getting Around in Avalon" for more details about bicycles.

ORGANIZED CAMPING

Young campers have been going to Catalina for years--Boy Scouts, Girl Scouts, and YMCA among others. These campsites are ideal for a getaway to sea, hills, and lots of fun. Young boys and girls have the opportunity to swim, snorkel, collect sea specimens with naturalists to explain, hike the surrounding hills, and just have a good time. They camp at Emerald Bay, Gallaghers Cove, White's Landing, Howland's Landing, and Buttonshell Beach. For more information, call the Chamber of Commerce in Avalon at (310) 510-1520.

AVALON RECREATION
BOATING

AVALON MARINAS

Mooring Information

Moorings are assigned on a first-come, first-served basis. Avalon has 400 moorings, and on a busy weekend, rafting (two boats tied together to one mooring) increases the boat population to as many as 500. Upon arrival, please stand by at the harbor entrance until a patrol boat assigns a mooring. Mooring fees are payable to the patrol boat or at the harbormaster's office. Don't depart without paying or you'll be charged double. On your day of departure, you must vacate the moorings by 9 a.m. If you arrive in Avalon on a busy weekend and find all moorings occupied, you can anchor for free in specified areas at the harbormaster's discretion. The Harbor Patrol maintains a 24-hour service year-round; there is no landing fee at Aval-

on, Descanso Bay, Hamilton Beach, or any Conservancy property. For more Avalon harbor information, call (310) 510-0535.

Note: Between Oct. 15 and two weeks before Easter, two nights' fees buy five additional consecutive nights if the moorings are available.

Services

Complete cooperation is necessary to keep the harbor and beaches clean. Harbor Department service boats pick up trash daily, free of charge, at approximately 10 a.m. and 2 p.m. Obtain plastic trash bags from the patrol boats or at the harbormaster's office. Leave the trash bag on the stern of your boat, making sure there's nothing near it that might be mistaken for trash and hauled away. You'll find a holding-tank pump-out station on float No. 5 in the southeast corner of Avalon Bay. You must shut off all generators and other noisy motors by 10 p.m. Shore boats and fueling service are available year-round. Shore boat fees to the Pleasure Pier are $2 pp for the inner harbor and $2.50 for the outer harbor. Some summers, enterprising Island kids operate a boat-to-boat shopping service from a small outboard. You can order almost anything and they'll deliver it to your boat for a price. Please anticipate your water needs because Avalon has a water shortage. Fresh water is available at the Chevron fuel dock and at float 5.

Gas Dock

The **Avalon Marine Dock** on Casino Pier in Avalon can supply all your boat fuel needs, tel. (310) 510-0046. Diesel fuel and regular gasoline and oil are also available at Two Harbors, tel. (310) 510-0303. Shipwreck Joey's next door on the dock serves breakfast, lunch, and snacks.

NUMBER OF MOORINGS ALONG CATALINA COAST

Avalon Bay	315
Catalina Harbor	85
Parson's Landing	2
Emerald Bay	97
Howlands	39
Big Geiger Cove	1
Cherry Cove	102
Fourth of July	42
Isthmus Cove	239
Empire Landing	2
Buttonshell Beach	7
Hen Rock Cove	25
White's Landing	17
Moonstone Beach	34
Toyon	9
Hamilton Beach	36
Descanso	4

AVALON MOORING FEES

Boats 39' and under	$15 per night
40' to 49'	$20 per night
50' to 59'	$28 per night
60' to 69'	$35 per night
70' to 79'	$43 per night
80' to 89'	$50 per night
90' to 99'	$58 per night
100' and over	$66 per night

MOORING OPTIONS

Besides Avalon, 17 other coves have moorings, and many others provide anchorage. For more detailed information about the other numerous coves on the Island, call the Camp and Cove Agency, tel. (310) 510-0303. The staff can tell you where to moor, what the prices are, the hazards, and if anchorage is available.

Note: Do not bring firearms, bow-hunting gear, or motorcycles to shore--all are prohibited. Fires are a real danger, and are not allowed except in designated camping and picnic areas. Make charcoal fires only (charcoal is available on the Island). Do not cut trees or shrubs or remove any artifacts you might find on shore or underwater.

Descanso Bay

A short distance from Avalon Bay (just west of the Casino), you'll find 47 moorings and anchorage in Descanso Bay. Keep dinghies out of the swimming area, and you may not land on the beach. Avalon has three dinghy docks: one on the gas dock at Casino Point, another between the Tuna Club and the Yacht Club, and one at the Pleasure Pier. Dinghies up to 14 feet may be tied to any of these docks for up to 72 hours. Don't leave removable motors or anything else loose, and be aware that even an entire dinghy can be a victim of theft. Stopping at any dock other than the dinghy docks mentioned is permitted only long enough to transfer people.

Hamilton Cove

Beyond Descanso Bay lie 36 moorings and un-

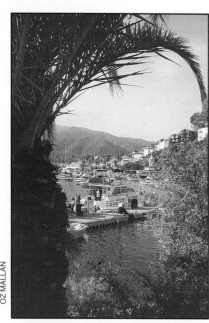

OZ MALLAN

Marine fuel dock

comfortable anchorage. The prewar seaplane terminal was built in this cove. Today, it is the home of a Mediterranean village of condos that climb the hillside. The architecture and design are lovely from a boat.

HARBOR SIGHTS EAST OF AVALON

Sightseeing along the coast both east and west of Avalon is an option open not just to boat own-ers. These are easy pleasant trips that you can accomplish in rented rowboats or outboard mo-torboats--check out Joe's Rent-A-Boat on the Pleasure Pier.

Lovers Cove

A short distance east of Avalon, there's a "no parking for boats" area. To encourage the growth of marinelife in this underwater preserve, there are no moorings; anchorage is prohibit-ed. Lovers Cove is reserved for swimming, snor-keling, and glass-bottom boat cruising only.

On the Way to Seal Rocks

Past Lovers Cove toward the east end lies Peb-bly Beach. Here the amphibian airport and ramp share the shoreline with the helicopter pad, boat yard, freight dock, Southern California Edison plant, Buffalo Nickel Restaurant, and the only gas station serving Avalon town. There are no moorings, and no anchoring is allowed.

Continuing past Pebbly you'll see one of Catalina's two rock quarries. This and the quar-ry at Empire Landing (in operation since before the turn of the century) have provided millions of tons of rock for Mainland seawalls and break-waters. The Los Angeles Light Breakwater is 90% Catalina rock, Pier J next to the *Queen Mary* contains three million tons, Redondo Beach and Port Hueneme breakwaters each contain 1.5 million tons, and Playa del Rey breakwater 750,000 tons. None of this seems to make a dent in the Catalina shoreline.

On past Jewfish Point lies a rookery for Cali-fornia sea lions. In the summer these rocks often swarm with seals--noisy barking, shiny bodies slipping on and off the wet rocks into the water. Boaters: Watch for submerged rocks in this area.

FISHING

Add boat to ocean, and you'll usually find a fish-erman. The water along the Southern California coast teems with sealife of all varieties. Visit-ing sportsmen revel in the knowledge that they have a good to excellent chance of catching a trophy in Southern California fishing beds. The biggest question is deciding what variety they want to go for.

Catalina is renowned for its excellent fishing, notably for marlin. The roar of the Avalon cannon alerts the town that another fisherman has brought a marlin into the Pleasure Pier at **Rosie's Fish Market.** Amidst crowds of visitors and fishing buffs, an Avalon ceremony follows: the big fish is hung on the pier's scale, a bottle of champagne is presented to the angler, and a photo is taken to record the exciting moment. Other fishermen bring in more delicious fish-- sea bass, rock cod, sand dabs, button perch, and sheepshead. If you're a lucky diver, you can find lobster and abalone.

You can rent tackle from **Joe's Rent-A-Boat** (on the green Pleasure Pier): still-fishing rods and trolling rods complete with lures and hooks. Bait also is available.

Note: Please respect the nonfishing areas-- Lovers Cove and the underwater park off Casino Point--and note the fishing seasons. If in doubt, ask the harbormaster at the end of the Pleasure Pier. You must have a valid California fishing license, available at Joe's-Rent-A-Boat and High Trade Traders, 415 Crescent Ave., (310) 510-1612.

FISHING TOURNAMENTS

Gold Cup Marlin Tournament starts with a cannon blast at 7 a.m. and off they go. And

The cannon booms and beachers rush to see a marlin hoisted onto the pier.

though the registration fees are costly, the prizes are flamboyant. The tournament has been held yearly since 1981. The winning marlin in 1995 weighed in at 234.5 pounds, and the prize winner collected $40,480. The **Tin Cup Tournament** prizes aren't nearly as grand, but every bit as much fun and cheaper to enter. The **Catalina Classic,** another highly competitive tournament usually held in September, also brings its share of excitement and takes lots of big fish.

Boats come from all over California and the fishermen make a weekend party of the event. For more information about the tournaments, call the Chamber of Commerce (310) 510-1520.

BOAT RENTALS

You can rent a variety of boats at **Joe's Rent-A-Boat** on the Pleasure Pier for trips to any one of the many coves along the Catalina coast, whether you want to fish, picnic, skin dive, or just sightsee. If you don't bring your own fishing tackle you can rent or buy most of the equipment needed at Joe's. Take a bright flashlight with you if you're planning to be out after sunset on a boat without running lights. Joe's is open Easter week through October. For reservations, call (310) 510-0455.

Note: Coast Guard regulations limit these small boats to six passengers.

Charter Boats
If you'd like to try for big fish and/or want to indulge in a little luxury, this is the way to go. Charters generally come with a skipper and, in some cases, a deck hand. Some provide you with lunch and drinks for the day. All have different rules and prices; most are negotiable.

Boat Stand Charters
Captain John Talsky takes custom fishing charters around the Island. He and his crew are long-time locals and want you to catch fish; if they aren't out there, your guide will tell you. Call for information, (310) 510-0455/2274.

Keeper Charters
The *Keeper* is equipped with reels and custom rods for catching marlin, yellowtail, tuna, and other deep-sea fish. The cost includes lunch, beverages, all fishing tackle, and tax; the only

OZ MALLAN

Joe's Rent-A-Boat stand on the Pleasure Pier rents boats and fishing equipment.

thing you need to bring is a valid fishing license. Call for prices and reservations at the **Catalina Island Inn,** tel. (310) 510-1623.

Tackle

What kind of fishing tackle to use? Choice of equipment grows every year. You can quiz 10 fishermen and get 10 answers to a simple question such as "What's the best tackle to catch a yellowtail?" Are you one who uses the same tackle whether fishing surf, pier, or live bait? Is your favorite the conventional reel or the spinning type? Brass, plastic, or chrome plate? How about the line? Is it 20-pound line, 50, or maybe 12? And then there's the rod, which can be eight feet or six feet. What's a beginner to do? One thing is to get a fellow fisherman to recommend a good tackle shop, find a salesperson who instills confidence, and start handling the options. As for price, you usually get what you pay for.

THE FISH IN THE SEA

Tuna Family

The variety of fish in Southern California waters is enormous. The tuna family includes, among others, albacore, yellowfin, bigeye, and bluefin tuna. These are all good eating fish, and many fishermen make sensational canned (or jarred) tuna from these big babies; wahoo is also a taste treat for tuna lovers. In the late 1940s and '50s commercial fishermen made a killing for several years with huge schools of albacore running between Catalina and the Mainland. For whatever reason, albacore are seldom seen in those same quantities in the '90s.

Flatfish

Sole, sand dabs, and turbot are all great table fare. Sand dabs, usually caught in water 200 feet deep or more, are particularly popular with local fishermen. Sand dabs are small fish that grow up to about a pound and that make great eating (once filleted); sole grow to about six pounds and turbot to about two pounds.

Sheepshead

This toothy fish, part of the wrasse family, can be a 30-pound catch. The young female is generally an all-over pink, and the male is more colorful with a white lower jaw, black head, and red and black striped body. But this is one of the fish (along with giant black sea bass and marlin, among others) that change sex during their development. As the small pink females grow, they begin to change color and sex.

Sheepshead dines regularly on shellfish in kelp and rock beds. Trimmings of mussels, squid, abalone, and shrimp make good bait. You can snag sheepshead in 60 feet of water, or the surf, or even at several hundred feet while you're fishing for rock cod.

Sculpin

Look out for this fish. Although it's great eating, and perfectly safe if you buy it in a fish market, when fishing--beware. The sculpin is the only venomous fish common to Southern California. Rather an ugly creature, it's rust and white with a high spiky dorsal. A bottom dweller, it seldom grows to more than three pounds and has a large mouth. The only safe way to handle this fellow is by grabbing the lower jaw with your thumb and forefinger. Though without teeth, the fish has spiny fins and rays that carry a toxic substance that, when introduced into a person, will produce severe pain, shock, and nausea; the only remedy seems to be time. They are good eating fish with fine white flesh, but catching them is better left to the experienced fishermen. The roe is poisonous.

California Spiny Lobster

This local lobster is found around Catalina and the other Channel Islands. The biggest ever caught was 35 pounds! Most of the time you're lucky to find one weighing five pounds. Lobster season begins the first weekend in October and ends the last of March. Spotting them is easy, grabbing them is more difficult. They live in rocky crevices by day, and by night they scavenge along the sandy ocean bottom. The best bet is capturing one at night; yes, a fishing license is required.

Barracuda

At one time this was a very common fish locally; overfishing and pollution have thinned the numbers. A 28-inch limit is helping the barracuda to make a comeback. This fish strikes both lures and bait, really goes for anchovy bait, and puts up a good fight. It shows up around Southern California in late January, lingering into February and March, and can be big: from seven to nine pounds, though the average size is four to six pounds.

Bonito

Bonito is an inshore fish that's found almost year-round. A good fighting fish, it can weigh from two to more than 12 pounds. Sometimes called the poor man's tuna, the fish is attracted to surface commotion--splashing--and tackle shops even sell lures called "bonito splashers." They strike at free-swimming anchovy bait as well as lures. Bonito is good eating when smoked.

Halibut

This bottom fish eats anything that passes it by, dead or alive. It's a lethargic fish that hides on the bottom after flipping sand over its body, and with bulging eyes just hangs around waiting for its prey. Another victim of overfishing in local waters, they were large in the past, up to 50 pounds. Nowadays a 10-pounder is a good size. There's a size limit of 22 inches as well as a bag limit of five fish. According to Charlie Davis, fishing guru of the Pacific coast, the halibut got its name in England, where in the early days all flat fish were called "butts." All butts were saved for priests, or "holy" men, thus *holybutts,* now halibut.

Kelp or Calico Bass

Found around reefs, rock jetties, breakwaters, and kelp beds, this bass grows to more than 10 pounds. It will take most live baits and a variety of lures, but especially likes anchovy, squid, and jack mackerel. It has a large mouth and a three- or four-pound bass can easily consume a bait that weighs half a pound. The favorite time to fish from a local breakwater is about an hour before and several hours after dark. The best fishing is when there's a full moon just a few hours after sundown. This is a great eating fish and cannot be sold; a protected species, its size limit is 12 inches.

Black Sea Bass

This is a historic old fish--historic in the sense that the old-time fishermen (including Zane Grey) caught these monster-sized fish frequently. Maybe they caught too many, because the fish are seldom seen any more. *If* you should come across one, let it be! These are protected fish and a large fine awaits those who catch it. The black sea bass is the largest of the bass family along the California coast. Very slow-growing, it can attain weights of 500 pounds. Since it's estimated that a 300-pounder is 20 years old, the 500-pounder is really a granddaddy.

White Sea Bass

Another favorite eating fish is the white sea bass. It grows to about 70 pounds, but a fish weighing 50 pounds is considered a prize catch. Though they're seen year-round, the best time to catch them is January through June. Live squid

OZ MALLAN

If you're a non-fisherman but want to see fish, take a trip on the Moonstone glass-bottom boat.

catch them is January through June. Live squid is a desired bait, and fishing after dark can be most effective, but sardines and Pacific green mackerel also do the job.

Note: Don't put your bare hand into the very sharp gills of this fish.

Marlin

Most fishermen think that once they've caught the big trophy, the marlin, they've made it to the big time. Anglers first caught marlin around Catalina Island at the beginning of the century. At that time they were almost exclusively caught with trolled flying fish. Though not considered a deluxe food fish in the States, it's been fished by the ton by the Japanese, who make a very popular wienerlike sausage in Japan. Overfishing has diminished the size of the fish. Marlin arrive in Southern California about July and stay as long as the water temperatures and food are to their liking, sometime as late as December. Marlins make for "fun" fishing. They spend most of their time close to the surface, and can be seen jumping if they're in the area. It's not unusual to see a marlin "sleeping" or "sunning" with its tail and the hump of the shoulders out of the water.

Along for the Ride

Many more varieties of fish make great sportfishing and/or terrific eating in Southern California. Fishing is great not only for the fisherman, but it's also a relaxing way to spend a day on the ocean for the nonangling companion.

But do make sure you bring a few things to stay comfortable: sunscreen, sun hat, lots of water or other beverages, ice, an extra shirt (a hot sun can burn right through a white T-shirt), motion sickness medication if it's a problem, first-aid kit, waterproof poncho, binoculars, and don't forget the camera and lots of film. Most serious fishermen carry protective gloves. Birdwatchers--bring along a birding book.

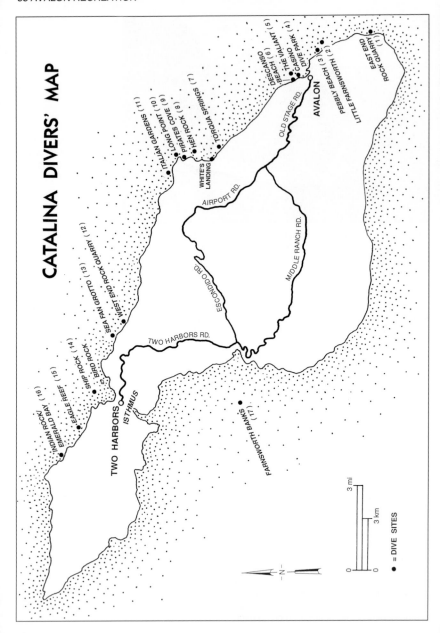

CATALINA DIVERS' MAP

EAST END ROCK QUARRY (1)
LITTLE FARNSWORTH
PEBBLY BEACH (2)
AVALON
DIVE PARK (3)
CASINO (4)
THE VALIANT (5)
DESCANSO BEACH (6)
TORQUA SPRINGS (7)
HEN ROCK (8)
PIRATES COVE (9)
LONG POINT (10)
ITALIAN GARDENS (11)
WHITE'S LANDING
OLD STAGE RD.
AIRPORT RD.
MIDDLE RANCH RD.
ESCONDIDO RD.
TWO HARBORS RD.
WEST END ROCK QUARRY (12)
SEA FAN GROTTO (13)
BIRD ROCK
SHIP ROCK (14)
EAGLE REEF (15)
INDIAN ROCK/ EMERALD BAY (16)
TWO HARBORS
ISTHMUS
FARNSWORTH BANKS (17)

3 mi
3 km
0
0
= DIVE SITES
N

KATHY ESCOVEDO-SANDERS

DIVING

DIVE ADVENTURES AND INSTRUCTION

Catalina's nearly transparent waters offer an enjoyable diving experience among its giant kelp forests, rocky reefs, and wrecks. Visibility is always better here than on the Mainland. Summer visibility averages 30-50 feet, while winter visibility can reach upward of 100 feet. Clarity depends on summer plankton blooms and winter storms; with both the water can get murky. Water summer temperature averages 67-72° F and 56-60° F in winter. Call the Avalon Harbor Department, tel. (310) 510-0535, or any Avalon dive shop to check on visibility and weather conditions. Certified divers, don't forget to bring your C-card.

Catalina's "wet" world is filled with marine life that's colorful, plentiful, and varied--fish, sharks, rays, algae, and kelp. Seals and sea lions appear frequently and on occasion a curious one will dive with you. The sharks you find in the shallow waters around the island are harmless; it's only in open ocean that you find the blue and mako sharks.

Excellent diving locations often lie within walking distance of the shoreline, eliminating tedious walks with heavy equipment over long beaches or rocky shores.

Dive Instruction

If your fantasy is to learn to scuba dive, you can combine a vacation on Catalina Island with an intensive certification course. Catalina is an ideal place to learn to dive with its clear, calm water and easy-access dive spots, and its abundant marine life makes learning enjoyable. Most of the many Catalina dive shops offer two-hour introductory dives to the noncertified, inexperienced diver. They give the amateur a chance to *sample* scuba diving in a protected environment, with no more than two divers per instructor. The dive shops all offer this dive at the same cost, $85 pp. You can complete certification in as little as three days.

Catalina Scuba Luv

This PADI five-star dive shop, 126 Catalina St, tel. (800) 262-DIVE, offers a laundry-list of services: introductory dives, open water certification, instructor development courses, and much more. A three-hour introductory dive costs $85. At Scuba Luv, the first hour is a one-hour classroom session that includes viewing an instructional video; you spend the other two hours in the water. With the extra instruction, neophytes enter the water with a lot more knowledge and added confidence.

If you plan to be certified on the Island, call

ahead for the books, do your reading at home and spend the next three days in the water with your instructor. Open water certification is $285 per person based on two or more in the class. All gear is included, and it is not mandatory to buy anything (although Scuba Luv carries a complete line of dive gear). Certified divers have many options: make a local orientation dive with a dive master who knows the area or take an underwater photo workshop, a rescue class, a night dive, video dive, deep dive, or even a shark dive.

King Neptune
Catalina Scuba Luv is also the home of two dive boats--the 65-foot *King Neptune* and the 32-foot *Prince Neptune*. The *King* offers three-tank dive days, 9 a.m.-5 p.m., which include tanks, weights, continental breakfast, lunch, snacks, and a soda fountain. The crew will find three sites with the best conditions equal to the divers' abilities. The cost is $85 pp. During lobster season the *King* makes frequent night dives, and divers usually come back with their limit. A one-tank dive costs $35, a two-tank trip costs $50--bring your fishing licenses. Live-aboard trips to San Clemente and the other Channel Islands are available for groups of six to 12. Call for prices.

Shark Diving
For those who like an adrenaline rush, the *King Neptune* offers shark dives. You'll head out to Captain Bob's secret spot in the channel. Energetic chumming attracts blue sharks and sometimes makos. About seven miles out, the crew kills the engines and places the cage in about 1,500 feet of water. Sharks can show up any time from 15 minutes to three hours after the chumming starts. When they're spotted, divers can climb into the cage; some divers opt to use it just as a handhold. Advanced and beginning divers both enjoy this thrill; watching the sleek grace of the blue shark is like an underwater ballet. The mako is a little more undependable; the cost is $199 pp.

Prince Neptune
Dive groups interested in eels can take the *Prince Neptune* trip to Pirates Cove, where Captain Steve feeds anchovies to a family of big eels. After offering a little instruction on how to feed eels and still hang on to one's fingers, Captain Steve videotapes divers feeding the multi-toothed sea serpents. The *Prince* carries a maximum of six passengers. Both the *Prince* and the *King* have heads (bathrooms) and hot showers. Dive packages are available and include transportation to and from the Mainland, hotel, and dive-boat trips. Call and ask for Tina, (310) 510-2350.

Catalina Divers Supply
You'll find this good dive shop on the Pleasure Pier, tel. (310) 510-0330, (800) 353-0330. It offers gear rentals, certification courses, intro-

night dive on the King Neptune

PATTI LANGE

OZ MALLAN

*Catalina Divers Supply
on the Pleasure Pier*

ductory dives, guided dives and boat dives. Look for the air station at the Casino Dive Park (at Casino Point), where you can fill your tanks or rent tanks and weights. The air station is open daily in summer and weekends only in winter. Snorkelers can find the snorkel-mobile parked at Lovers Cove; it's open daily in summer to rent snorkel gear. Another dive boat, the *Cat Dive,* offers a two-tank dive for $65, which includes tanks, weights, drinks, and snacks; a head and shower are on board. Bring sun screen and hats, as there's not much protection from the sun on deck.

Argo Diving Services

Argo offers big adventure with small groups. The small boat *Argo* runs two-tank dives for $100 pp, which includes tanks, weights, food, and drinks. The price is a little higher than that of some of the other dive boats, but you'll go to the best dive sites around the Island and you will have the option to dive with divemaster Jon Hardy and to pick his brain.

The *Argo* also runs shark dives, generally with a maximum of four people, $250 pp. And, for something a little different, the *Argo* goes on blue-water expeditions: you head out to sea,

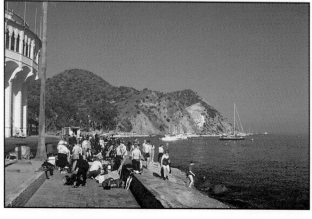

OZ MALLAN

*Diving Casino
Underwater Park*

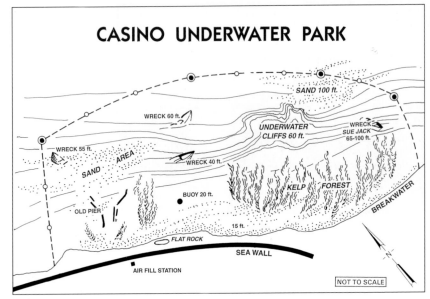

CASINO UNDERWATER PARK

SAND 100 ft.

WRECK 60 ft.

UNDERWATER CLIFFS 60 ft.

WRECK SUE JACK 65-100 ft.

WRECK 55 ft.

SAND AREA

WRECK 40 ft.

KELP FOREST

BREAKWATER

BUOY 20 ft.

OLD PIER

15 ft.

FLAT ROCK

SEA WALL

AIR FILL STATION

N

NOT TO SCALE

looking for whales, dolphins, and anything else exciting that's out there, and then jump in with snorkel gear to swim with the animals; cost is $149 pp. Call (310) 510-2208 for more information and reservations.

DIVE LOCATIONS

The following are some of the more popular dive spots on Catalina and are easy to reach. Almost all lie on the lee side of the island. The "weather" side of the island offers some great diving, but currents and surge are a lot stronger than on the lee side and dives, of necessity, tend to be a lot deeper.

Experienced divers will find dive trips and good information about the weather side from any of the dive shops on the Island. The number beside each destination matches the dive sites shown on the Dive Map.

Avalon Harbor Cleanup Dive
Most of the time, Avalon is off limits to scuba diving, except for the yearly **Avalon Harbor Cleanup Weekend** (usually in February). The dive serves two purposes: divers get rid of the

debris that is dropped or thrown over the side for a year, and the money raised (through registration fees) is used to benefit the Catalina Hyperbaric Chamber at Two Harbors. Divers come from everywhere to participate, and it's always a good party after the cleanup work is done. In the town plaza afterward, prizes are given and drawings bring surprise gifts. The $25 registration nets: one dive-fill, a commemorative T-shirt, and a "special" hotel price. For more information call the Catalina Island Chamber of Commerce, (310) 510-1520.

Casino Point Marine Dive Park (4)
Established in 1965 by the City of Avalon as a reserve, this dive park is the only spot within the city limits where scuba diving is permitted. Depths range 15 feet-100 feet with great variations of sea life. Spear fishing and taking of marine life are prohibited. During the Avalon Harbor Cleanup, members of the CCD (Catalina Conservancy Divers) set up a temporary underwater naturalist trail in the park. Trained research divers are on hand to explain the bright markers placed along the trail to identify many marine organisms varying from moray eels and octopi to

scallops and brown cup corals. The Casino Point Marine Park in Avalon is free and open to everyone.

East End Rock Quarry (1)
This is boat access only and just a short trip from Avalon. Anchor at the crane or in the general area. Either direction is good; plan the dive depending on the current. Big boulders mingle with smaller rocks, and kelp beds drop off to a sandy bottom starting about 50 feet. You'll see lots of horn sharks, moray eels, and lobster here--but you need a "lobster-magnet" to get them out of their rocky homes. Besides the usual calico bass, garibaldi, and perch, the unusual scythe Butterfly fish has been spotted at 45 feet.

Little Farnsworth (2)
Accessible by boat. You need a depth finder to find the pinnacle, which is small and circular. The top sits in 70 feet and drops to 115 feet. Little Farnsworth lies just off the power plant. It's a good place to look for nudibranches and a variety of small fish critters hiding in the rocks.

Pebbly Beach (3)
This one is beach accessible. The best entry is at Pebbly Beach, just before you come to the fence and the first buildings (Catalina Freight Line). Expect to see a lot of sea anemones, starfish, and sand. The bottom slopes from ankle deep to 100 feet-plus. A slow-moving dive, it's good if you're studying the pace of starfish.

Descanso Beach (6)
This beach-accessible dive is available only when tourist season slows. The Harbor Department bans diving here during the summer, when too much boat traffic makes it hazardous. Check out the reef between Descanso Bay and Hamilton Cove; it's home to a thick healthy kelp forest and lots of fish, lobster, and other marine life.

The reef starts in about 20 feet of water with rocks covered in algae; the kelp starts soon after. A sandy bottom borders the kelp forest, and it's a good place to see stingrays and occasional bat rays.

Don't be shocked to find an accumulation of "Budweiser fish"--beer cans and bottles. Yes, it's true, some boaters are not "harbor-broken." Do you suppose they toss the Bud cans on the floor of their houses, or in their yards, or over their neighbor's fence?! (The city sponsors a harbor dive cleanup every year. It's a great party; want to volunteer? See above.)

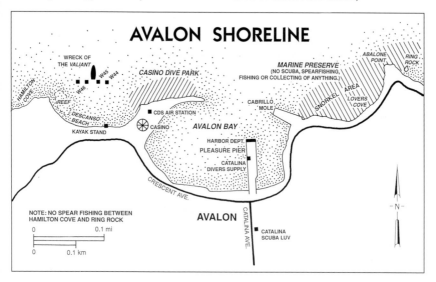

Torqua Springs (7)

Named after a Native American chief and home to a natural spring that at one time supplied Avalon with its fresh water, this dive spot lies west of Avalon, past Toyon Bay and before Moonstone Cove. A "U"-shaped reef and kelp beds house this shallow dive spot. Closer to shore small rocks and algae sit in 20 feet of water; in the kelp forest and rocky crevasses you'll drop to 45 feet and then find sand in 50 feet.

Lobster and horn sharks are everywhere (at least before lobster season starts). This is a good easy spot, but it has a tendency to murk up easily. Look for the bald eagles on the cliffs above.

Hen Rock (8)

The prominent rock covered with bird droppings west of White's Landing denotes this dive site. It's a good dive for the new diver, as you can stay within a 40-foot depth and not miss out on anything. Horn sharks, lobster, scallops, and calico bass are common here. A sandy bottom starts about 40 feet and is a great spot to find stingrays and bat rays. You'll see a tunnel at 20 feet. This site can murk up easily; in summer you might have to wait your turn to anchor since it's such a popular spot.

Pirates Cove (9)

Tucked in on the Avalon side of Long Point, this cove provides good anchorage. For a shallow dive, swim 20-40 feet toward Camp Fox. This is a good site to spot some of the half-dozen resident eels (they are BIG!). A natural cave opens above the water line and at just the right angle, you can observe the shape of Catalina. You'll see very little kelp here, mostly grasses and algae.

Long Point (10)

The tip of land that you see extending seaward past the light beacon and that runs eight miles across the Island names this spot. There's good anchorage in Pirates Cove. Submerging, you'll find deep vertical cliffs plummeting to 100 feet. Kelp beds, thick with marine life, grow all around the point. The biggest concern here is the boat traffic, mainly during the summer. Carefully plan your dive so that you surface closer to land

Divers come from all over California to dive on Catalina.

rather than in open ocean, where you will face lots of boat traffic and a strong current.

Italian Gardens (11)

Locals disagree as to which is the real Italian Gardens. The pebbly beach just west of Long Point is sometimes called Italian Gardens, as is the cove just beyond that.

The second cove is what we'll refer to. Depths range from 20 feet to 100 feet, with a steady drop-off that creeps up on you if you're not watching your depth gauge. This is a great night dive--you'll see horn sharks everywhere, lobster, great schools of perch, eels, and urchins. Visibility can be excellent.

West End Rock Quarry (12)

This encompasses a large area, but anchor near what's left of the old platform. Rocky boulders house calico bass, garibaldi, moray eels, and sea cucumbers. You'll hit a sandy bottom about 65 feet--look for rays and flat fish.

Sea Fan Grotto (13)

Just west of the west end rock quarry, this dive spot offers swim-through caves and many sea fans. Big rocks, some sandy areas and some kelp make for pretty scenery--bring a camera. The swim-throughs lie in 20-40 feet but the bottom can drop off quickly.

Ship Rock (14)

This is the larger of the two rocks offshore of Two Harbors. From a distance, the rock looks much like a regal ship under full sail. Ship Rock is a beautiful dive. It offers a reef, which many boats find by surprise with a thud (some sink). Anchor in the area between the rock and the reef. It's possible to dive around the entire rock; just beware of currents.

Depths range from 15 to 60-plus feet. A thick kelp forest surrounds the rock; rocks and boulders house many marine specimens. Closer to the reef, you'll find remnants of sailboats and masts.

suiting up

Eagle Reef (15)

Look for the buoy markers that warn of the shallow rocky reef. Depths range from 30-125 feet. This is an interesting dive--reef and kelp hide a rich selection of marine life. Currents can be strong and in summer you'll face a lot of boat traffic.

Indian Rock/Emerald Bay (16)

Indian Rock lies in Emerald Bay and makes a good shallow dive and great snorkeling; it's perfect for the beginning diver. Depths around the rock average 20 feet, sometimes shallower. Schooling fish, sea hares, and garibaldi are part of the marine scene common here. Head toward the west end of the Island and you'll find a sand flat in 30-40 feet of water; it's a good spot to look for bat rays and stingrays.

Farnsworth Banks (17)

This one is boat access only and you'll need a depth finder to find the banks. This is a deep dive and recommended for experienced divers only. This area is known for its flashy purple hydra coral (which is protected, so take only pictures).

DIVING THE WRECKS

In the underwater park directly off Casino Point, several wrecks have been placed near some of the world's finest kelp forests. Artificial reef areas have been established to provide additional fish habitats. In this same area are deep underwater cliffs and pinnacles waiting to be explored. The park is often used as the underwater backdrop for Hollywood films.

Note: Removal of game and specimens from the underwater park is prohibited, as is salvaging artifacts placed there to serve as subject matter for photography. Spearfishing is also illegal.

The *Valiant*

A short distance from Avalon in Descanso Bay lies the wreck of the *Valiant,* on the outer edge of the Descanso Bay Moorings. With both boat and beach access, the remains of this 163-foot yacht lies in Descanso Bay, just outside the dive park. Bring a dive flag, and you'll need a (free) permit to dive this spot (get it from the harbor-master). Swim to mooring can #W45, follow the anchor-chain down, and you will drop right to it. It sits in a sandy bottom, but the wreck is home to algae and some kelp, lots of fish, nudibranches, and lobster. Some even say the owners' jewels were never recovered. Depths range from 75 feet to 110 feet.

The *Catalina Islander* newspaper covered the sinking in 1930:

The palatial yacht was 163 feet long and carried 3,000 gallons of fuel . . . it recently made a 7,500-mile cruise to the Pacific. . . . The explosion occurred while the owner, Mr. Charles S. Howard, and his guests were at dinner Saturday evening, December 13. The vessel carried a crew of 22 who were also on board at the time. . . . Anchored some 500 yards from the pier at the Hotel St. Catherine, the explosion reverberated through the town of Avalon. . . . Immediately following the blast, flames shot out from the huge hole in the starboard side near the engine room . . . the fire department responded immediately but the vessel was too far from the pier to be reached . . . the flames illuminated the sky for miles.

The *Valiant* burned for three days and then sank. Divers still occasionally find small coinlike tokens that say "good for one drink MV Valiant," an inside joke among guests who sailed during Prohibition days. One of the most costly shipwrecks in Catalina waters, its valuable metals were salvaged long ago. But it's reported that more than $75,000 in cash and gems went to the bottom, and no one has ever claimed to have found it!

You must obtain a (free) permit from the Harbor Department to dive the Valiant or any other spot within city limits, with the exception of the underwater park off Casino Point.

Sue-Jac

A more recent shipwreck (1980) is the *Sue-Jac*. This modern 70-foot schooner went down during a severe northeaster while bystanders watched Los Angeles County's Bay Watch crew rescue all aboard--three crew members and one dog. The *Sue-Jac* sank gently and came to rest on a 90-foot-deep slope, bow down, almost in one piece. An experienced diver can swim through an entrance into the cabin and then out the skylight--an exciting dive destination.

Other Wrecks

These are not common dive sites, but offer intriguing information for the romantic sea rover. Several galleons are rumored to have sunk near Catalina, some supposedly carrying huge treasures--none has ever been recovered. Many believe that in 1598 a Spanish galleon struck a rock and sank with a reported $2 million in bullion and artifacts. In 1602, some of the goods from the wreckage were found on Catalina shores, and in 1850 what may have been part of its hull was found off Ship Rock in six-plus fathoms. In 1852, a Spanish frigate sank near the Island with a $1.2 million cargo. In 1920, the *North Star* sank; in 1924 the *Taurus,* a 551-ton U.S. schooner, went down; 1926 took the *William G. Irwin* to the bottom; and in 1929 the *Charles F. Crocker,* an 860-ton U.S. barkentine, foundered. The list continues with the USS *Koka* sinking in 1937. Ten years later, in 1947, the *Rossino II* hit bottom off Catalina Head. Basic NOAA charts show some spots by wreck symbol with "PA" (position approximate). If you're a devoted treasure seeker, break out the old history books; you'll find records of many more ships just waiting to be salvaged.

SPECIAL DIVERS' ACCOMMODATIONS

A few hotels encourage diving clientele by providing facilities for storing and cleaning equipment. It's smart to mention your equipment when making reservations.

Bay View Hotel

This older hotel has men's and women's showers and toilets on each floor. It offers washdown facilities for dive gear, outdoor shower, barbecue pits, jacuzzi, and accommodates groups up to 150. Courtesy car on request. Ask about winter rates; 124 Whittley, Box 1017, Avalon, CA 90704, tel. (310) 510-0600.

Seaport Village Inn
This one offers views, beach one-half block away, color TV, spa, sundeck, free coffee, one- and two-bedroom family suites with kitchen, studio suites, and transportation from boat. Group and package rates are available. In Avalon, call

(310) 510-0344, in San Diego call (619) 571-0663, in Southern California, call (800) 2-CATALINA.

Hermosa Hotel and Catalina Cottages
This very old hotel has storage space for gear, is close to everything, and is the cheapest around; rooms cost as little as $35. Now, don't expect a whole lot and you won't be disappointed. It's on Metropole Ave., tel. (800) 666-3383, (310) 510-1010.

MORE WATER SPORTS

Swimming and Snorkeling
Swimming and snorkeling are great water sports around Catalina Island, and they're free.

Many coves around the Island are well-suited for swimming and snorkeling--but in Avalon you can snorkel only in Lovers Cove. It's a great place for a scenic romp through the looking glass--lots of animals swim in this protected cove.

Middle and South Beaches are the most crowded, and both have lifeguards on duty during daylight. North Beach access to the ocean is by steps down onto a rocky beach, and during high tide there is no beach, just water. This is not a good place for young kids alone.

Snorkel Catalina
If you want an escorted snorkeling experience, a guide takes adults and kids under 12 to snorkeling spots around the bay; mask and fins are included in the price. For six snorkelers, one and a half hours, rates are adults $24, kids $19; make reservations at Joe's Rent-A-Boat on the Pleasure Pier, tel. (310) 510-0455.

Wave Runners
Catalina Jetski rents Yamaha Waverunners, singles and doubles available by the hour ($45-55) and half hour ($55-65). Explore the hidden coves of Catalina; instruction is available. Take the shoreboat at the green Pleasure Pier to **The Float** at Hamilton Cove. Reservations are recommended, tel. (310) 510-1922; buy tickets at **Video Postcard**, 101 Pebbly Beach Rd.

Water-Skiing
Avalon's lee side offers calm ocean water where the water-skiing is ideal. You must bring your own equipment and boat. Avalon Harbor areas are well-marked and the speed limit for all boats and dinghies within the harbor is 5 mph or "wakeless speed," whichever is less.

Paddleboards
Avalon's calm, clear, surf-free waters are perfect for exploring the bay on a board. Rent one on the Pleasure Pier at Joe's Rent-A-Boat; cost is $5 per hour plus $2.50 deposit.

Para-Sailing
Experience a thrill of a lifetime, and enjoy the most spectacular view of Catalina as you soar overhead. You have no need to get wet as you'll be taking off and landing directly in the boat. Simply stand there as the wind fills the para-sail and gently lifts you into the sky. **Para-Sailing Catalina With Island Cruzers** is next to Brown's Bikes across from the basketball courts; tel. (310) 510-1777.

Kayaking
You'll see the **Wet Spot,** tel. (310) 510-2229, just before you reach the boat dock on the Cabrillo Mole. Here you'll find kayaks, pedal boats, wetsuits, snorkel gear, and beach equipment for rent; it's open summer only.

Descanso Beach Ocean Sports also rents kayaks and snorkel gear, and you'll find food, drinks, and beach-side service too. Ask about customized kayak trips; you'll find it at Descanso Beach, three minutes' walk beyond Casino Point, tel. (310) 510-1226.

Ocean Safety

The usual precautions apply: don't swim alone in isolated places, and don't take small children to rough surf areas, especially if there isn't a lifeguard. Familiarize yourself with the beach before splashing into the surf. In Avalon the surf is usually gentle during the summer, but at Pebbly Beach and on the Island's back side the surf is much stronger and there are no lifeguards. While swimming, if you feel yourself being pulled out to sea, don't panic and don't wear yourself out trying to swim to shore. Instead, swim parallel to the beach in either direction; usually after swimming three or four yards you'll be out of the undertow--then swim to shore. Pebbly Beach especially is noted for undertows.

GROUNDED SPORTS

RIDE AND RUN

Biking

You'll find lots of fine places to bike on the Island. In Avalon, bike to Pebbly Beach, to the Casino, to the Wrigley Memorial Gardens, or just up and down the streets of Avalon to peep at the houses. If you want to go out of town, get a free bike permit at the Conservancy Office at 125 Claressa Ave., and then take off for the hills, up past the Chimes Tower and through the "gate" at Hogsback, and you can go as far as you are able. You can bring camping gear, or you can make it a roundtrip day adventure.

Horseback Riding

Catalina Stables and Kennel is on Avalon Canyon Rd. just past the golf links on the left side of the street. You can ride the picturesque mountain and valley trails on a Western saddle. An active group of Catalina riders uses a pony ring. Rentals are available by the hour or day, with one-hour guided rides at $30, two hours for $45 pp. Call (310) 510-0478.

Running

The Island is a great place to run, with lots of flat roads, gentle rises, and steep hills--take your choice. Catalina is the scene of several popular

biking at the summit

PATTI LANGE

Exercising the horses at Catalina Stables.

running events each year, among them a triathlon that includes a run into the hills, a bike ride into the hills, and a swim across the bay.

LINKS AND NETS

Golf

The nine-hole, 32-par Catalina Golf Course offers a challenge to all golfers, duffers and experts alike.

The course, with its narrow fairways hugged by rugged hills, is considered tricky. Tall eucalyptus trees spill welcome shade across the grass, while thick groups of scattered fig trees provide a juicy fruit snack in late summer, yours for the taking. Out-of-bounds is tall dry grass and brambles. Be prepared for an up-and-down climb.

The course is kept in good condition--though occasionally a wild boar makes his way onto the green and digs in the tender grass, but the patient attendants make quick repairs. The course has a small putting green but no driving range.

The first three holes were built by the Bannings in 1892; they added four more, and by 1894 there were nine holes.

Catalina is believed to be one of the first golf courses in the United States. Old photos at the museum show the busy fairways with women playing golf in flouncy dresses, button-top shoes, and Gibson Girl hats.

In years past, this was the scene of the Bobby Jones Tournament, Bobby himself participating. Many celebrities played the course over the years.

Since 1968, the Catalina Golf Course has been the site of the prestigious Catalina Junior Golf

Several running events take place yearly.

Tournament. Held the weekend after Easter Sunday, the tournament attracts talented juniors from all over California. Several young adults on the pro circuit today began their careers playing in this tournament--Amy Alcott and Craig Stadler to name two.

A pro shop sells the basics: clubs, balls, gloves, hats, and tees. Rentals include clubs and motorized carts. Pro Frankie Hernandez gives lessons in the off-season, group or private.

At the old pitch and putt course on the street just below the Country Club is the **Sand Trap,** a great outdoor sandwich shop that also serves cold drinks, breakfast and barbecue-your-own dinners.

To reach the Country Club, walk to the end of Sumner Ave. and up the small hill (well-marked with a sign that says Catalina Visitors Country Club). This is where you pay your greensfees; call (310) 510-0530 for more information. Greens fee: $20 for nine holes, $10 golf cart rental for nine holes.

Tennis

Laykold tennis courts are available (free) throughout the summer at the Avalon School Grounds in Falls Canyon. From mid-September to mid-June, the courts are available before 9 a.m. and after 2:30 p.m. Bring your own equipment.

At the Catalina Visitor's Country Club you'll find Pacific Pave tennis courts. You can rent rackets and balls. The courts are lit for night use. (For directions to the Country Club see "Golf.") Fees

are: $10 hourly, racket rental is $1. Reservations are a good idea, up to 24 hours ahead, tel. (310) 510-0530

HUNTING

Catalina's 40,000-acre hunting site is rich with mule deer and wild boar. Hunts are determined by the "hatch," and the average season supports about 42 hunts from mid-October until mid-December. Only eight hunters at a time hunt the 40,000-acre reserve. Mule deer is the primary game and wild boar the secondary game. You may arrange exclusive hunts for a limited number of other exotic game, such as Spanish mountain goat, black buck antelope, or American bison.

Licenses

You will need to obtain a California G-14 zone either-sex tag to hunt on Catalina Island. To hunt pig as well as deer, have a pig tag in your possession. Tags are available from the California Department of Fish and Game in Sacramento. You must have your tags in hand when you arrive since they are not available on the Island.

Gear

You may use rifles only (.270 and up recommended); scopes are highly recommended. No handguns, archery, or assault rifles are allowed. Blaze orange vests are *required*. Other clothing should include heavy-duty boots. Bring a

Catalina bison

OZ MALLAN

set of field glasses, a good supply of ammunition, and a warm jacket.

Terrain
The landscape varies from hillsides--some steep, some gentle--to open fields, wooded canyons, and steep rocky mountains.

Package Prices
Land-packages are available that include food, lodging, on-island hunting vehicles and transportation, guide service, and game cleaning and packaging ready for return shipment to the Mainland. It does not include transportation to and from the Island.

There's always a waiting list of hunters for the Island hunts; names are drawn from a pool of applicants. Call Kathleen King at

Two Harbors, (310) 510-0303, for detailed information, including prices.

Lodging
Hunters will find the Banning House Bed and Breakfast very pleasant lodging within a few minutes' walk to the ocean, Doug's Harbor Reef Bar and Cafe, and general store.

The Conservancy
You will be hunting on Catalina Conservancy land and all profits go to help the nonprofit organization. The hunting program is carefully managed, and you may hunt only introduced animals. By removing these exotic species, which have severely damaged the Island's flora, hunting guests are helping to restore and enhance Catalina's native plants and animals.

AFTER DARK

It's perfectly safe and highly recommended to meander Avalon's streets after dark. This is a magic time of dancing lights, shimmering sights, and the moon rising dramatically from behind Mt. Ada. Take a romantic walk along Pebbly Beach Road to Abalone Point (aptly named Lovers Cove) for a glimpse of Avalon after dark. Stroll along the serpentine wall of the waterfront; follow the front street, Crescent Ave., past the Tuna Club and the Yacht Club to the Casino. Be sure to take a boat ride over the black silky water for a glimpse of flying fish, or stargaze on a harbor cruise.

ENTERTAINMENT

Movies
The **Casino Theater,** tel. (310) 510-0179, presents first-run movies that change weekly. It offers two showings--7 and 9:30 p.m. Winter season there are two showings only on Friday and Saturday night; admission is adult $7, senior $4, child $3. Get there when the box office opens at 7 p.m. (or earlier if it's a popular film--there'll be a line); this will give you a few minutes to inspect the monumental art-deco murals painted more than 50 years ago by John Beckman. When the movie is over, stroll around the

BOB SALISBURY

Bob is one of the local boys who continues "to make good." Bob is an outstanding musician and frequently plays the Page organ for Avalon visitors before the first movie on weekend evenings. Those who dine on weekends at the Channel House will hear him play his baby grand piano. Bob's choices of music cover the entire spectrum of today's music. He has several CDs for sale in gift shops around town; you can also buy them at the Channel House Restaurant.

theater to the edge of the seawall for another impressive view of the bay and glimmering Avalon town. During the summer, Bob Salisbury plays the Page organ Friday and Saturday nights before the first showing.

Dances
About 10 times a year the big-band sound comes to the world-famous **Casino ballroom.**

These events generally begin at 8:30 p.m. and last until 1 a.m. or on Saturday afternoons from 12-4 p.m.

The 20,000-square-foot ballroom, which accommodates 1,200 dancers, is veneered with seven hardwoods laid over cork for an ideal dancing surface. The open balcony encircling the ballroom presents a breathtaking view of stars, moon, and sea. The bar serves liquor, and food is sometimes available. For special dances, such as on New Year's Eve and other special dates, an excellent meal is catered in the ballroom. Prices vary according to the event. Drinks average $4. Call the Avalon Chamber of Commerce, tel. (310) 510-1520 or (310) 510-2000, or your local Ticketron office for scheduled bands and ticket information. The Casino ballroom is available for private parties, tel. (310) 510-0244.

Live Theater
Avalon's amateur theater group is called ACT, **Avalon Community Theater.** This energetic local company presents several productions during the year. Popular with visitors and hometown audiences, the plays are staged at Tremont Hall (at the end of Tremont St.) and admission is generally adult $6, child $2.50.

GETTING MARRIED ON CATALINA

Catalina *is* the Isle of Romance. And as such more and more couples choose to get married on the Island. Pick a hilltop or a cove, and more than likely a wedding can be planned around it. Newspapers all over the country are filled with curious weddings; couples have tied the knot in hot-air balloons, on boats at sea, sky-diving, on horseback; even Catalina'a famous marine gardens were the location of a "watery wedding." The happy couple (in complete scuba gear, wet suits plus a floating white veil for the bride) were wed underwater with witnesses and videos. Guess what they did for their honeymoon-- they spent a week scuba diving.

Getting Married By The Sea
Even for traditionalists-- couples who just want the "usual" with flowers and bridal gown --Catalina has everything to offer including several companies who will coordinate the whole thing.

Weddings By The Sea suggests a variety of settings from which to choose: garden spots, courtyards, hotel patios, as well as beautiful vistas around the Island. If a couple wants something unique, these wedding specialists are full of ideas. They will assist with coordinating music, photography, video, catering, and flowers. For more information call Anne Marshall, (310) 510-0436, Box 2173, Avalon, CA, 90704.

Another choice is **Island Romance.** They will make all arrangements to ensure that special day on Catalina will be all that it can be. Contact Nancy Russel, wedding and group coordinator, Box 2096, Avalon, CA 90704, tel. (310) 510-2096.

Note: The Inn on Mt. Ada is available for weddings, including all the rooms if you reserve in advance, tel. (310) 510-2030. Don't forget the wedding license!

Added Touches
For wedding pictures there are a couple of good local choices: **Avalon Studio Arts'** photographer Tony Sanders, tel. (310) 510-0824. **Wedding Photographs By Melinda,** tel. (310) 510-8344. For catering contact **Casino Ballroom Catering,** (310) 510-7400. Wedding cakes can be made by **Mama's Bakery & Deli,** or **Avalon Bake Shop.** Check out local florists: **Catalina Floral Design,** tel. (310) 510-0529 and **In Paradise,** tel. (310) 510-2143. Need a ring? **Catalina Gold Co.** at the Metropole Marketplace has a great selection. Any number of restaurants in town are perfect for a reception--and there's always the Casino Ballroom.

JAZZTRAX

What a great name for a lively weekend event in Avalon (actually you have two weekends to choose from). Anyone who is a jazz lover will enjoy such greats as Richard Elliot, Craig Chaquico, Greg Vail, Tuck and Patti, Nelson Rangell, and on and on. The festival is generally in October (Chamber of Commerce has exact dates). The venue is the stunning Casino Ballroom, with high-tech sound, room for lots of folks, choice of seating, tables available. Several artists play each day. For more information call (619) 535-0899 or the Catalina Chamber of Commerce, (310) 510-1520.

Nightclubs

Avalon's nightspots come alive after the sun goes down. The **Channel House Restaurant,** 205 Crescent Ave., tel. (310) 510-1617, at the Metropole Marketplace advertises "light jazz" evenings, seafood, steaks, fabulous bar, patio and decor. **The Galleon** restaurant and bar across from Middle Beach (also on Crescent Ave.) sports a small sidewalk cafe, a great crowd-watching spot, but you'll find the action inside; in the summer you have a chance to get up and sing with the help of karaoke--a machine that gives your singing *star quality.* Don't forget the **Chi-Chi,** 107 Sumner, for a lively afternoon or evening of live DJ music and dancing seven nights a week all summer.

Luau Larry's stages loud live music on Friday and Saturday night; one-man-band Bobby Johnston sings a little of Dylan, Buffet, Marley, and reggae--don't forget to try a wiki wacker (the house drink)! Plan to spend at least one evening of your vacation at the **Catalina Comedy Club** next to the Glenmore Plaza Hotel, tel. (310) 510-1400. You'll catch good featured comedians from the Improv and HBO, to name just two; prices vary depending on the artist.

The Blue Parrot, on Crescent Ave., tel. (310) 510-2465, offers a tropical atmosphere and light blues music in the summer.

Sportsmen, don't despair! For that baseball game or early season football exhibition game you just can't miss, rush to **J.L.'s Locker Room,** 126 Sumner Ave., tel. (310) 510-0258. This is Avalon's only sports bar, with five large-screen TVs dedicated to sports viewers. Drinks are approximately $3.50; the bar is open 10 a.m.-2 a.m., cash only. If you just want a quiet spot to share a late-evening espresso with a special person, drop by **C.C. Gallaghers,** 523 Crescent Avenue, tel. (310) 510-1278.

The Arcade

Avalon's arcade, the **Mardi Gras,** 225 Crescent Ave., tel. (310) 510-0967, is like most arcades everywhere--it has all the latest electronic games, is well-lit, and generally crowded with young kids.

Miniature Golf

Golf Gardens is open every day from April through October and weekends during the winter. This 18-hole park is in a one-acre garden set back one block from the beach. Enter from the Island Plaza. Rates for adults and children, $5.25 pp. It's open 10 a.m.-9 p.m. summer, 10 a.m.-4 p.m. winter, tel. (310) 510-1200.

Browsing Avalon

Since daytime in Avalon is taken up with myriad outdoor activities, evening is the perfect time for a stroll through the shops.

The **Metropole Marketplace** is a browsers' paradise with 30 shops, several clothing stores, gift shops with Catalina souvenirs, and an art/gift shop where you can find original drawings and paintings of Catalina. For an after-dinner treat, the **Catalina Cookie Company,** home of the "killer brownie," sells home-style cookies and luscious old-fashioned handmade chocolate turtles and fudge. Or for ice cream go to **Catalina Ice Cream** parlor. You might prefer to walk up a flight of stairs to **The Blue Parrot** for a drink or dinner on the outdoor patio and enjoy the view over the harbor. After leaving the Metropole Marketplace, wander up Crescent to the **El Encanto Mexican Marketplace,** with its bubbling fountain, Latin atmosphere, shops, and restaurants. All along Crescent Ave. clothing and gifts shops offer perfect souvenirs, clothes, or original art.

EVENING CRUISES

Shore Boat

The shore boat is an important service for the boating community. The several shore boats that dock at the Pleasure Pier run every hour, shuttling passengers to and from their boats. This is also a fun way to spend an hour sightseeing on the bay; you'll get a close-up view of the many vessels that visit Avalon Harbor--the small fishing boats, the super-deluxe powerboats docked in the outer harbor, and the sleek-lined sailboats. Fares for the inner harbor are $2 pp, for the outer harbor, $2.50, to White's Landing, $5, children $1. Hours vary with the season; in summer the boat generally runs 7 a.m.-2 a.m., in winter weekday hours are 8 a.m.-10 p.m., winter weekends 8 a.m.-midnight.

Harbor Cruise

The shore boat travels to White's Landing three times a day at 3, 6, and 9 p.m., May through September, for $10 RT. For those mooring their boats at White's Landing, it's an opportunity for a night out on the town. The boat also offers a harbor cruise around Avalon Bay for $2 adults, $1 children.

Flying Fish

A boat trip on the *Blanche W* to see the flying fish leaves the Pleasure Pier every evening at dark. These trips start in May and continue into September, when the warm Pacific lures the four-winged fish to the waters surrounding Catalina. The boat is an open launch equipped with a 40-million-candlepower searchlight. Attracted by the light, these unusual fish glide as far as 50 feet along the water. They often fly over the boat and have even been known to land in a viewer's lap. The species found in Catalina waters grows 19-24 inches in length and can weigh 1.5 to 2 pounds--Goliaths compared to the tiny flying fish common in the South

Pacific. It has a blue back and silver belly, with practically transparent fins that serve as wings. When the wings dry out, the fish plummets back into the water.

The *Blanche W* motors north along the Island's coast, the powerful light playing up and down the steep cliffs that edge the water. Be sure to bring a sweater or light jacket because the ocean air after dark can be chilly--even in summer. The trip lasts one hour; tickets and reservations are available from the visitor's information center on Crescent Avenue. For more information and schedules, call (310) 510-2000 in Avalon.

Underwater Gardens

Visiting the graceful creatures of the deep at night is an adventure. On an evening trip you may see a hungry sea lion swimming swiftly through the water, chasing after the flying fish that are attracted to the brilliant underwater light. Here's a good opportunity to see certain species of marinelife that hide or sleep during the day, such as the Catalina lobster.

The *Emerald* and the *Starlight* semi-submersibles make evening runs to Lovers Cove and treat passengers, surrounded by thick clear windows, to a glidelike ride through the midst of intriguing sealife. The brilliant light and delightful taste treats bring gangs of fish thrashing and diving.

Trips leave the Pleasure Pier several times daily; tickets and reservations are available at the Visitors Center, or at the Island Plaza kiosk. The *Oceanview* is a glass-bottom boat equipped with a powerful light that shines down around its glass wells. A powerful diesel-driven craft, its four sheets of laminated quarter-inch glass allow an unusually clear view of the marine environment.

The boat operates year-round, with night trips as long as the weather permits. Make reservations and buy tickets on the Pleasure Pier.

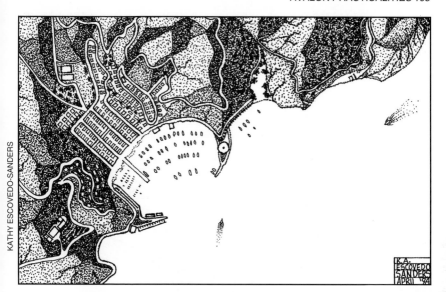

KATHY ESCOVEDO-SANDERS

PRACTICALITIES

ACCOMMODATIONS

The variety of accommodations on Catalina can be as luxurious as your wallet and taste dictate. You can stay on top of a hill with its invigorating walk and views, or you can remain on the "flats"--close to all downtown activities and just a short walk from the beach.

Note: with the exception of Banning House Lodge Bed and Breakfast Inn, and winter camping cabins at Two Harbors, the only lodging on the Island lies within Avalon city limits.

Many hotels offer package deals. During summer most require a two-day weekend minimum stay, and on holiday weekends a three-day minimum. Condominiums and houses, which offer kitchens, are also available. Make reservations as early as possible for summer stays and don't hesitate to visit Avalon in the winter. Winter rates, which begin the middle of October, are cheaper, the weather is usually

beautiful, and you'll find fewer tourists, giving Islanders more time to show you what their Island is really like. A city ordinance states that children (under 18) cannot occupy an overnight accommodation unless accompanied by a parent or guardian.

SERVICES AND RESERVATIONS

Many hotels serve free coffee or breakfast, some provide transportation to or from the mole or heliport, and some have jacuzzis, patios, and barbecues. During the summer, reservations will ensure a room; in the winter you could chance it and probably get a room that suits you. The Avalon Chamber of Commerce, tel. (310) 510-1520, handles a simple one-call system; it has a good list of current reservations available. Make one call and the staff will tell you what's available and in turn transfer your call to the hotel of your choice. Rates are quite fluid in today's economy and Catalina is definitely affected by the seasons--call and double-check for the most current prices. Add an eight and

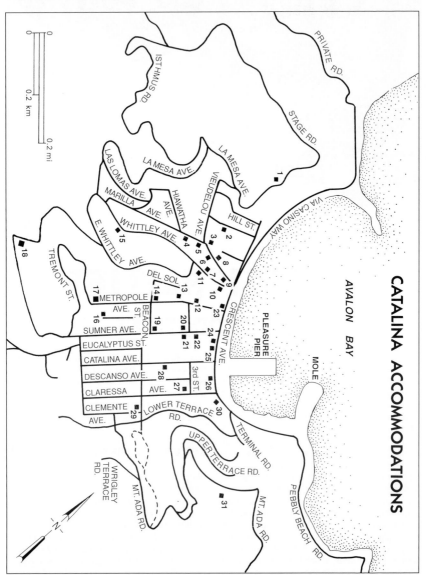

CATALINA ACCOMMODATIONS

CATALINA ACCOMMODATIONS

MAP #	NAME	PHONE	RATES	TRANSPORT	OCEAN VIEW	RESTAURANT	CONTINENTAL BREAKFAST
20	Atwater Hotel	(310) 510-2500	$55–130	no	no	yes	no
	Banning House	(310) 510-0303	$55–180	yes	yes	no	no
10	Bayview Hotel	(310) 510-2848	$40–60	no	yes	no	yes
11	Buena Vista Hotel	(310) 510-0340	$80–130	no	yes	no	no
14	Casa Mariquita	(310) 510-1192	$80–275	yes	yes	no	no
5	Catalina Beach House	(310) 510-1078	$35–135	yes	yes	no	yes
18	Catalina Canyon Hotel	(310) 510-0325	$69–135	yes	yes	yes	no
13	Catalina Cottages	(310) 510-1010	$35–100	no	no	no	no
12	Catalina Island Inn	(310) 510-1623	$75–185	yes	yes	no	yes
19	Catalina Lodge	(310) 510-1070	$79	yes	no	no	yes
30	Catherine Hotel	(310) 510-0170	$75–100	no	yes	yes	no
8	Cloud 7	(310) 510-0454	$40–130	yes	yes	no	yes
24	Edgewater Hotel	(310) 510-0347	$65–265	no	yes	no	yes
3	El Rancho Hotel	(310) 510-0603	$40–75	no	yes	no	no
4	El Terado Terrace	(310) 510-0831	$55–120	no	yes	no	yes
21	Glenmore Plaza Hotel	(310) 510-0017	$89–400	yes	yes	yes	no
15	Gull House	(310) 510-2547	$110-145	yes	no	no	yes+
7	Hotel Catalina	(310) 510-0027	$50–110	no	yes	no	yes
22	Hotel MacRae	(310) 510-0246	$42	no	yes	yes	yes
23	Hotel Metropole	(310) 510-1884	$89–295	yes	yes	yes	yes
32	Hotel Monterey	(310) 510-0264	$65-165	no	yes	yes	yes
11	Hotel Villa Portofino	(310) 510-0555	$65–275	yes	yes	yes	yes
8	Hotel Vincente's	(310) 510-1115	$89–235	no	yes	no	yes
25	Hotel Vista Del Mar	(310) 510-1452	$65–275	yes	yes	yes	yes
31	Inn on Mt. Ada	(310) 510-2030	$250–620	yes	yes	yes	yes
16	La Paloma	(310) 510-1505	$45–165	yes	yes	no	no
28	Old Turner Inn	(310) 510-2236	$100–180	no	no	no	yes
26	Pavilion Lodge	(800) 626-5440	$59–169	no	no	no	no
27	Seacrest Inn	(310) 510-0800	$65–185	yes	no	no	yes
2	Seaport Village Inn	(310) 510-0344	$69–189	yes	yes	no	yes
17	Hotel St. Lauren	(800)645-2479	$40–210	no	yes	no	yes
1	Zane Grey Hotel	(310) 510-0966	$55–125	yes	yes	no	yes

Add 8.5% tax.

a half percent city bed tax to hotel prices you are quoted.

Remember, prices quoted are the hotels' bottom prices, and they go up from there.

HOTELS

Picturesque Hotels

El Terado Terrace stretches across a small canyon, each unit with a complete kitchen. You'll have a stunning view from **Zane Grey Hotel,** the historical former home of the late Western novelist and big-game fisherman and now a bed and breakfast. The **Glenmore Plaza Hotel,** built in 1887, is charming and boasts that Teddy Roosevelt slept here; for a special occasion stay in the cupola suite (round bed included). The **Catalina Island Inn** was built in 1906, and the turn-of-the-century flavor has been tastefully preserved. Another with yesteryear charm, the **Hotel Catalina** is one of the older hotels in town and reflects its past.

Modern

Some of the more modern accommodations include attractive **Seaport Village,** which offers small rooms to suites with all the conveniences, including a jacuzzi; some have lovely views of the harbor.

When you call, ask about its package deals, including transportation from the Mainland. **Hotel Villa Portofino** has a beachfront location, queen- and king-size beds, some suites with ocean view; it's downtown and close to all activities. You'll find an excellent restaurant and bar on the premises.

Try **Hotel Vincente's,** where all rooms have king-size beds, refrigerators, color televisions, heat, and fans. Suites have ocean views.

Luxury

Avalon luxury hotels are not that much more expensive than the average hotel and well worth the splurge. The **Hotel Vista Del Mar** is one of Avalon's newest hotels; it's in the center of town on Crescent Ave. overlooking Avalon Bay and the beach.

Upscale rooms include cable color TV, a wet bar, refrigerator, air-conditioning, telephones, fireplaces, and some are equipped with jacuzzis.

Continental breakfast is served in the cool green atrium.

The pink **Hotel St. Lauren** was designed to resemble the old circular building that was built on the same spot at the turn of the century. The lovely new structure has amenities the old homestead probably never dreamed of, such as jacuzzis, rooms for the handicapped, an elevator, smoking and nonsmoking rooms, color TV, phones, video rentals, honeymoon suites, and conference rooms. Guests are invited to a continental breakfast with an ocean view--all of this a block from the beach. Ask about year-round packages. No pets are allowed.

Note: ask for a room in the back; those in the front hear the passing traffic all night.

The new **Hotel Metropole** has 45 rooms offering various amenities depending on whether you choose standard, superior, or suites. The standard rooms are nice, suites are really outstanding. Your choices include jacuzzi, ocean view, balcony, fireplace; an elevator serves the upper floors. Some rooms look over the busy

Hotel Metropole

OZ MALLAN

OZ MALLAN

Old Turner Inn B&B

and continental breakfast is free. The Pavilion's 72 rooms are just "14 steps" from South Beach and the blue Pacific, and from all downtown activities and restaurants. It provides baggage delivery to and from the transportation terminal at the Cabrillo Mole. Rates are variable according to season, from a low of $49 to a high of $149. For hotel information and reservations, call from California (800) 446-0249.

Budget

Although the **Bayview Hotel** is diver-friendly, it's just as friendly to nondivers. The simple family-oriented hotel offers continental breakfast. For reservations, call (310) 510-2848 or fax (310) 510-1204. Ask about family rates.

The **La Paloma,** tel. (800) 310-1505, (310) 510-1505, is a shady group of bungalows with patios and barbecues off the main drag with 1940s charm. The new part of the hotel, **Las Flores,** offers luxury rooms with double whirlpool tubs, refrigerators, and coffee-makers.

The older hotels are few in number so make summer reservations as early as possible; many rooms have shared bathrooms.

BED AND BREAKFAST

Avalon boasts five outstanding bed and breakfasts. Guests frequently call **The Inn on Mount Ada** the star of B&Bs in California. This is the former William Wrigley Jr. home, a Georgian colonial style "mansion" built on a hill overlooking Avalon Bay. The home was built in 1919 after the Wrigleys bought Catalina Island, and beautifully refurbished and renovated to accommodate visitors of the 1990s. Innkeepers Susie Griffin and Marlene McAdam have created a luxurious, pleasant home reminiscent of the Wrigley era. Each bedroom is comfy and attractive; some have fireplaces. The house is inviting and decorated with antiques and comfortable furniture. The views are spectacular-- Ada Wrigley loved it because she could watch the sun rise *and* set. The public rooms are many and spacious, including a formal living room and dining room, expansive terrace, a cozy sun room always stocked for help-yourself snacks, including homemade cookies, fresh fruit, hot and cold drinks. Wine and hors d'oeuvres are served at cocktail hour. A hearty

Metropole Marketplace, with fountains and plants, shops, cafes, and the buzz of the crowd. The hotel provides transportation to and from the mole or heliport. Packages are available, and price includes continental breakfast. For more information, call (800) 300-8528 or (310) 510-1884.

Moderate

The newly built **Casa Mariquita,** tel. (800) 410-1192, is Spanish-styled, comfortable, and shiny clean. Rooms offer a/c, refrigerator, cable TV, telephone, and continental breakfast. It's conveniently located on Metropole, one block to the beach.

Downtown

The **Pavilion Lodge** in 1991 was the recipient of a $1.8 million renovation and remodeling transformation. The hotel now has air-conditioning/heating, nice bathrooms, comfortable room furnishings and bright colors for all units. A lovely garden courtyard is lined with chaises longues,

THE INN AT MT. ADA

On the top of a hill overlooking Avalon Bay, chewing gum tycoon, William Wrigley Jr's lovely Georgian "cottage" is now one of the most acclaimed bed and breakfasts in California.

His love and enthusiasm for the Island's beauty is apparent in the design of the house. It boasts breathtaking views from almost every room and especially from the broad luxurious terrace.

One favorite story tells how he had a window cut into his cottage so he could watch the activity on the baseball diamond where his Chicago Cubs took part in spring practice. Fact or fiction? The house was warm and

OZ MALLAN

OZ MALLAN

A VIEW FROM ABOVE

OZ MALLAN

OZ MALLAN

inviting and today's guests feel the same pampering hospitality of the past.

Every Christmas season the Inn is open to the public for a grand tour, a cookie and wassail party (no admission is charged, proceeds from raffles go to the Catalina Museum). If you happen to be on the Island during the Christmas holidays, do attend; the house is always beautifully kept, but for this event it becomes a Christmas fairyland.

"Catalina" breakfast, deli lunch, and gourmet dinner are included in the price, as is the use of a golf cart.

All six rooms have beautiful views and different prices. No smoking; children over 14 are welcome. Want to have a wedding party? The Inn is available. Reservations year-round are a must; call (310) 510-2030.

The "Old" Turner Inn is a quiet country setting in the heart of Avalon near the beach. Completely renovated, the inn is convenient to all the activities of town. The Old Turner Inn offers five guest rooms (four with wood-burning fireplaces), handmade linens, and lovely antique furniture. Guests enjoy a superb continental-plus breakfast buffet, and the inn serves wine and snacks in the afternoon. Bikes are available for touring the island. Rates are $110 to $175. You'll find it at 232 Catalina Ave., tel. (310) 510-2236; the mailing address is P.O. Box 97, Avalon, CA 90704.

Gull House, 344 Whittley Ave., offers two suites with separate entrances, living room, and in the rear-yard patio a small pool, spa, and barbecue. Owners Hattie and Bob Michalis give special attention to anniversary and honeymoon couples. The roomy suites are comfortable and offer much privacy. Continental breakfast is served each morning under an umbrella on a cheery patio. Rates are $125-135; the inn is closed approximately November through April. For more information and reservations, call (310) 510-2547 or write to P.O. Box 1381, Avalon, CA 90704.

Catalina Island Seacrest Inn offers a cozy romantic getaway with free continental breakfast, in-room fireplaces, whirlpool spa for two, and nonsmoking rooms. Ask about wedding packages that include boat or air transportation. It's a block from the beach at 201 Claressa, Box 128, Avalon, CA 90704, tel. (310) 510-0800, fax (310) 510-1122.

Zane Grey Pueblo, tel. (800) 3-Pueblo, (310) 510-0966, offers one of the best views in Avalon. The home was built by author Zane Grey in 1926 in the Hopi Indian style. Grey lived here and did some of his writing here. The pueblo offers a swimming pool, multiple patios, queen beds, coffee, tea, and toast for breakfast, and a courtesy taxi will meet you when you arrive. Ask about winter rates.

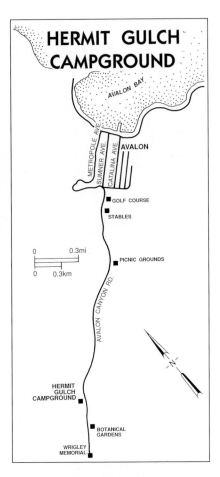

CAMPING

The cheapest way to stay in Avalon is to bring your tent and camp at the **Hermit Gulch Campground,** or set up camp in an Indian tepee camp or tent cabin; Hermit Gulch rents camping equiment. The complex can accommodate 200 people and is handicapped-accessible. Rates are $6 pp per night. It's a one-mile walk from the mole past the golf course on Avalon Canyon Rd., or take a tram from the plaza, $2. Call the campground for a tram schedule at (310) 510-8368.

Hermit Gulch Campground

Campers will find lighted restrooms, flush toilets, coin-operated indoor hot showers, vending machines, fire rings, picnic tables, barbecues, and a group campfire area. This is a great place for a family reunion. Tepee package prices are available, as are off-season discounts. Reservations are necessary. Call (310) 510-TENT, (310) 510-8368.

OTHER RENTALS

Many visitors save on vacation costs by renting a house or condo and sharing it with another family or group. The condos are all fairly new and in many cases offer a swimming pool. Most of the rental cottages are older, but some are larger than many of the condos. More houses and apartments are available each year. If you're interested in this option, several good property managers offer long lists of houses, apartments, and condos. **Catalina Island Vacation Rentals,** 119 Sumner Ave., tel. (310) 510-2276, offers houses all over town plus a good selection of Hamilton Cove Condos. Accommodations rented through one of these companies usually offer telephones, microwaves, televisions, and linen service. Call Beach Realty, tel. (310) 510-0039; or Hunt & Associates Realtors, tel. (310) 510-2721.

busy Avalon Bay

AVALON 10:40 to 6:00
Seafood
Open 7 Days a Week

SHRIMP	3.00
SCALLOPS	3.50
ABALONE	4.50
CALAMARI	3.50
ABALONE STEAK	4.50
ABALONE BURGER	3.00

DIET 7-UP
DIET ROOT BEER
MILK
CHOC. MILK .65
O.J. .65 LRG. 85

Coke

ABALONE SANDWICH   ABALONE BURGE
3.00
FILET OF CHICKEN   ROSIE'S REAL CHEDD
BREAST SANDWICH   CHEESE FRESH FISH SA
SWORDFISH   SWORDFISH SANDWI
4.00   2.25

KATHY ESCOVEDO-SANDERS

FOOD

In Avalon, eating can be a gratifying dining experience or merely the exercising of a necessary daily habit. The town offers walk-away hotdog stands, carry-out tacos, fresh shrimp cocktails in paper cups, and chocolate-covered frozen fruit, as well as culinary delights at a variety of first-class restaurants. As of this printing the big chain burger takeouts haven't yet invaded the Island, but Kentucky Fried Chicken/Taco Bell has made a breakthrough! You'll find little difference in price between comparable restaurants in Catalina and Southern California. If in some instances you notice the prices are slightly higher on Catalina, remember that you're on an island; everything you eat starts out on the Mainland and must be barged across the ocean.

The Way to Start Your Day
Don't be a lay-a-bed; get up early and get out to the **Casino Dock Cafe** (it opens at 7 a.m.). Get a hot *cuppa* (of your choice) and sit on the dock and watch the sun and harbor come to life. Look around. You'll see lots of Islanders; they know how to enjoy their special Island. Breakfasts

are simple but good! Try the "porthole," --eggs, avocado, and bacon grilled on an English muffin--or one of the many other choices. Place your order inside. Watch the buoys on Casino Point, and along with the seagulls, pelicans, and cormorants, you'll see a long-legged white egret that looks a little out of place, but happy. It's fun to watch the boaters as they rise and start their vacation routines in the quiet morning harbor. The cafe serves breakfast and lunch, from 7 a.m. until 4 p.m.

FROM ETHNIC TO RED WHITE AND BLUE

Mexican Fare
Several good Mexican restaurants have atmosphere to match. **Mi Casita** on Claressa Ave. serves excellent Mexican food in a pleasant south-of-the-border atmosphere. The full bar serves margaritas and the specialty of the house, a fruity "cazuela" drink, is big and potent. Moises and Estella are from Guadalajara

and go out of their way to please. Mi Casita is open for lunch and dinner. For a family-style cafe and a quick spicy lunch go to **Coyote Joe's,** at 113 Catalina Ave., or on the front street, try the **Topless Tacos**--prices are good, but the tacos are tiny.

A few breakfast houses, such as **Joe's Place,** the **Pancake Cottage,** and **Sally's Waffle Shop,** open for the early fishermen and serve hearty lunches.

Dining with a View
The **Busy Bee** offers a great view of the bay, boats, and Casino along with full cocktail service, and it grinds its own beef for delicious half-pound burgers. Another outdoor cafe, **Coney Island West** at the **Metropole Marketplace,** offers the best hamburgers in town (really!) and crowd-watching tables where the pigeons strut close by hoping for a small crumb.

Outstanding Dinner Houses
Channel House is one of the nicest in town; it serves lunch in the summer. But dinner is special, either inside or out. Ambience is crystal and candlelight, with romantic piano music in the background, played by Bob Salisbury during the season. Channel House serves good steaks, excellent German dishes, and gourmet desserts. It offers full bar service. **Armstrong's** specializes in the freshest seafood (try the swordfish in season!!) mesquite-broiled, a great selection of

shellfish, outdoor seating, full bar, and a pleasant atmosphere. **Pirrone's** also offers a complete continental menu (including eggplant parmesan), cocktails, lunch, and a buffet brunch at which customers design their own omelettes.

Doing Italian
Italian-food lovers have several choices. The exquisite **Ristorante Villa Portofino** serves dinner year-round, offers full cocktail service, and features Northern Italian cuisine (pasta seafood dishes are served in light herb sauces). The warm romantic atmosphere invites lingering over a Frangelica or cappuccino and tiramisu. **Antonio's Pizzeria and Catalina Cabaret** serves tasty pizza and creative sandwiches with lively entertainment suitable for the whole family. **The Prego,** with soft, candlelit interior and Italian dishes (best garlic toast in town), is reminiscent of a small Italian trattoria in Florence; it serves beer and wine.

Eclectic and Good
Those who like spicy old favorites should try **The Blue Parrot**--great tropical setting and American food with a Caribbean flair. Cajun prawns with linguini and seafood stew are good starters for fish lovers. You'll find it upstairs in the front part of the Metropole Plaza.

The meat-and-potato gang has many choices for dining on juicy steaks and tender prime rib dinners, many with salad bar. For a lively

OZ MALLAN

Casino Dock Cafe

evening of eating, drinking, and karaoke go to **El Galleon.** Chinese food is great at **Mr. Ning's Chinese Garden,** 127 Sumner Ave., next to the Atwater Hotel.

At the El Encanto, check out the **Landing Bar & Grill.** Downstairs try its gourmet pizzas and one of the many draft microbeers or go upstairs for the chicken piccata or the fresh fish of the day. Outdoor upstairs seating overlooks the bay; the bar offers live music on the patio on the weekends. On the coldest nights, sit by the fireplace and enjoy a hot toddy.

Barbecue it Yourself

Every evening the **Descanso Beach Club,** the **Buffalo Nickel,** and the **Sand Trap** fire up their giant barbecues and invite the public to bring their own steaks, fish, or whatever to roast over the hot charcoal. The cost is about $6.95 for a buffet of salads, baked potatoes, corn on the cob, and lots of trimmings, bread and butter; beer, wine, cocktails, and all drinks are extra.

FAST FOODS

At **Original Antonio's Pizzeria,** 114 Sumner, expect genuine pizza, gourmet sandwiches, beer and wine--even some of Mamma Mia's "day-old" spaghetti plus jukebox music of the 1950s. Antonio's offers food to go; for delivery call (310) 510-0060. It's open daily year-round.

For anyone who's been coming to Avalon for very long, the best place for Avalon seafood will always be **Rosie's** place on the Pleasure Pier! An open-air take-out restaurant, it specializes in fish and chips--cooked to perfection --and a great walk-away shrimp cocktail. If you're cooking yourself, this is the place to buy locally caught fish. Fisherman will find bait, have their gamefish cleaned, and bring their fish to be weighed here at the official weigh station for those big marlin--you know one's caught every time the cannon booms out across the bay; tel. (310) 510-0197.

On a sunny sidewalk patio, enjoy **Coney Island West,** "my choice" as the best hamburger in town, plus hot dogs, fish and chips, milk shakes, and a cold glass of beer or wine. You'll find it at the street side of the Metropole Marketplace.

Lori's Good Stuff is open 11 a.m.-4 p.m. behind Joe's Place at the foot of the Pleasure Pier on Catalina Street. Lori knows the real meaning of scrumptious fresh fruit shakes and serves thick meaty sandwiches along with healthy salads and special iced teas.

For tasty, generous submarine sandwiches, salads, and the Island's "best" cheesecake, go to **Mama's Bakery & Deli** in the Metropole Marketplace.

Bay of the Seven Moons is the nearest thing to a health-food store in Avalon. Along with a good selection of bulk grains, nuts, spices, and natural foods to go, customers will enjoy the tried and true espresso bar and occasional live music in the shady courtyard of the Metropole Marketplace, tel. (310) 510-1450.

A LITTLE BEYOND AVALON TOWN

The strolling visitor will enjoy breakfast (Saturday

Buffalo Nickel

OZ MALLAN

and Sunday only), lunch, and dinner at the **Buffalo Nickel** at the heliport in Pebbly Beach. The breakfast burrito is a local favorite. Buffalo dishes include buffalo chili, buffalo burgers, and buffalo steaks, all made with Catalina-grown buffalo. If a mile walk doesn't appeal to you, the Nickel offers free transportation back and forth to Avalon; call (310) 510-1323.

Take a stroll toward the stables and stop off at the **Sand Trap** (formerly the Pitch and Putt golf course) and have a tasty lunch alfresco. Customers have a choice of excellent sandwiches, omelettes, and special "soft" tacos, beer and wine. It's open evenings for private parties and Do-It-Yourself Barbecues, and it's open year-round for breakfast and lunch, 7:30 a.m.-3 p.m.

Farther out of the city at Catalina's Airport-in-the-Sky, visitors will find the **Runway Cafe,** open 8 a.m.-4 p.m. year-round. Vacationers who want a change of pace can enjoy a ride into Catalina's interior from Avalon on an airport van or tour bus. Or pilots can fly via their own planes. One of the Runway specialties is buffalo burgers.

Two Harbors Dining
If you'd like a chance to go to Two Harbors for dinner, take the *Blanche W* on a five-and-a-half-hour trip down the coast. The boat departs at 4:30 p.m. for a 14-mile sightseeing cruise along Catalina's stunning coastline on a comfortable 90-passenger motor vessel to Two Har-

bors at the Isthmus. This is a special evening of romantic cruising under the stars, and you arrive at Two Harbors for a look around and a carried picnic, or splurge on a good dinner at **Doug's Harbor Reef.** This trip gives you an opportunity to see the fauna that make Catalina unique. On the outgoing passage you'll enjoy the birds, the mountains, maybe a buffalo, a goat, a fox, and the setting sun, the conviviality of fellow passengers, and of course the comic crew. On your cruise back to Avalon, scan the seas for flying fish, aided by the *Blanche W*s 40-million-candlepower searchlight. It's great fun to watch the silvery-finned fish skim along the wave tops. Be sure to bring a jacket for the return trip. If can get chilly on the ocean at night. Boat fare ($25) does *not* include dinner. Get full information and make your reservations for this trip at the Catalina Visitor's Information Center across from the green Pleasure Pier or call (310) 510-2000.

SWEETS AND OTHER GOOD STUFF

On the corner of Crescent and Claressa, poke your head into **CC Gallaghers**. Here you'll find a wonderful shop filled with the trendiest, the coolest gifts, and in the far corner you'll find Avalon's only full-service espresso bar. Take your choice of lattes, cappuccinos, au laits, cold frappes, and great brioche, croissants, scones,

CC Gallaghers

OZ MALLAN

TONY SANDERS

TONY SANDERS

Make your dream of meeting that reclusive artist come true. The work of fine-art photographer Tony Sanders hangs in the company of such greats as Ansel Adams, Irving Penn, R.C. Gorman, and Henri Cartier-Bresson in many important collections and galleries across the United States and Europe. He's known for exceptional black and white photographs, shot with the 8x10 view camera, of ancient architecture such as Stonehenge, Anasazi Cliff Dwellings, Spanish missions, and the pyramids in Egypt. He keeps his studio/gallery at 310 Beacon St. in the historic bungalow once occupied by the famous skipper, Captain Eddie Harrison. Sanders displays his work in September at the Catalina Art Festival and is very well received. For more information call (310) 510-0824.

and sinfully rich pastries--oh yes, the shop does sell a fat-free cheesecake that would fool anyone. Take your goodies out into the small sidewalk cafe and enjoy.

Just up Claressa past CC Gallaghers, the **Sweet Shoppe** features a complete soda fountain along with a tantalizing display of pastries and candy, but best of all, the tastiest ice cream in town. **Big Olafs,** next to Armstrongs on Cres-

cent, sells giant ice cream cones and other ice cream specialties.

Are you looking for something really sweet? Try **Lloyd's** (an Island institution) on the corner of Crescent Ave. and Sumner, and watch *real* taffy being pulled on machines that have been operating since before WW II. There's a difference between real saltwater taffy and the imitation. Try a bag and *you'll* be the expert.

top: Avalon's Casino
bottom: Catalina's west end

top: Catalina buffalo
bottom: Catalina Yacht Club

Lloyd's also sells freshly made chocolate fudge, divinity, and pralines, and mails all of them to anywhere in the world.

In the Metropole Marketplace you'll find the **Catalina Cookie Co.,** with mouth-watering home-style cookies, candies, great coffees (brewed or beans), and last but not least, this is the home of the Killer Brownie.

PICNICS

You can use the barbecue pits, free of charge, along the mole on your way into town, close to where the boat disembarks. A pleasant one-mile walk past the horse stables on Avalon Canyon Rd. brings you to another picnic area ($1 pp, expect to pay a $100 refundable deposit) with tables and large barbecue pits. Toilets are available. Ask at the Chamber office on the pier, at the Visitor's Information Center, 605 Crescent across the street from the Pleasure Pier, or call (310) 510-2500 for information.

Bring your picnic basket or cooler over on the boat, or shop at one of the two grocery stores in Avalon: **Fred and Sally's Market,** 117 Catalina Ave., or **Von's Market,** 123 Metropole. Fred and Sally's sells tasty barbecued chicken and ribs; call early--they sell out fast. Both of these markets are not only well-stocked with food, but also with crowds of people in the narrow aisles.

SHOPPING

AVALON ARTISANS

Art Shops
Upton's House of Wood was originated by the late Avalon artist Bud Upton and his son Roger. Bud was a prodigious artist who painted scenes from all over the Island. He captured eras in time and small vignettes of the Catalina panorama from many years past until he died in 1989 at the age of 88. The quaint wooden house in the House of Wood window was just one of his clever creations and his sense of humor is evident in his "infamous" gold buffalo chip. As well as original paintings, carvings, and knickknacks, the shopper will find unique Catalina-made souvenirs. The shop, 517 Crescent Ave., is open daily during the summer.

Don't miss a stop at the **Off White Gallery,** a showroom for several of Catalina's most talented artists. You'll see watercolors by Frank Loudin, oil paintings by Denise Burns, locally designed and handcrafted gold jewelry by Dave Stein, and bronze sculpture by J. Quillan. On the corner of Crescent Ave. and Whittley at Hotel Villa Portofino, it's open year-round.

While strolling through the Metropole Marketplace, make a stop at **Perico Gallery** for something different again--pen and inks, watercolors, and prints of Catalina created by local artists. You'll also find a superb collection of Catalina bird tiles.

Browse through **Tonya's Art Gallery** with original paintings and sculptures in the El Encanto, another place where it's easy to spend time window-shopping.

GLITTER SHOPS

Gold and Silver
The **Catalina Gold Company** sells wonderful chains and unusual pieces created by talented artisans. The shop also deals in pearls and diamonds. Rumors are that the gold prices here are *much* cheaper than on the Mainland. You'll find it at the Metropole Marketplace, open year-round. **Patricia's** is a gallery of handcrafted gold and silver jewelry. Many of the silver pieces come from Taxco, Mexico, and included among the fine gifts are handblown glass and art tiles. It's just inside the arch at the El Encanto, tel. (310) 510-1448.

UPSCALE GIFTS

Trendy
Allow time to browse in a marvelous shop filled with surprises in every corner. Look up and around, and down under, and in every cranny.

CC Gallaghers, 523 Crescent Ave., on the corner of Claressa, is a gourmet, bed, bath, and wine shop. And it doesn't stop there; it sells clever educational children's toys, unusual decorator baskets, exotic dried flowers, excellent books, and too much more to try to list. As one Island visitor put it, this is a museum for the shopper. Don't miss the espresso bar in the corner, and its small outdoor patio. The shop is open year-round.

More Gift Shops

Don't miss the Conservancy's **Catalina Nature Co.** Here you'll find gifts galore that are charming and ecologically correct. The **Hen House Gifts,** in the Island Tour Plaza, offers a large selection of fun things, including unusual children's jewelry, Nativity scenes, chimes, music boxes, T-shirts, bears, and dolls. It's open daily from Easter through October, weekends in the winter; tel. (310) 510-1912.

Catalina Design Center, 125 Sumner Ave., offers handmade jewelry, woodwork, ceramics, windsocks, Pacific Coast jewelry and crafts, and lots more.

Look for **Le Bouquet de Catalina** in the Post Office arcade building, tel. (310) 510-1278. You'll find flowers, balloons, dried floral arrangements, and lovely glass designs. At **Sherri's Stationery and Gifts,** 205 Crescent Ave., tel. (310) 510-2984, shoppers will find a selection similar to most Mainland Hallmark shops. **Catalina Confetti,** tel. (310) 510-2511, offers a little bit of everything, including candy and fudge.

Two's Company of Avalon is a shop filled with elegant gifts and outstanding made-in-Catalina items; at the Metropole Marketplace.

WHAT TO WEAR?

Clothing Stores

Men and women can find an excellent choice of active sportswear and shoes, including most of the big names, at the **Catalina Island Department Store,** 421 Crescent Ave., opposite the Pleasure Pier. It sells a great selection of shorts and tops, sporty dresses, trendy sweatshirts and sweaters for those cool evenings on the water.

One of Avalon's upscale men's shops, **Buoys**

Arty signs direct the way.

and Gulls, 407 Crescent Ave., offers quality resort, yachting, and beach attire. **Catalina Gear,** 226 Crescent Ave., carries men's and women's active wear and accessories, including such brands as Patagonia.

Carlotta's Mexican Shop has been offering charming clothing, jewelry, and accessories from Mexico, Guatemala, and Indonesia for many years in the same location at the El Encanto.

Visit Peggy's Gifts and Souvenirs, next to Leo's Drug Store, 104 Sumner Ave., for a great selection of hats, bags, and shirts. Wander on up to 233 Sumner Ave. for a spree at the **Whale's Tale.** At this fashionable boutique, shoppers will find feminine fancies, finery, and gifts, including jumpsuits, swimwear, and exclusive dresses.

Shoes

Catalina Department Store and **Buoys and Gulls** offer good selections of sporty footwear.

FOR THE KIDS

Children's Shops

Looking for that special gift for the little ones? In Avalon you'll have so many choices that your problem will be making a decision. At the **Toy Attic,** 119 Claressa, you'll find a variety of toys, games, books, and beach and water toys. As for dolls, choose from quality Madame Alexander or Raikes and Gund Bears. The well-dressed child shops at **Melody's,** 106 Sumner Avenue. The selection offers children's clothing from infants and up.

The Sand Box Children's Boutique, 519 Crescent Ave., is jam-packed with all the best names in children's clothing and more. Even the kids hate to leave. Sizes are infant and up. **Catalina Kids,** 201 Crescent Ave., dresses the kids, infants and up, in T-shirts, chic beach outfits, and smart accessories.

INFORMATION AND SERVICES

Chamber of Commerce

This office, at the foot of the Pleasure Pier, offers helpful information on just about any Island-related subject; it's especially helpful for making hotel reservations by providing a list of daily hotel vacancies. Ask for a free directory of businesses in Avalon. It's open daily from 8 a.m.-5 p.m., tel. (310) 510-1520.

News Media

A local paper, the **Catalina Islander,** is published once a week. You can buy it at many shops in town. This small newspaper is mailed to thousands of Mainlanders who enjoy keeping up with Catalina activities. A classified ad section often lists summer and winter housing rentals. Another local paper, the **Avalon Bay News,** is available every Thursday. Both papers include Island news and feature stories focusing on Island history.

You can buy Mainland newspapers such as the **Los Angeles Times** at Sugarloaf Bookstore, tel. (310) 510-0077, and at several racks around town and on the mole.

OZ MALLAN

Avalon Hospital

public showers

OZ MALLAN

Bookstores

The **Sugarloaf Bookstore,** 403 Crescent Ave., carries a tremendous collection of magazines, guidebooks, best-seller fiction, paperbacks, cold drinks, candy, beer, wine, and ice cream. **R. Franklin Pyke Bookseller,** 228 Metropole Ave., tel. (310) 510-2588, carries books from cheap (secondhand paperbacks) to expensive (local history and fine collector's items), chart guides and maps, both old and new, and early local photos and postcards. It buys and sells Catalina pottery and displays local artwork. It's open Tues.-Sun. and by appointment; credit cards accepted.

Hospital and Paramedics

Avalon Municipal Hospital, 100 Falls Canyon Rd., has an efficient emergency room, a fully equipped lab, and X-ray facility. One full-time doctor is a permanent resident of Avalon, and during the summer interns come to the Island to help out. At least 20 doctors are on call when in town. In case of a serious emergency, call 911 or (310) 510-0700 for an ambulance. In extreme situations the Medivac helicopter can transport emergency cases to several hospitals on the Mainland in about 25 minutes.

Working hand in hand with the local medical staff, Avalon's highly trained paramedics have saved hundreds of lives with their quick response to emergency situations. *Bay Watch,* the Los Angeles County lifeguard vessel docked at the Avalon Mole, is manned by paramedics

who handle boating and other water-related emergencies.

For the Bends or a Toothache

The Marine Science Center at Two Harbors has one of the few hyperbaric chambers on the Southern California coast, to treat divers with the bends (nitrogen poisoning). For simple complaints you can be treated at the Avalon Clinic, 100 Falls Canyon Rd. (part of the hospital complex), tel. (310) 510-0096. If a sudden toothache won't wait until you go home, call resident dentist Dr. B.A. Calise, 204 Metropole, tel. (310) 510-0322, in Avalon.

Water

Avalon has good, clean water straight from the sky and the sea. Yes, Catalina has a desalination plant that provides 25% of the Island's water. The plant at Pebbly Beach is state of the art, and soon may increase the amount of sea water converted and then mixed with the Island's existing water-delivery system.

Mail

You can reach the post office, tel. (310) 510-0084, in the **Atwater Hotel Building** either from Metropole St. (across from Von's) or from Sumner Ave. (next to the Atwater Hotel). If you plan to stay on the Island for more than a day or two and would like to receive mail, have it addressed to you care of General Delivery, Avalon, CA 90704. There's no mail delivery in Avalon; it all comes to post office boxes or the general delivery window. Mail deposited by 3 p.m. will leave Avalon the same day. Mail drops are on the corner of Crescent and Metropole and in the post office. Helicopters bring **Federal Express** mail to the Island from Long Beach.

Telephone

For all parts of Catalina the telephone area code is 310. You'll find public telephone booths in the post office arcade, the plaza, and on the green pier. Calls to Orange County and Los Angeles County are usually less than $1 for three minutes. Western Union: tel. (800) 325-6000, in Avalon (310) 510-0600.

Restrooms

You'll find men's and women's public restrooms in Avalon at the foot of the Pleasure Pier, Boat Terminal Mole, Bird Park, Casino walkway, Island Plaza, and at Pebbly Beach. At the Buffalo Nickel look for the sign that says "Buffalo Heads." A drinking fountain sits on each end of Middle Beach.

Public Showers

At the foot of the green Pleasure Pier and along the Casino walkway, coin-operated showers are open to the public. Bring your own towel, soap, and a quarter for each three minutes of shower you desire. On middle beach, free saltwater showers are available to rinse the sand off.

Lockers

If you're just visiting for the day and need someplace to leave your gear while swimming or eating, storage lockers are available at the Island Plaza and on the mole.

Groceries

Try **Von's Market,** 123 Metropole Ave., or **Fred and Sally's Market,** 117 Catalina Ave. Ask about grocery delivery for a fee.

Laundromat

You'll find **Catalina Coin Wash** in Metropole Marketplace beyond the Cookie Company, and **Cottonwood Coin Laundry** at 220 Metropole Ave., tel. (310) 510-1244.

Dry Cleaners

Avalon Bay News, 117 Whittley Ave., tel. (310) 510-1500, doubles as a dry-cleaning depot. It sends clothes to the Mainland to be cleaned. Turnaround time can be lengthy but it's a great convenience otherwise.

Pharmacy

Leo's Drug Store, 401 Crescent Ave., tel. (310) 510-0189, fills prescriptions. Leo's is well-stocked with camera supplies, film, gifts, and other sundries.

Hardware

Chet's Hardware is Avalon's general store and

OZ MALLAN

Avalon's gas station in Pebbly Beach

carries a little bit of everything, from household goods to fishing supplies. It's open year-round in the Atwater Arcade opposite the post office, tel. (310) 510-0990.

Banks
The **Southern California Bank** offers Touch and Go ATM service at 303 Crescent Ave., tel. (310) 510-2265. It's open weekdays 9 a.m.-3 p.m., Saturday 9 a.m.-noon. You'll find another ATM on Catalina Street next to the Visitor's Center.

Credit Cards
Business is run much as it is on the Mainland; most businesses accept credit cards. Many do not accept personal checks, but most will accept well-known traveler's checks with proper identification.

Fishing Business and License
Avalon Boat Stand, on the Pleasure Pier, for years has been the familiar spot for fishing supplies and small talk; tel. (310) 510-0455. Check at **Chet's Hardware** store, in the Atwater Arcade opposite the post office, tel. (310) 510-0990. If you want your gamefish cleaned and fileted or mounted, check with **Rosie's** on the pier. She's also the official fish weigh-in station.

Government
Many visitors are surprised to find that Catalina is in America, and a tax-paying, sixth-class city of Los Angeles County, state of California. The Los Angeles County Health, Fire, and Building Inspection departments provide services for Avalon and Catalina Island. The city receives its police protection under a contract from the Los Angeles County Sheriff's Department. Avalon has jurisdiction for three miles out to sea, including moorings, sanitation, and police protection. It functions under a city council with an appointed city manager, and the voters directly elect the mayor.

The Law
Although the police department is run by the Los Angeles County Sheriff's Department, Avalon has a resident judge and administers a jail and courthouse.
Note: Drinking of any alcoholic beverage on

CAMERA CARE HINTS

Take a few precautions with your camera while traveling. At the beach, remember that a combination of wind and sand can really gum up the works and scratch the lens. On 35mm cameras, use a clear skylight filter instead of a lens cap so the camera can hang around your neck or over your shoulder, always at the ready for that spectacular shot that comes when least expected. And if something is going to get scratched, better an $18 filter than a $300 lens. It also helps to carry as little equipment as possible.

If you plan to spend time in small boats that put you close to the water, keep the cameras temporarily in Ziploc bags when not in use. Don't *store* cameras in plastic bags for any length of time, because the moisture that builds up in the bag is as damaging as being in the rain. It's always wise to keep cameras out of sight when camping. Put your name and address on the camera. Chances are if it gets left behind or stolen it won't matter whether your name is there or not, and don't expect to see it again; however, miracles do happen. You can put a rider on most homeowner's insurance policies for a nominal sum that will cover the cost if a camera is lost or stolen.

the beach or city streets is prohibited by city ordinance. This is vigorously enforced. Avalon has a local attorney if you should need one; call G.J. Sanders, tel. (310) 510-2903.

WHAT TO TAKE

Clothes
Go simple. Dress to suit your lifestyle. There isn't a place on the Island that requires a tie. Sundresses and shorts are acceptable everywhere, as are Levi's and T-shirts. Take at least

one swimsuit, and a sweater or a light jacket for the boat ride; it can get cool on the water once the sun goes down. Sandals are good for pavement and hot sand, and a good pair of walking shoes will carry you comfortably over the hiking trails around Avalon or the interior. Avalon has laundromats, so you needn't take your entire wardrobe.

Bring your children's favorite beach toys and flotation vests or arm rings for safety. Don't forget beach towels. See "A Kid's Adventure" for more details.

Winter Visits

If you're visiting Avalon in the winter, the weather is much the same as it is along the coast of Southern California: about 56-63° F and an average yearly rainfall of 14 inches, nearly all of it occurring between mid-October and mid-April. If you plan to be outdoors a lot, bring warm clothes and a raincoat. Fall and spring are really gorgeous times of the year in Catalina.

Photo Equipment

Catalina is a photographer's paradise. There's a picture to take wherever you look: the bay, the Casino, the purple hills, a buffalo, or sun worshipers on the beach. Bring an ample supply of film--it's cheaper at your favorite discount store on the Mainland. However, if you run short, camera supplies (including rentals) are available at many Island locations, including **Leo's**

Drug Store on the corner of Sumner and Crescent and **Island Photo & Video,** at 121 Metropole, tel. (310) 510-2614; processing here is a little more pricey than on the Mainland.

Pets

If you plan to bring your pet with you to Catalina, it travels free on the boat but must be leashed and muzzled; check with your carrier ahead of time. On the plane pets require a regular-priced ticket. For convenience and in an effort to keep Avalon as clean as possible, the Avalon Humane Society has provided a fenced-in area for your pet to relieve itself alongside the roadway on the Casino side of the bay. Check the Avalon map.

Avalon also has some regulations pertaining to your pets in town. For a helpful pamphlet containing excerpts of the municipal code concerning animals, ask at the chamber of commerce office at the foot of the Pleasure Pier, or write to the Avalon Humane Society, Box 1584, Avalon, CA 90704.

Note: Pets are not allowed on Crescent Ave. or any beach at any time! Pets must be on leashes when on Avalon city streets.

Insurance and ID

Carry proper identification and a medical insurance card with you. If you need to use a medical facility, your card will expedite matters, just as it does on the Mainland.

GETTING TO CATALINA

DEPARTURE TERMINALS FROM SOUTHERN CALIFORNIA

Catalina Island lies within easy reach of Southern California. Several boat lines depart from various handy locations (Newport Beach, Long Beach, and San Pedro). You have a choice of two boating destinations on Catalina: Avalon or Two Harbors. If you're in a hurry, there's helicopter service to Pebbly Beach or charter flights to the Airport-in-the-Sky. Reservations are a must on all transportation to (and from) the Is-

land. Even with reservations you should arrive at all debarkation points at least an hour early to buy your ticket and check in. If you already have a ticket, it must be stamped before you get in line to board. Being early also allows time to park your car. Parking is ample at each location; the fees vary. On the Mainland, you can make transfers between air and boat terminals via Super Shuttle, tel. (213) 777-8000, or Super Express, tel. (213) 670-7080. You may bring as much luggage as you like, but keep in mind that on all boats passengers handle their own. For a more detailed description of boat rides to Catalina, see "A Kid's Adventure."

TRANSPORT COMPANIES SERVING CATALINA ISLAND

Catalina Express
The newest and fastest Catalina Express boats take just one hour and 10 minutes. They provide comfortable, airline-style seats. Drinks and snacks are available. The Express departs from San Pedro and Long Beach. At the Port of L.A., the San Pedro Terminal has been renovated into a beautiful, state of the art, ADA approved, earthquake proof structure offering all the amenities passengers could want.

From either Long Beach or San Pedro, roundtrip fares for the Express boats run adults $36, seniors $33, children 2-11 yrs. $27, under two $2. Group rates apply for 20 or more. Ask about the Captain's Lounge, which seats eight, by reservation only; it's $40 one way for the room in addition to the regular fare and includes a bottle of champagne. The Express offers an

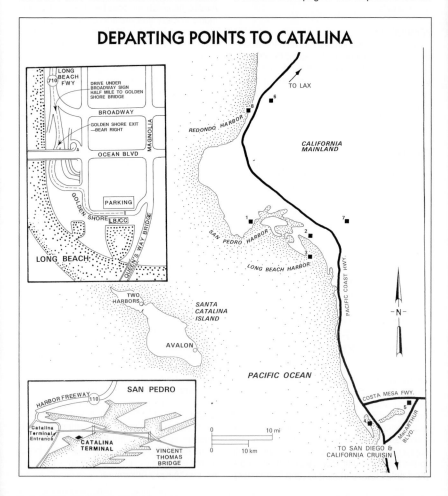

DEPARTING POINTS TO CATALINA

early-morning trip originating in Avalon and Two Harbors during the summer. The charge for bicycles and surfboards is $3 one-way. For roundtrip reservations and schedule, call Catalina Express, tel. (800) 995-4386, (310) 519-1212.

Catalina Cruises

This older line leaves from the Long Beach Catalina Terminal daily. The cruise between Long Beach and Avalon on Catalina Cruises takes approximately two hours, part of which is a tour through massive Long Beach Harbor, past the permanently docked *Queen Mary.*

Fares: adult $26 RT, child under 12 $22, child under two $2. Group rates on request. Bikes and surfboards are permitted for $3 (space available), but only at specific sailing times. Wheels must be removed and attached to the frame. Ask about other sports equipment, including scuba gear.

Each three-deck ship carries 700 passen-

and wine. During the summer, Catalina Cruises offers a minimum of four scheduled roundtrips a day, with weekend variations; ask about departures that go to Two Harbors. After November, call for the winter schedule. For reservations and schedules (800) 228-2546 from the Long Beach area. Credit cards are accepted. You'll find a small cafeteria, upstairs restaurant, and gift shop at the Catalina Terminal in Long Beach.

Catalina Passenger Service

From mid-March through November (limited service December through mid-March), *The Catalina Flyer* departs Newport Harbor each morning at 9 a.m., and departs Avalon 4:30 p.m. Fares are adult $35 RT, child 12 and under $16.50 RT. Credit cards are accepted. If you're bringing a bicycle, mention this when making reservations; the fee is $7, RT. *The Catalina Flyer* is a fast catamaran with sundeck, full-service cocktail lounges, and a private stateroom for

DEPARTURE POINTS TO CATALINA

1. Catalina Air Sea Terminal (San Pedro to Avalon and Two Harbors) Take Harbor Fwy. South (110) to the Terminal Island-Long Beach exit to Harbor Blvd. Follow signs to Catalina Terminal entrance across Harbor Blvd.

From Long Beach take Ocean Blvd. west to the Harbor Boulevard exit from the Vincent Thomas Bridge.

2. Catalina Terminal (Long Beach to Avalon and Two Harbors) Go south on the Long Beach Fwy. (710), turn off at Downtown Long Beach exit to Golden Shore exit and follow signs to terminal.

3. Helicopter Service (Long Beach to Avalon) Go south on the Long Beach Fwy. (710) to Harbor Scenic Dr. exit, last exit before Queen Mary. Turn left at bottom of exit ramp and go 100 feet

past stop sign. Heliport is small building on right, on ocean side.

4. Newport Boat Terminal (Newport to Avalon) From Pacific Coast Highway (Hwy. 1) turn south on Newport Blvd. to Balboa Blvd. Travel two miles on Balboa Blvd. to Balboa Pavilion on left.

5. John Wayne Airport (Orange County to Avalon) From 405 Freeway, exit Century Blvd. West, follow signs for departure to terminal six. Check-in counter near Republic and Delta.

6. Long Beach Municipal Airport Charter Service (Long Beach to Avalon) San Diego Freeway (405) to Lakewood Blvd. North turn-off. Turn left at second traffic light (Douglas Dr.) off Lakewood Blvd. to airport terminal

gers, with tables and chairs on the inside and wooden benches on the open decks. Two snack bars sell light snacks and drinks, including beer

groups. On board are a small snack bar, comfortable inside seats, open deck, and video games. The trip between Newport and Catalina

Catalina Express

OZ MALLAN

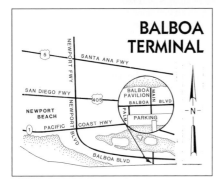

BALBOA TERMINAL

takes 75 minutes. For reservations call Catalina Passenger Service, 400 Main St., Balboa, CA 92661, tel. (714) 673-5245.

Island Express Helicopter Service
Call (800) 2-AVALON, (310) 491-5550 or (310) 510-2525, offers daily flights between Long Beach (at the bow of the *Queen Mary*), the

Sea/Air Terminal in San Pedro, and Avalon. Adult roundtrip ticket is $110. Commuter books, good for one year, are $247.50 including tax for five one-way tickets.

You're allowed one bag; extra luggage is allowed only if space is available. Island Express offers courtesy van service in Avalon and free parking in Long Beach.

Island Hopper/Catalina Airlines
The Island Hopper is a small independent that flies daily year-round between San Diego and Catalina. During the summer the airline flies a 10-passenger plane, in the winter a five-passenger plane. It departs from Montgomery Field in San Diego to Airport-in-the-Sky. Fares range from $200 OW for a single passenger to $75 OW pp if there are three or more passengers on board. One small suitcase per passenger, please. For information call (800) 339-0FLY or (619) 279-4595, or write 3760 Green Curtis Dr., San Diego, CA 92123.

Catalina's West End And Interior

KATHY ESCOVEDO-SANDERS

TWO HARBORS

In 1602, when Vizcaino approached the mountains of Catalina rising out of the Pacific, the explorer was certain he had reached two islands. From a distance, the bulk of land on the east end of Catalina appears to taper to a low point. Here the sea seems to separate the east end from the small nub on the west end. Actually, there is no separation, only a low-lying neck. A half-mile-wide isthmus just 50 feet at its summit, it comprises the narrowest section of Catalina Island. The ocean side of this isthmus is Catalina Harbor, the most protected harbor on the Island; the channel side is Isthmus Cove. This area is now called Two Harbors, 14 miles by ocean and 23 miles by road from Avalon.

HISTORY

For many years, Two Harbors, at one time called Union Harbor, was also referred to as the "Isthmus." It is the site of some of the most intriguing Island history.

Allegedly, this is where one of the largest groups of Indians lived, and where the Vizcaino expedition observed the still-sought "temple," or *yuva'r*. Its description fits the worship of Chingichnich that was the religious custom of most of the Gabrielinos at the time. You can still see the sinkholes of the gold mines that flourished at the Isthmus, Cherry Valley, and Fourth of July Cove in the 1860s. The Civil War barracks, built in 1863, are still in use by the Isthmus Yacht Club. Most of the roughnecks of the gold rush (though gold was never found) were driven out after the arrival of the Union volunteers. (See "History" in the main "Introduction" for details.) The wreck of the nefarious Chinese pirate ship *Ning Po* is buried under the mud here.

Fact or Fiction?

The history of Catalina abounds with legends. In most cases there is a minutia of truth. But as time passes and the stories are repeated, they take on the embellishments of each storyteller. Most pirates and smugglers did not keep diaries, or, if they did, none has ever been found. Still, some stories persist; accept them for what they are, legends that may or may not be historically accurate.

Buried Treasure

The brig *Danube,* out of New York, was wrecked in 1824 on the rocks near San Pedro. Samuel Prentiss and other survivors made their way to the San Gabriel Mission. There Prentiss found an old Gabrielino Indian called Turie, alleged to be a chieftain from Catalina Island. The 70-year-old Indian, close to death, welcomed Prentiss's friendship. Before he died, Turie told Prentiss about Island Indians who had buried rich treasure beneath a tree on Catalina. He sketched a crude map, which launched the legendary treasure hunt of Sam Prentiss.

Prentiss returned to the site of the wreck in San Pedro, and from the salvage of the *Danube,* he built himself a small vessel and set sail for Catalina. In the middle of the channel he was caught in a severe storm. Everything he owned was washed overboard, and it was all he could do to keep himself alive in the small boat. The treasure map was buried at the bottom of the sea, but the dream was not forgotten. Prentiss made it to the Island, remembering only that the treasure was buried at the base of a tree. He built a small cabin overlooking Emerald Bay. For the next 30 years he hunted sea otter, fished, and spent every extra moment searching for his treasure. Gripped by the dream of riches, he sold firewood from the trees he cut down and dug up in his relentless quest for the mysterious treasure.

He is purported to be the first white man to die on Catalina Island. Today, near where his cabin stood, you can see the wind-grazed tombstone erected by Joseph Banning, one of the early owners of Catalina:

> *In memory of*
> *Samuel Prentiss*
> *A native of Massachusetts*
> *Came to California in 1824*
> *Died on Catalina 1854--Age 72.*

Apparently he never found the treasure. Keeping his secret almost until the day he died, ultimately sharing it with Santos Louis Bouchette, giving rise to another bit of Island lore.

Bouchette

Santos Louis Bouchette was the son of one of the survivors of the *Danube* shipwreck. When Prentiss shared his secret with this young man, it stimulated within Bouchette's heart the same urges and desires about the treasure that had consumed Prentiss for 30 years. Bouchette also began the search, but he was luckier than Prentiss--or maybe wilier. In the midst of his treasure hunt he stumbled across rich veins of silver, lead, and gold. Some tell the story a little differently, saying that Bouchette "salted" the mine to encourage heavy financial backing from out-

SCI CO.

Cat Harbor in the early 1900s

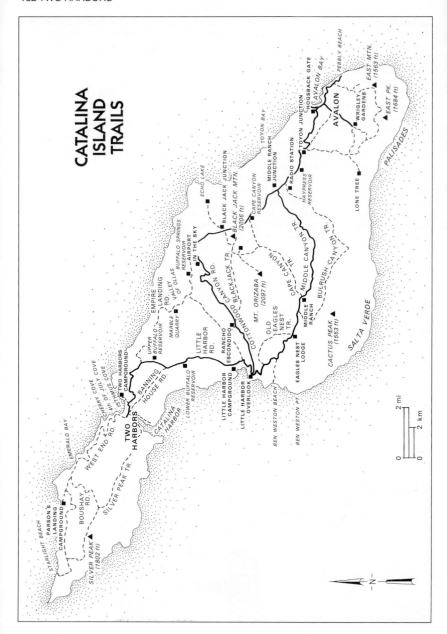

CATALINA ISLAND TRAILS

siders. Whether this is true or not, his mine was incorporated under the name of Mineral Hills Mines Company, and it became his real treasure.

Bouchette operated the mine for some years. On one of his many cross-channel trips to the pueblo of Los Angeles, after a whirlwind romance, he came back to the Island married to a French dance-hall girl. The story goes that she didn't like the rough life the miners led, so Bouchette built her an elaborate house one mile from Johnson's Landing, furnishing it with English mahogany furniture and a plate-glass mirror from France that cost him $1000. He kept borrowing money to keep his mining venture solvent, and continued to prospect around every tree even remotely likely to be the one that guarded the treasure of Turie, the old Indian chief.

After some time his wife was apparently still dissatisfied--or could Bouchette have finally found Samuel Prentiss's long-coveted Indian treasure? For one day in the spring of 1876 Bouchette and his wife were seen loading silver ore and a few provisions into their sailboat, and they were never seen again.

Gold

Francisco Lopez, a Mexican youth, has been credited with discovering the first gold in California, near Newhall in 1842. While digging up a wild onion he found a gold nugget entangled in its roots. However, according to Catalina leg-

end, Captain George Yount, a friend and associate of Samuel Prentiss, discovered an outcropping of gold-bearing quartz in a canyon near Two Harbors in 1830, a full 12 years before the strike at Sutter's Mill that started the California gold rush. Yount was deeply involved in otter hunting, and he forgot about the bit of quartz he had chipped off and stuffed into his pocket in Cherry Valley until the Sutter's Mill find. He returned to the Island three times over the years trying to rediscover, without success, the location of the gold quartz he was so sure he had first seen.

In a fit of depression, the sea captain shared his frustrating story with gold miners on the Mainland, and they began the gold stampede on Catalina Island.

Stories vary concerning the amount of gold found. Some say there was a lot, but the cost of mining was prohibitive. Others say the quality of the ore was not high. In 1873, after discovering the difficulties involved in using burros to get ore out of Silver Canyon, an English syndicate forfeited its dreams and a $40,000 down payment to George Shatto.

The First Tourists

The Banning brothers, who owned the Island from 1892 to 1919, made one of the first changes to the landscape of the Isthmus. They could see its potential as a fishing paradise, so to encourage tourists they built a fishing bungalow on the hill between the two harbors in

Old barracks that housed Union soldiers during the Civil War

1910. As the Bannings and then the Wrigleys developed the Island, the Isthmus, now called Two Harbors, also grew--but not in the same manner as Avalon.

As more people discoved Catalina, Two Harbors remained a harbor only for those who could indulge in the luxury of yachting. This limited traffic during the 1920s and '30s to the elite. Christian's Hut, a Polynesian-style resort with a tropical-beach atmosphere, was a gathering spot for the affluent, glamorous film celebrities of that era. The Isthmus was a place where they could get away from autograph seekers and socialize with others who shared their status. The "star" status is far less important now, though some years ago everyone was thrilled when John Wayne brought his large yacht, the *Wild Goose,* to Two Harbors.

Today, Two Harbors quietly bustles with campers, boaters, and vacationers who enjoy the serenity of low rolling hills and the fresh breeze that skips across the narrow strip of land from the Pacific Ocean side of the Island.

Movie Making

Many films were shot at Two Harbors, especially in the days of the silents when the noise of the elements was unimportant. The shaggy palm trees and clear blue water met by a smog-free sky also were the backdrop for several talkies: *Mutiny on the Bounty, Treasure Island, The Sea Witch, McHale's Navy,* and later, in 1976, *MacArthur.*

For many years the *Ning Po,* a nefarious Chinese junk built in China in 1773, was an attraction at Catalina Harbor. With an unsavory history, including piracy, smuggling, and destruction at sea, it was rebuilt by an enterprising businessman for use as a Chinese cafe at the Isthmus, where it was also a prop in several movies. The builders of this camphor and ironwood ship used no nails in its construction; each joint was carefully fitted. The *Ning Po* stood as a monument to the genius of the Chinese shipbuilding industry. It was ultimately destroyed by the sea and lies buried beneath the mud in Catalina Harbor.

SCI COMPANY

The ship Hesperia *was used in making Robert Louis Stevenson's* Treasure Island, *filmed in 1935.*

Catalina Marine Science Center

Operated by the University of Southern California's Institute for Marine and Coastal Studies, the center conducts courses through USC and other universities in the marine sciences both at undergraduate and graduate levels. At Two Harbors' Big Fisherman Cove, the center was established in 1968 through a Santa Catalina Island Company gift and lease of 45 land acres and 360 acres of sea floor. The National Geographic Society has used the center to film (among other subjects) lobster moulting (lobsters shed their skins as they grow). Scientists from all over the world occasionally gather to study the sea and Catalina's undeveloped surroundings.

Buildings include laboratories, dormitories for students, and a hyperbaric chamber for emergency treatment of divers suffering from the bends (open to anyone along the Southern California coast who needs it).

Occasionally groups of 15 or more can prearrange a guided tour, which will include an illustrated lecture about the research at Catalina Marine Science Center, a viewing of the award-winning documentary about the kelp forests of Catalina, a visit to the touch tank, and a walking tour of the laboratory and the hyperbaric chamber; the tour takes two hours. The complex is a pleasant 2.2-mile hike from the center of Two Harbors, or take the shore boat that leaves from the Two Harbors dock. Ask at the Two Harbors Office, or call (310) 743-6792.

The area along the waterfront of the Marine Science Center is a marinelife refuge. The public is not allowed to anchor a boat, to fish, or to take anything away, and the moorings are for Center use only.

Note: In case of a storm, the moorings in front of the Science Center are available to boaters in distress.

For information about the program offered to marine-science students, write: Resident Director, Catalina Marine Science Center, P.O. Box 398, Two Harbors, CA 90704-5044, tel. (310) 510-0811. (See below.)

RECREATION

OZ MALLAN

Even the buffalo enjoy the views of Two Harbors.

SIGHTS

If Two Harbors is nothing else, it's a laid-back relaxing place to spend some meditating time. Walk over to Cat Harbor (about a quarter mile), and you'll pass the old Union Army Barracks. It's hard to imagine that there were once Union soldiers on the alert in this peaceful cleft of Catalina's isthmus. Cat Harbor is a very deep protected harbor that captains used for centuries to seek shelter from storms and to repair their ships; even today it's a harbor of refuge from nasty northeastern storms. Picnic tables along here make it a pleasant place to stop. This is not a good swimming area.

Back on the lee side of Two Harbors the beach is broad and palmy, with sand, picnic tables, and a very calm surf. This is a perfect place for little kids to swim. Many activities take place

BIRD ROCK HISTORY

Most everyone recognizes Bird Rock, a large white mound that boaters can see from some distance at sea. Few people know that Helen Webb once bought this landmark with Civil War scrip. It was her intention to build a seasonal gambling casino, and she believed that eventually the government restrictions would be lifted. She clung to her deed, but alas, never built her casino. Perhaps her descendants are still waiting? Though a casino wasn't built, the tiny islet continues to be home to thousands of birds, whether it's "in" season or no.

on this beach throughout the year. Or bring your beach-back and read a good book under the gentle rustling palms.

Two Harbors Visitors Services
This is a user-friendly office that will give you information on just about anything to do with Two Harbors and Avalon. Call (310) 510-7265 or fax (310) 510-0244.

Day-Trippers
A day-trip from Avalon on the shuttle bus leaves you plenty of time to explore Two Harbors, take a swim in exceptionally clear water, and enjoy a leisurely lunch at the Snack Bar. Some opt to bring a lunch and picnic either at the beach or at Catalina Harbor (a short hike past the old Union Army barracks), where you'll find wooden tables, barbecue grills, water, and public restrooms (coin-operated showers at Two Harbors only). You can reserve the Isthmus Beach bandstand area, with tables, benches, and barbecue pits, for private groups by calling (310) 510-0303. Two tennis courts are available to the public for an hourly fee. A volleyball court on the main beach is open to the public--free.

Nature Hikes
Day-trips from Two Harbors offer several exploration adventures. Naturalists lead nature hikes, pointing out nature's unique exhibits, explaining the area's colorful history, and helping you explore the plant and animal life surrounding the Two Harbors area. Hikes are conducted regularly, and walking tours can last two to three hours; wear good walking shoes and bring water. Cost is $15 and up per person, depending on the length of time. For groups, these hikes can be custom-designed to fit the interest of the party, and an appropriate naturalist will be available (summer only). For information and reservations call (310) 510-2800.

Island Safari
If you're spending several days at Two Harbors and want to see more in the company of a nat-

Cat Harbor

OZ MALLAN

Two Harbors pier

uralist, an Island safari van will take passengers into the rugged interior. This is an opportunity to see spectacular views of the formidable cliffs and rolling sea as well as a close-up look at Catalina wildlife, including buffalo that wander the hills. Trips are available to a wide range of destinations in the interior of the Island and vary from ancient Indian middens to a hidden waterfall to the site of an Indian village where visitors can see a soapstone quarry with half-carved Indian bowls, just as they were left hundreds of years ago. Two and a half-, three- and four-hour tours are available, starting at $18 pp (summer only). Check with Two Harbors Visitors and Information Office, tel. (310) 510-2800.

On Your Own
For independent explorations, take the Two Harbors Catalina Safari shuttle bus to either the airport, Little Harbor, or Black Jack Junction. One-way fare is $14.50 per person for adults, $10.25 for children. For schedules and information call (310) 510-2800.

WATER SPORTS

If you've come to Two Harbors for diving, you won't be disappointed; about 75% of all boat-divers off Catalina choose the west end. Snorkeling is excellent in any of the remote coves or kelp beds at the west end of Isthmus Cove. See "Diving" for more details.

Ocean Kayaking
Sit-on-top kayaks are great for beginners. The company, tel. (310) 510-7265, offers hourly rentals, sales, instructions, and guided tours to secluded easy-access coves and bays nearby.

Catalina West End Dive Center
The dive center offers a laundry list of choices: dive packages, scuba/snorkel trips on board the *garibaldi* or the *Sea Bass,* PADI certification classes, resort dives (for those with no experience), gear rental, and air fills. The dive center is a full-service dive shop. Rent an Aqua-View paddleboard; it's fun for exploring the bay's underworld from the surface of the water. For detailed information, call or write the center, tel. (310) 510-7265, fax (310) 510-0244, Box 5044, Two Harbors, CA 90704.

Snorkeling Safari
For the snorkeler who would like to see Catalina's offshore marinelife, one of Two Harbors' leading underwater guides leads a two-hour snorkeling excursion. Snorkelers meet at the dive center at the foot of the pier, from where the "captain" takes them by boat to some of the richest marine habitats on the west end for shallow-water snorkeling. Explorers will investigate areas of shell-lined octopus lairs, the brilliant orange garibaldi's nesting grounds, and can often observe the sea hare *(Aplysia vaccaria),* largest sea snail in the world, which can grow to the size of a basketball. Rates are $12 pp, with

gear included $16 pp. The dive shop rents all dive equipment along with Aqua-View paddleboards. For more information, call (310) 510-0303.

Scuba Diving Safari
Scuba divers, ask about the two-hour dive trip onboard the *Garibaldi,* a boat designed for dive trips. It takes divers to a variety of spots on the west end of the Island; advanced divers will have the opportunity to dive at more spectacular spots on the windward side of Catalina. The fee is $30 pp. Bring your own regulator and your C-card; all other equipment is available for rent at the dive center.

Fishing
Many fine eating fish swarm around the Two Harbors area. Although not the easiest to capture, lobster and abalone are two big favorites (check out fishing seasons and limits.) For a good list of the fish found in Catalina waters, see "Fishing" in the Avalon chapter.

West End Cruising Club
Boaters who visit Two Harbors no longer have to pay a landing fee. The club is still active and members pay a yearly fee of $15. The money helps the club fund the multitude of activities it sponsors, including beach parties with big bands, theme parties, and fish and steak barbecues. Planned activities include dinghy races, volleyball tournaments, and wildlife seminars. Once a year, members get together and have an underwater and shoreline cleanup in the Isthmus harbor. Doug's Harbor Reef Restaurant and Saloon is the scene of many cocktail parties and catered events on the beach. The Cruising Club offers special cruises, and a subscription to the *WestEnder* bulletin (plus a lot more).

The Fourth of July is a special time, with a magnificent children's summer festival and flamboyant fireworks display over the bay jointly sponsored by the West End Cruising Club, Fourth of July Cove, and others; it's open to the public. If you've never watched fireworks on an island, it's an experience you won't soon forget: flashing lights reflecting off black water, the smell of explosives mixed with fresh sea air, and at the end--a cacophony of sounds from the boats as they blast horns, dingers, and bells

--a thank-you for the great display. For more information about the West End Cruising Club, call (310) 510-0303 or write Box 5044, Two Harbors, CA 90704-5044.

ANNUAL EVENTS

In **February** President's Day Weekend kicks off the season.

In **April** the Easter celebration includes an Easter sunrise service, an egg hunt, spring camping, and spring hiking with the naturalist to discover spring wildflowers.

In **May** the Cinco de Mayo celebration is a colorful event with music, dancing, and a piñata.

June brings out the best-dressed of shipwreck cronies and a chance to compete in the shipwreck stew-making contest, plus scavenger hunt, music, and dancing.

In **July and August,** besides fireworks, there are dinghy races and DJ dancing under the stars.

loading scuba tanks for a day of diving around Two Harbors

October is the time when all buccaneers search for treasure, swashbuckle around the beach, and enjoy the Buccaneer Ball. This is usually the weekend that all divers heave to and clean up the harbor.

BOATING AND HARBOR INFORMATION

MOORINGS AT TWO HARBORS

Isthmus Cove
This large cove has 249 moorings available and anchorage for 100. Transient moorings are on a first-come first-served basis. Pay your mooring fees to the patrol boat or at the harbormaster's office at Isthmus Cove. You may anchor outside of established mooring areas, except under special weather conditions, at the discretion of the harbor patrol. You may not raft boats in mooring areas unless the harbor patrol permits you to. The speed limit within all mooring areas is five miles per hour or "wakeless" speed, whichever is slowest; this includes dinghies. Keep your neighbor happy--no generators or other motors before 7 a.m. or after 10 p.m. Carry a bright flashlight when traveling after dark in a dinghy skiff or inflatable raft that does not have navigation lights.

Little Fisherman's Cove
Moorings here are counted as part of those of the Isthmus Cove. The southwest shore is leased to the Channel Cruising Club; the south shore offers camping sites (Two Harbors Campground, reservations necessary through Catalina Island Camping). The southeast shore is leased to King Harbor Yacht Club.

Big Fisherman's Cove
This is the home of USC Marine Science Center. Do not use the ramp, dock, or two moorings as they are for research use only. This entire area is now a marinelife refuge. For more information call Bill McFarland, director, tel. (310) 510-0811. The diving-bends recompression chamber at the Science Center is open to anyone who needs it. For emergencies only, call (310) 510-1053.

BOATING SERVICES

Shore Boat
During the summer, five shore boats run regularly between Fourth of July, Cherry, Big Fisherman's, and Isthmus coves. During the winter, they're "on call"; three blasts of a horn and a wave during the day, three blasts and a flashing light at night will summon a shore boat. All shoreboats monitor channel 9 VHF. When calling, give them your mooring number and cove name. It helps if you use a flashing light at night when you see the boat approaching. Fees are: Isthmus Cove $1.25 per person, Fourth of July, Big Fisherman's, and Cherry Cove $1.50 pp.

Dinghy Dock
Floats on the Isthmus pier are for loading and unloading passengers. Dinghy docks are provided at the Isthmus Cove and Catalina Harbor for dinghies up to 13 feet. Tie them with a long bowline.

Trash
You'll find trash cans at the end of the dinghy dock at Catalina Harbor and on the southwest side of the Cove Agency office at Isthmus Cove. During summer, a trash collection boat (familiarly called the "salad boat") operates in the Two Harbors, Fourth of July, Cherry, Howland's, Emerald Bay, and White's Landing areas; it will accept your trash and recycling bags for 75 cents. In winter, harbor patrol boats will accept your trash bags for 75 cents. If all else fails, take your trash with you. The fine is $500 and/or six months in jail for trash thrown over the side.

TWO HARBORS PRACTICALITIES

LODGING

Banning House Lodge
The history-rich Banning House was built in 1910 by Judge Joseph Brent Banning (son of Phineas Banning). At the beginning of the century, the house served as a holiday home for the Banning family and their Mainland friends. The Bannings built a dirt road from Avalon and brought tourists on stagecoaches to the Isthmus, where they stayed in a tent village on the beach. Over the years the Banning House has housed a variety of guests, including Hollywood stars and other celebrities who used it as a hotel while filming at the Isthmus during the early Wrigley days.

This all changed in 1941 with the beginning of WW II. At that time the U.S. Coast Guard took it over and used it for officers' quarters. After 1946 the Lodge was used variously as a dude ranch, girls' camp, hunting lodge, and employee housing. In 1987 Doug Bombard (lifelong resident of Avalon and Two Harbors) began restoring the building into a turn-of-the-century delight.

Set on the top of a small knoll, the house enjoys views of both Isthmus Cove on the lee side and Catalina Harbor on the windward side of the Island. Today the Banning House Lodge is operated as a bed and breakfast inn with 11 charming rooms available by reservation only. Each room has unique decor suggesting the history of the era. Continental breakfast is served in the "oak period-piece dining room" from 8-10 a.m. Guests can walk (or take the shuttle) to the beach and small village of Two Harbors. Each room has a view. For rates and reservations write to Box 5044, Two Harbors, CA 90704-5044, tel. (310) 510-2800.

Catalina Elderhostel Program
A popular program specifically designed for older adults, Elderhostels let members develop new interests or expand current curiosities. Those 60 years and older (a companion can be as young as 50) enjoy inexpensive, short-term academic programs at educational institutions around the world. On Catalina Island the program is held at the Catalina Marine Science Center at Two Harbors. While at the Center, participants have the option of taking five different classes, though the requirement is only one. Offerings include a study on how Catalina's Indians used the underwater world, the Japanese art of *gyotaku* (fish printing), a seminar on a selected topic about conservation--and much more.

Accommodations are in the second-floor housing complex. While taking part in the program, participants will walk several times a day to and from the waterfront research area and between buildings, with steep roads to and from. Double-occupancy rooms share bathrooms with up to four people. Registration costs, six nights' accommodations, all meals from Sunday evening through Saturday breakfast, five days of classes, and a variety of extracurricular activities are included in the tuition; transportation to and from the Mainland is not included. For more information contact Elderhostel, 75 Federal St., Boston, MA 02110-1941, tel. (617) 426-8056.

CAMPING AND CABINS

Year-round camping is available on Catalina's west end, with camping cabins, tent-cabins, and campsites. **Camping Cabins** are basic cabins available only in the off-season, which begins in October. Each room houses two people and comes equipped with either twin bunk beds or a double bed, and guests supply their own sleeping bags or bedding. Rooms have a refrigerator, heater, electrical outlets, and ample storage space. Separate community bathrooms for men and women offer sinks, toilets, mirrors, electrical outlets, and hot coin-operated showers. A communal kitchen has four two-burner propane stoves, tables and chairs, two large gas barbecue grills, and cleanup areas.

Cabins are clustered in groups of seven around a large deck area. These clusters are ideal for group meetings. Plenty of fresh-water outlets around the camping cabins make it convenient to rinse off diving gear. The cabin rate is $39.50 per night weekends, $25 Mon.-Thursday. For reservations and information, call (310) 510-2800 or write Box 5044, Two Harbors, CA 90704-5044.

Tent-cabins are sturdy wood-framed, with wood decks, canvas roofs, and shaded porches. Cots and mattresses are supplied; you bring your sleeping bag. Available only in summer and fall, they sleep 6-10 people; cabin rates are $60 per night. The improved Two Harbors Campground is a quarter-mile-long walk on a narrow bumpy path from Two Harbors; carrying too much can be a problem. The rangers provide a gear-hauling service, and for $1 per item ($10 minimum) they will haul ice chests, heavy backpacks, etc. Other rental camping equipment, such as propane, butane, charcoal, lanterns, tents, and campstoves, is available at the campground. The campsites ($6.50 pp per night) lie on a hillside that slopes to the blue water. On site are barbecues, picnic tables, toilets, cold showers, sun shades, and fire rings. Fires are a real danger; restrict all fires and smoking to the barbecue and fire ring areas only. Water is provided at each site; family and group campsites are available. For reservations, call **Catalina Island Camping,** tel. (310) 510-2800.

Parson's Landing Campground, open year-round, is about seven miles farther into the west end, and transportation is provided by the Two Harbors shore boat, summer only; $15 per person up to six, then $5 each additional person.

Restrictions

All groups must be accompanied by an adult (at least 18 years old) who will assume full responsibility for the group at all times. Campers must stay in assigned camping areas. Plant collecting, woodcutting, or removing any natural feature is strictly prohibited. Trash cans are provided. Motorcycles, archery equipment, fireworks, and firearms are prohibited anywhere outside the city of Avalon. No pets are allowed in the campgrounds. Keep it quiet between 10 p.m. and 7 a.m.

Bear in mind that the Coast Guard prohibits passengers onboard the cross-channel vessels from carrying propane, charcoal, gas stoves, and lanterns. All are available to rent from the campground ranger at Two Harbors. Bring a flashlight and a canteen if you plan to hike.

EATERIES

Just a few feet from the beach, **Doug's Harbor Reef Restaurant and Saloon** serves fine steak and seafood in a South Seas atmosphere. Doug's is close to the foot of the pier in the center of Two Harbors village; it opens for dinner.

mooring at
Two Harbors

OZ MALLAN

The outdoor bar/patio area has two television sets for sports viewing, and a live band or a DJ plays every weekend during the summer. A satellite dish and cable bring in entertainment from around the world. The **Snack Bar** is open for breakfast and lunch serving sandwiches and snacks. Doug's Harbor Reef Restaurant also caters for special events, boaters, and beach parties.

SERVICES AND SHOPPING

Two Harbors is a small village of fewer than 200 year-round residents. But, visitors find most everything they need, only not in very large quantities. The village moves at a slower pace than the Mainland, and that's how most Islanders want to keep it. The one-room schoolhouse is the only one left in Los Angeles County. Children from kindergarten through the fifth grade attend school in the rustic small building, which was built with a lot of help from Mainland visitors. Each day, the older children are bused into Avalon for junior and senior high school. Catalina schools operate under the Long Beach Unified School District.

General Store
Two Harbors General Store, tel. (310) 510-0303, ext. 217, stocks a little of everything: most of the essential grocery items along with sundries, ice, liquor, clothing, household supplies, marine supplies, and fishing supplies and licenses. Don't forget the lending library; this is the spot to bring your "already-read" paperbacks. For large-group grocery orders, call at least two weeks in advance and they'll be waiting for you when you arrive.

Two Harbors Marine Fuel and Repair
The shop, tel. (310) 510-7265, sells inboard and outboard gas and diesel and offers engine repair and other boating services; dry storage is available for boats 24 feet and under.

Health and Help
Two Harbors has no medical facilities. However, some of Los Angeles County's highly trained paramedics operate a fast boat, the *Bay Watch Isthmus*. It carries all the high-tech equipment of

an ambulance and is based year-round at Isthmus Cove. The *Bay Watch I* is based in Avalon. With these two medical evacuation boats and the Avalon Municipal Hospital, plus an airvac helicopter between the Island and the Mainland, Catalina possesses a highly effective emergency system for land or sea accidents. For diving accidents, a hyperbaric chamber is available at the Marine Science Center in the Two Harbors area at Big Fisherman Cove.

GETTING THERE

From the Mainland
There was a time when the only way to Two Harbors was by private boat; today it is easily accessible via several routes. Both the speedy Express boats and the fastest Super Express depart from the **San Pedro Air and Sea Terminal** and the **Express Terminal** in Long Beach

CAMPING SUPPLIES

As a camper you know what food and clothes will fit your lifestyle. The following is a checklist of other things to consider taking on your camping trip to Catalina Island:

✔ flashlight
✔ extra batteries
✔ sunglasses
✔ pen/paper/cards/book
✔ knife
✔ extra pair of broken-in shoes
✔ lightweight tent
✔ lightweight sleeping bag
✔ something to anchor a windbreak
✔ camera/film
✔ waterproof matches
✔ water supply
✔ canteen
✔ extra pair of glasses
✔ toilet paper
✔ Chap Stick
✔ water purification tablets
✔ towel
✔ Calmitol ointment (good for burns, bites, and rashes)
✔ snake-bite kit

(near the bow of the *Queen Mary*) on a regular schedule every day, year-round. These boats feature stabilizers to smooth out the trip, individual airline-type seats, and an attendant to serve you snacks and drinks.

For reservations and schedules, call (213) 519-1212; groups of 15 or more call (310) 519-7957, elsewhere in California (800) 540-4753. Roundtrip fares on the **Express** are $36 adult, child 2-11 $27, senior $33. Ask about the Captain's Lounge, a comfortable salon that accommodates private parties of up to eight people for $40 in addition to the regular ticket price (includes a bottle of champagne).

Catalina Cruise Line
Another large passenger boat to Two Harbors, Catalina Cruises, operates on a regular schedule throughout the year. During the summer, it makes two trips daily to Two Harbors. Call for the winter schedule, tel. (310) 253-9800 or (800) 228-2546; roundtrip fares are $26 adult, child under 12 $22, under two $2.00, senior $24.

From Avalon
The *Shoreliner* cruise is a popular way to travel to Two Harbors from Avalon. The boats hug the coast from Avalon and give visitors an opportunity to leisurely view the mountains, which drop to the sea and often are alive with wild goats. Depending on the time of the year, passengers will see flying fish, porpoises, sea lions, and whales, along with pelicans and other seabirds fishing the coastal waters of Catalina. The ship passes numerous small coves, some with private schools, Scout camps, and many filled with boats. These coves are favorite destinations for diving enthusiasts and Mainland boaters. Adult one-way fare (in either direction) is $12.50. Many travelers enjoy taking the *Shoreliner* one way and the Safari Bus the other, which gives them the opportunity to see the rugged Catalina interior.

Note: Those bringing bicycles and surfboards to the Island aboard passenger boats from the Mainland pay a $3 fee each way.

Catalina Safari Bus
The Safari Bus shuttle provides daily scheduled bus transportation between Two Harbors and Avalon with stops at Little Harbor, Airport-in-the-Sky, and Black Jack Junction. The bus leaves from Avalon's Island Plaza, 213 Catalina Street. The fare is $14.50 OW, $29 RT. For schedules (group rates available) call (310) 510-2800, or write Box 5044, Two Harbors, CA 90704-5044. The drive takes passengers through the Catalina Conservancy and gives first-timers a view of the undeveloped lands of the reserve and the stunning wildlife of the Island, including herds of roaming buffalo. (See "Fauna" in the Introduction.)

OZ MALLAN

Little Fisherman's Cove with the Marine Science Center

KATHY ESCOVEDO-SANDERS

HIKING AND CAMPING

IN CATALINA'S BACKCOUNTRY

HIKING

Backpacking is a real adventure in the rugged hills of Catalina. Be aware of the interior's mountainous terrain and allow enough daylight to reach your destination. The network of undeveloped trails running across Catalina varies in type from goat trails and footpaths to jeep trails and fire roads. However, the Conservancy asks that you keep to designated trails. No streams have potable water, so take an ample supply; there's safe drinking water at all the improved campsites. Be prepared for very few commercial

contacts such as stores (general store at Two Harbors), and you'll find only a few phones along the way (phones all noted on hiking map).

Hikers should carry first-aid kits. Remember, you'll be sharing this outback with wild animals: bison, wild boar, deer, and rattlesnakes. Expect to encounter poison oak. Even in winter, when the branches are bare, a brush against them will cause a reaction if you're sensitive. You need a hiking permit (free) before you begin your trek into the interior. These are available at the Conservancy Office, 125 Claressa St., Avalon, tel. (310) 510-0688; at Two Harbors; and at Airport-in-the-Sky.

A few tips to first-time hikers on Catalina: good hiking shoes are important, and the weather can differ between the interior and the coastal sections of the Island, varying as much as 30°. Wear layers of clothing. The days may be hot, and wearing shorts and a T-shirt is comfortable, but the evenings (even in summer) usually cool down, and long pants and a heavy sweatshirt feel good. If you're traveling around the Island in fall or winter, bring a waterproof poncho. Don't forget to bring sun protection, e.g., a hat and sun-block lotion.

HIKING TRAILS

Route out of Avalon
You can start your trip in Avalon--trails and roads lead from there to within one mile of the west end of the Island. To hike out of Avalon, go toward the Casino on Crescent St., turn left on Marilla St., right on Vieudelou St., and then take a last left onto Stage Road. A paved street, it's the main road out of Avalon into the interior; expect lots of vehicular traffic. This first part of your trip is a hilly climb from the first turn on Marilla. Please note the hiking map.

Silver Peak Trail to Parson's Landing
(10.1 miles--strenuous.) This is a backcountry trail for the experienced hiker. Use a compass. On this hike, you'll get sensational views of the mountains meeting the sea. Campsites are available at Parson's Landing, but reservations are necessary through Camp and Cove, tel. (310) 510-0303.

Two Harbors to Parson's Landing
(6.8 miles, 0-5% grade.) This is all dirt, fairly level, a comfortable walk with beautiful views of the ocean. The trail takes you past the Scout camps.

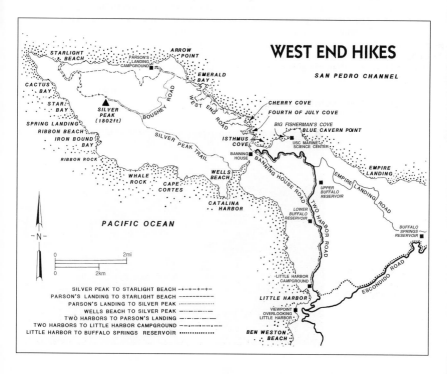

Little Harbor to West Summit
(4.3 miles, 5-10% grade.) This is a gradual uphill dirt trail, moderately difficult: you travel uphill for two miles.

West Summit to Two Harbors
(2.5 miles, 10%-plus grade.) This dirt trail is mostly downhill from West Summit to Two Harbors. It takes you past the turnoff to Fisherman's Cove, USC Marine Center, and Little Fisherman's Campground. While at Two Harbors notice the Isthmus Yacht Club, formerly the old Civil War barracks.

West Summit to the Airport via Empire
(7.0 miles, 5-10%-plus grade.) This is an undeveloped dirt trail. It goes up and down and takes you past the old Empire Landing rock quarry, where you can get water. It's uphill to the airport, a moderately difficult hike.

Airport to Little Harbor Overlook
(5.8 miles, 10%-plus grade.) This road is all dirt and downhill. It passes through the Wrigley family's Rancho Escondido. The trail parallels Cottonwood Canyon. If you want to detour through Cottonwood, turn left at the airport to hit Cottonwood Canyon. Water is available at Little Harbor. Watch out for wild pigs.

Little Harbor Overlook to Little Harbor
(1.2 miles, 5-10% grade.) This dirt trail is all downhill. Be aware of vehicle traffic through here, including tour buses.

Ben Weston Junction to Little Harbor Overlook
(2.3 miles, 10%-plus grade.) This trail is mostly uphill--about two miles of it. You'll see the location of a WW II gunnery station at the top. From here the view of the coast and Little Harbor is breathtaking.

Old Eagles Nest Trail
(2.6 miles, 5-10% grade.) This is an undeveloped loop trail that begins at the old Eagles Nest stagecoach stop and meets the main road into Little Harbor. Hill climbing is involved; it's moderately difficult.

Cottonwood Trail
(5.5 miles, 5-10%-plus grade.) This is a moderately difficult undeveloped trail.

Black Jack Junction to Black Jack
(1.5 miles, 5-10% grade.) This dirt trail is a gradual upgrade. The turnoff to the campground is marked. Black Jack is Catalina's second-highest peak at 2,010 feet. Old mine shafts dot the area. You'll find a telephone at the junction.

Black Jack Junction to Airport
(2.5 miles, 5-10% grade.) You'll see some lovely views on this moderately easy hike. Runway

Islanders bring their luxury camping outfits to Little Harbor.

OZ MALLAN

Cafe and water are available at the airport. Lots of buffalo roam the area.

Middle Ranch Junction to Black Jack Junction

(2.7 miles, 0-5% grade.) This is fairly level walking along Catalina's China Wall.

Middle Ranch to Black Jack via Cape Canyon

(4.4 miles, 5-10% grade.) This difficult dirt trail is all uphill. The last mile and a half is very steep. Cape Canyon is a pleasant hike, giving you a good look at Catalina farming.

Note: The Conservancy asks that you do not cut through crops. The second bump gate is the trail marker turnoff.

Middle Ranch to Ben Weston Junction

(2.4 miles, 10%-plus grade.) The dirt road on this moderate hike passes the Camp Cactus turnoff (old Army camp). Turn at the Ben Weston Junction for the beach.

Middle Ranch Junction to Middle Ranch

(4.8 miles 0-10%-plus grade.) This all-dirt road runs downhill. You'll see lots of buffalo and maybe deer. Stay to the side of the road--tour buses and other vehicles pass this way.

Bullrush Canyon Trail

(7.5 miles, 5-10% grade.) Hardy trekkers call this undeveloped dirt trail the best hike on the Island. You'll see lots of scrub oak and wildlife; the trail is downhill and level.

CENTRAL ISLAND HIKES

Summit to Middle Ranch Junction
(2.0 miles, 0-5% grade.) This is a slurry road, and it's a fairly level, moderate hike. Behind Haypress Lake are two others called Hidden Lakes, gateway to Silver Canyon--and to lots of poison oak. Taking a left at the third lake takes you to Silver Canyon.

Avalon to East Summit
(3.2 miles, 10% grade.) This is all uphill. The road is slurry and lined with eucalyptus trees. You'll enjoy great views, though it gets quite steep in places. When you reach the summit, stop to admire more superior views.

Empire Landing Road from Two Harbors
(6.2 miles--moderate.) Leave Two Harbors on the surfaced main road to Avalon, and break off to an abandoned dirt road, which leads to the Airport-in-the-Sky.

Hiking to Little Harbor from Two Harbors
From Doug's Harbor Reef Restaurant and Saloon, walk to the main road toward Avalon and follow it up and over the hills past upper Buffalo Reservoir and into Little Harbor. For the highly experienced hiker in excellent physical condition, there's another strenuous trail to Little Harbor by way of the old Banning House Road, which cuts off about a mile from the Banning House. Follow Banning House Rd. for 3.2 miles until you run into graded, dirt Little Harbor Rd., where you turn right. Following that for another 1.9 miles brings you to Little Harbor Campground. (Beware of rattlesnakes.)

Bouchette/Boushey Road
(2.1 miles--strenuous.) This dirt road connects

CATALINA CAMPSITES

PRIMITIVE
Emerald Bay (H)(SB)
Ripper's Cove (SB)
Starlight Beach (SB)
Little Gibraltar Rock and
  Cabrillo Harbor (H)(SB)
Italian Gardens (SB)
Goat Harbor (SB)

IMPROVED
Hermit Gulch Campground (H)(V)
Black Jack (H)(V)
Little Harbor (H)(V)
Two Harbors Campground (H)
Parson's Landing (SB)
For details phone (310) 510-0303
Accessible by:
      SB = Shore Boat
      H = Hike
      V = Vehicle

Silver Peak Trail and Parson's Landing. For the hardy hiker only.

Organized Nature Hikes
These treks offer you the opportunity to explore the plant and animal life surrounding the Two Harbors area. The Conservancy conducts nature hikes upon request during the summer only. Contact the Two Harbors office. It also gives slide lectures at various times on the beach at Two Harbors.

CAMPING

On Catalina you'll find two types of campgrounds: primitive and improved. Primitive camps have no facilities whatsoever; improved sites include toilets, fire rings, and barbecue pits. Some have showers, most have phones, some are accessible only by boat (B), some by shuttle (S), some by hike-in (H), and a few by shore boat (SB) from Isthmus Cove at Two Harbors. The five improved campgrounds are all accessible by road. Of the six primitive sites, five are accessible by boat only on a first-come first-served basis (see hiking maps). Little Fisherman's, Parson's Landing, and Emerald Bay, at the west end near Two Harbors, no longer require landing permits.

When camping on the beach where fresh

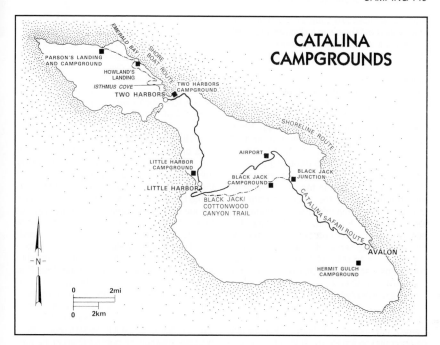

**CATALINA
CAMPGROUNDS**

water is scarce, use sea water to wash dishes and even yourself. Liquid Ivory or Joy detergents both suds well in salt water. It takes only a small squirt to do a good job. (A rub of soap on the bottom of pots and pans before use over an open fire makes for easy cleaning of the pots after cooking.)

For a map of the areas described, send a stamped legal size self-addressed envelope and $1 cash to the Los Angeles County Parks, Box 1133, Avalon, CA 90704.

Note: Fires are permitted at improved campsites *only.*

Getting There

From the Island Plaza in Avalon, catch the (seasonal only) shuttle bus to Hermit Gulch Campground (in Avalon), Airport-in-the-Sky, and to all the improved campsites in the interior. Reservations to the interior are required.

For more information and seasonal schedule, call (310) 510-2078, (310) 510-0143, or (310) 510-0303.

IMPROVED CAMPGROUNDS

Catalina Camping

Most of the campsites on Catalina (except Hermit Gulch Campground) are managed by the Two Harbors company Catalina Camping; Box 5044, Two Harbors, CA 90704.

Hermit Gulch Campground

Hermit Gulch Campground is the closest camping area to Avalon and is within walking distance of all the town attractions. It's easy to reach by walking up Sumner Ave. through Avalon Canyon. Follow the sign that says "Avalon Canyon Road." From the sign it's 1.5 miles inland on the Memorial Park Road. Operated by the SCI Company, the campground can handle 200 people. Attractively landscaped with tall shade trees, the campground offers fresh water, coin-operated inside hot showers, lighted rest-rooms, picnic tables, barbecue pits, vending machines, and a public phone; no electrical hookups, no pets, no wood fires. Fees are adult $7, child under 6 free; groups of 20 receive a discount. For reservations call (310) 510-TENT; check into the ranger's office upon arrival.

Black Jack
Mount Black Jack, at 2,006 feet, is the second-highest peak on Catalina (the highest, at 2,097 feet, is Mt. Orizaba). It's the site of old Black Jack Mine (lead, zinc, and silver). Black Jack Camp, 10 miles from Avalon and 15 miles from Two Harbors, sits at 1,500 feet. It is the principal inland camping area on Catalina, set in a lovely, protected pine forest. Some vantage points in the camp overlook the channel side of the Island toward the Mainland. The camp offers accommodations for 75 campers. Facilities include water, toilets, fire rings, barbecue pits, public phone, and shuttle bus service to Black Jack Junction. Fees are adult $7, child six and under 50 cents. For reservations call (310) 510-7265, fax (310) 510-0244, or write Box 5044, Two Harbors, CA 90704.

Little Harbor
Some campers say Little Harbor, the primary campground on the Pacific side of Catalina, is also Catalina's most picturesque and historic. Bring your camera for spectacular views from Indian Head Point above Little Harbor. Much of the history of the Catalina Indians has been brought to light in a deeply stratified archaeological site overlooking the twin bays of Little Harbor (see "History"). In 1894 Dr. O.T. Fellows built an inn here as a stopover for stagecoach passengers visiting the Island. The inn has long since gone, but the old stage road, still used today, meets the sea at its twin harbors: the smaller one (Little Harbor) a placid anchorage, the larger one (Shark Harbor) a surf-pounded strand that offers exciting beachcombing possibilities (especially after a storm) and excellent bodysurfing.

Little Harbor Campground is built on the site of an ancient Indian village. A good base for day-hiking to a variety of destinations, it's seven miles from Two Harbors and six miles from Black Jack. Though on the windward side of the Island, the camp sits in a protected patch of flat land close to the road and the

ocean. Little Harbor campground can accommodate 150 campers, with toilets, cold showers, barbecue pits, fire rings, picnic tables, phone, and shuttle bus service. It offers excellent swimming, diving, and fishing. Fees are adult $7, child six and under 50 cents. For reservations, call (310) 510-7265, fax (310) 510-0244, or write Box 5044, Two Harbors, CA 90704.

Two Harbors Campground
This privately owned campground is a half mile from Two Harbors on a bluff overlooking the rocky beach and crystal-clear waters of the cove. From here you can see right down to the bottom and watch the variegated hues of blue and green continue for some way out to sea. It's a good base from which to explore the many trails and coves of the west end. You'll find a general store, dive shop, restaurant, bar, and many other activities available thanks to the close proximity of the West End Cruising Club (see "Two Harbors"). The campground accommodates 250 campers, with toilets, cold showers, fire rings, barbecues, picnic tables, phone, swimming, fishing, and diving. Since it is illegal to carry combustible materials on public transport, be prepared to buy charcoal and lighter fluid from the park ranger. Fees are $6 pp, payable at the Camp and Cove office at the foot of Two Harbors pier. For reservations, call (310) 510-7265, fax (310) 510-0244.

PRIMITIVE CAMPSITES

Camping is permitted at six different coves on the lee coast of the Island. These completely undeveloped sites are not maintained by any agency and provide little more than a flat area to lay out your sleeping bag. Pay your fees ($3 pp per day) to Conservancy rangers, who will find you. First-come, first-served. For more information and reservations, call (310) 510-7265, fax (310) 510-0244, or write Box 5044, Two Harbors, CA 90704.

Emerald Bay/Sandy Beach
The cove of Emerald Bay is leased to the Corsair Yacht Club, and part of the beach and sur-

Quality tours since 1894

For the best Catalina Island has
to offer, look for the "Saludos Girl"
emblem at our ten ticket
locations -- your guarantee of
quality sightseeing tours. The
memories will last a lifetime.
*For detailed information,
see pages 71 - 76.*

Santa Catalina Island Company

310-510-TOUR
Money-saving overnight
packages which include *Discovery
Tours* on the next page.

It all adds up to fun and value, too!

With *Pavilion Lodge Packages*, one call arranges everything -- including round trip boat from San Pedro, Long Beach or Newport Beach, two nights' hotel accommodations at Pavilion Lodge PLUS the *Inland Motor Tour* (into Catalina's wilderness) and the NEW *Undersea Semi-Submersible Tour!*

◆ ◆ ◆
AAA

Midweek packages from
$105 - $195
Weekend packages from
$128 - $233

Per person. Price determined by season and choice of boat. Rates to 3/97. Some restrictions. Includes tax.

800-626-7496
Santa Catalina Island Company

rounding area is leased to the Boy Scouts of America for use as a summer camp. However, public camping is available in a primitive campsite on Sandy Beach. Accessible by boat or by road from Two Harbors, Emerald Bay, too, has exceptionally clear water and its share of Catalina's colorful past. Samuel Prentiss was the first white man to build a house on Catalina, here at Emerald Bay. He is buried on the hill overlooking what almost became the mining town of "Queen City" during the gold frenzy of 1863-64. Today this out-of-the-way area continues to provide a tranquil retreat for the explorer who prefers the peace of a grassy hillside sloping down to a spacious Robinson Crusoe-style beach.

Ripper's Cove
This excellent primitive campsite is accessible

Find a little cove, take a little snorkel, and have a little picnic.

only by boat. The sandy bottom provides good anchorage, and the sloping grassland behind the beach provides vigorous safe and scenic hiking.

Starlight Beach
This small beach lies one mile short of Land's End, the westernmost tip of Catalina Island. Access is by boat only. The diving is excellent in the transparent waters of this cove.

Little Gibraltar Rock and Cabrillo Harbor
The small leased camp at Cabrillo Harbor is operated by the Long Beach Council of Boy Scouts as a summer camp. The harbor also contains a primitive campsite for public use. Access to the interior from the beach is very difficult because of the rough terrain. Boat-in only.

Italian Gardens
Named for the many Italian fishermen from San Pedro who successfully fished here some years back, this is a long beach with access by boat only for primitive camping and terrific diving. You cannot hike into the interior from the beach.

Goat Harbor
This is a rugged geological area. A sandy beach offers primitive camping. The cliffs are dangerous. Access to the interior from the beach is very difficult because of the rough terrain. Surprisingly, you will find two deluxe yurt cabins set in a secluded cove. Access is by boat only.

OZ MALLAN

THE OTHER CHANNEL ISLANDS

KATHY ESCOVEDO-SANDERS

INTRODUCTION
THE LAND

Eight islands form the Channel Islands group, which extends off the California coast in a chain from Santa Barbara south to the Oceanside area. All share similar geologic origins, but each has evolved over the millennia into its own special environment with its own history. Geologists disagree about what once they believed to be fact: that from 70 million years ago to less than 20,000 years ago, the four northern Channel Islands were one colossal "super-island" connected to the Mainland by a land bridge. The theory was that the Anacapa end of this supposed island was joined to the Mainland at Point Mugu and was part of the Santa Monica Mountains. Earlier scientists believed that a land bridge might have existed because of the presence of land animals; the bridge gave them a logical explanation for how the fauna traveled to the islands. Many other theories now being studied would be plausible explanations for the presence of wildlife on the islands without a land bridge.

Other geologists believe that the islands were formed 14 million years ago when volcanic activity along the Southern California coast was at its maximum. Islands, peaks, and ridges rose out of the sea, only to settle again as the volcanic activity subsided. Ultimately, this left what we now call the Channel Islands. With the coming of the Ice Age more than a million years ago, freezing water and subsequent melting eroded the offshore peaks. Geologic stresses from all the changes caused buckles, folds, fractures, and tears in the earth. Cliffs rose, ridges slid into the sea, and islands appeared and disappeared into the ocean.

Geology buffs, while traveling around the Channel Islands, study the cliffs, bluffs, terrain, and underwater floor. In most cases it's rugged and craggy with horizontal and vertical strata

155 FLORA AND FAUNA

and flat terraces above and below the sea. To a scientist this tells the story of many changes in ocean levels over the centuries. A relatively shallow submarine shelf at an average depth of 300 feet extends three to six miles around each of the islands. Here, the mingling of the cold current of the north with the warmer countercurrent of the south, along with the unique topography of the ocean bottom, contribute to making this one of the richest marine environments in the United States.

FROM THE SMALLEST TO THE LARGEST

Santa Barbara Island . . . . . . (one square mile)
Anacapa Island . . . .(1.1 square mile)
San Miguel Island . . . .(14 square miles)
San Nicolas Island . . . .(22 square miles)
San Clemente Island . . . .(56 square miles)
Santa Catalina Island . . . . . .(75 square miles)
Santa Rosa Island . . . .(84 square miles)
Santa Cruz Island . . . . (96 square miles)

FLORA AND FAUNA

ON LAND

Coreopsis
All eight Channel Islands have many natural similarities. On each of the islands many of the same plant communities thrive. One of the most common, coreopsis, also called sea dahlia and

sunflower tree, has been variously described as a dwarf or miniature tree. The grotesque, odd plants average two feet in height but can grow as tall as 10 feet. In the fall, the clustered plants, bare of blossom or leaf, look like a dwarfed, misshapen, mysterious forest, all black and brown with knobby branches. But with win-

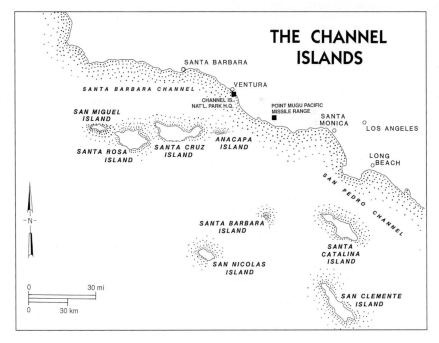

THE CHANNEL ISLANDS

ter rains, a change spreads over the hills; delicate fernlike fronds begin to appear. By spring, the plant blooms profusely (depending on the amount of winter rainfall) though just for a short time, bearing brilliant yellow/orange flowers; this splash of color carries clear to the Mainland.

Coreopsis grows on all of the islands but San Clemente, spreading a bright carpet along the gentle hills of Santa Barbara Island, poking up even from craggy pockets and crevices of Anacapa and San Miguel. The Hyder family (settlers who began raising sheep and rabbits,) burned the coreopsis first. Then their rabbits destroyed most of the coreopsis on Santa Barbara as it returned in the spring. Rabbits ate all the greenery they could reach, and then even girdled the trunks, ultimately destroying the plant trunks and their bright flowers.

However, the coreopsis is a weed that is hard to kill forever, and they are seen once again, now that the rabbits are gone.

Cactus

The **prickly pear,** an *Opuntia* species, is a common Channel Island cactus, growing over much of the southern part of California and on into Mexico.

The oval, disk-like pads are edible, as is the fruit--the pear. The plant bears beautiful satiny-yellow blossoms that wither and drop as the fruit begins to develop. The fruit becomes sweet and juicy if allowed to ripen on the plant, and is commonly eaten not only on the Channel Islands but also in Mexico, Central America, and parts of Africa. An account given in *The Diary of a Ship Captain's Wife* by Margaret Holden Eaton, who lived on Santa Cruz Island with her husband and baby girl from 1909, tells of making syrup for pancakes from the prickly pear. The trick is to peel the spines very carefully; then the fruit is ready to enjoy. Oddly enough, sheep were known to eat the pear, prickly spines and all. The land was severely overgrazed--that's real hunger!

Another relative of the species growing on the islands is the **cholla cactus.** It's shaped differently from the prickly pear but is just as deadly with its curled barblike spines. It too produces a flower, a delicate blossom sprouting at the joints. Long trails of **snake cactus** hang from rocky walls and canyons on the islands.

tuna cactus

Wildflowers

The purple **blue-eyed grass flowers** have six graceful petals with yellow starlike centers. The **western thistle** blooms a bright pink on top of its feathery tassel. After a rainy winter, spring bursts forth on the islands, and even the sand dunes come alive with blue **lupine** and golden **California poppies. Dudleya,** grayish green and similar to common ice plant, grows side by side with the orange-blossomed **mimulus,** or monkey flower, on the steep walls of rocky southern-exposed cliffs. White **morning glories** steadfastly climb over and around **sea cucumbers** and **island sage. Ferns** and **mosses** grow at the bottom of steep canyons.

Island Fox

The unique island fox, a relative of the Mainland gray fox, is an inhabitant of the six larger Channel Islands (not Anacapa or Santa Barbara). The animal differs from his Mainland relative in several ways. It's small--about the size of a house cat; in fact it has many feline characteristics, a scampering movement, and a yowl resembling a domestic cat's. It lives on a diet of mice, fish, birds and their eggs, crabs, fruit, insects, berries, and yes, even prickly pears. The fox has little fear of humans and a great curiosity (another catlike characteristic); it will stop and give you a good look if you meet on a mountain path.

There's no certainty about how it arrived on the islands. One possibility is that it rafted on a tree trunk washed out to sea from the Mainland during a heavy rainstorm; another is that it could have been brought to the islands by Indians traveling from the Mainland. The fox suffers from the introduction of "exotic" grasses. Wild oat seeds (the kind that stick on your shoelaces when you hike the hills) get into the foxes' eyes and blind them. The island fox is just a little different on each of the Channel Islands--a bit bigger or smaller with slight color variations.

Rodents

The **white-footed mouse,** also known as the deer mouse, is endemic to the particular island it inhabits and is an important part of the food chain. Its chief predator is the fox. The rodent

Channel Island fox

has white undersides, oversized feet, a hairy tail, and wide ears. It eats a varied diet--seeds, bark, twigs, fruit--and if it can get into a camper's tucker, it recognizes gourmet heaven. The mouse reproduces readily and survives nicely in the nooks and crannies of the rocky coastline, meadows, or sandy shore. It lives on all eight of the Channel Islands. As with the fox, each island has developed a subspecies with subtle differences. Those on Santa Rosa and Santa Barbara have even developed their own varieties of ticks and fleas.

Other small rodent relatives living on the islands are the **meadow mouse** and the **harvest mouse.** The **island shrew** must be extremely shy, since it has been spotted only a couple of times in more than a hundred years. The **ground squirrel,** also part of the island family, lives in underground burrows in the meadow areas.

Wild Goats

This feral animal was introduced to the islands sometime during the Spanish era. Historians believe that domestic goats were dropped off so the ships' crews would have fresh meat the next time they passed through. It doesn't take many generations for the goat to revert to its wild stage, and it reproduces quickly; the female generally delivers two kids a year.

On Catalina and San Clemente the goats increased freely for many years, building up large free-running herds. They are destructive animals with voracious appetites. Once ecologists began to see the need to preserve these islands in their natural states, many of the goats were hunted or removed. On Catalina the occasional hunt keeps the herds down to a reasonable number. On San Clemente, the Navy Wildlife Biology staff has been trying to rid the island of the animals through hunts and bodily removal to Mainland sites. The staff has had not only the spritely goats to contend with (they can scamper up the tiniest trail and walk sideways where few humans dare to tread), but also animal lovers who believe that goats have a right to life on San Clemente. So while the environmentalists and the animal lovers argue, the goats keep right on reproducing and devastating the landscape with their natural eating habits.

UNTANGLING A PELICAN FROM YOUR LINE

1. Keep reeling! Although it'll struggle and flap its wings, remember you know what's best. As large as the bird appears, it only weighs about six pounds and is quite harmless if handled correctly.

2. When you've got the bird close enough, grab the closed bill and hold it securely with one hand. The inside edges of the bill are sharp, but unless you rub your hand up and down the edge, a pelican bite will not hurt you.

3. Fold up the wings into their normal closed position and hold them there. This quiets down the bird and it should stop struggling.

4. Turn the bird's head around so it lies along the middle of it's back (that's how pelicans sleep) and the bird is easier to handle. Tuck the pelican under your armpit, or between your legs while removing the fishing line and hook. But remember, keep a firm grip on the bird's bill. Certainly it would be easier for two people instead of one, but one person can do it.

5. The most important thing you can do for the bird is cut off every bit of fishing line. Do not throw scrap pieces of line into the water to ensnare another bird or wrap around a boat prop shaft.

6. If the hook is embedded in the pelican's flesh, try to cut off the barb and back the hook out. Or cut off the loop end of the hook and push the rest of the hook through. If you lack wire cutters, remove the line from the hook and push it forward. Do not rip the hook out; if it's impossible to remove the hook, leave it in. Pelicans do not seem to get infections and the bird's skin will heal around the hook.

7. If the hook has been swallowed and the line is very long and hanging out of it's bill, you will need the help of another person to hold the pelican's bill open (wear gloves) while you cut the line off as short as possible. If you're alone, just cut the line at the edge of the bill.

8. Set the bird down, step back a few feet and release it. You just did a very good deed for one of mother nature's favorites.

DIANA LASICH HARPER

BIRDS

Pelicans

An enormous variety of birds nest on the rocky cliffs and shores of the Channel Islands. Here it is easy to see that the **brown pelican,** only a few years ago in danger of being destroyed, is now flourishing. These large birds fly in a wedge formation, gracefully flapping their wings close to the wave tops. Spotting a fishy morsel, they dive into the sea and, forgetting all grace, scoop up as many fish as their large beaks will hold, and flop into a crumpled heap on the water's surface.

Not too long ago, pelican reproduction slowed to a point of concern. Eggshells were so thin they could not support the weight of the brooding mother, cutting down dramatically on the number of chicks hatching each year. Researchers discovered that DDT caused the problem; it contaminated the small fish that the pelican fed on. The pesticide accumulated in the tissues of the bird, eventually reaching such high levels that it affected, among other things, the shells of the eggs. Since DDT has been banned, the pelican has made a remarkable comeback and lives in large healthy numbers on Channel Island rookeries.

Pelicans have a few bad habits that get them into other troubles. One is trying to steal fish from fishermen--often right off the hook. If a pelican should get caught on your hook, *do not* just cut the line at your end. If you do, you're condemning the bird to death; the line almost always ends up wrapped around the bird's body, including his wings, leaving him helpless, unable to fly, and doomed to starvation. Don't be afraid to reel the pelican in.

DIANA LASICH HARPER

Other Birds

Along with a flourishing brown pelican rookery on Anacapa Island, thousands of other birds have found that the Channel Islands are nirvana. Little outside influence disturbs the birds, and the relatively shallow near-shore waters around the islands supply 11 species of breeding seabirds with a rich food source of fish and invertebrates. On Santa Barbara, bird enthusiasts will find the largest colony of **Xantus' murrelet** and **black storm petrels** in the U.S. These timid seabirds are usually noticed only on or above the open ocean; they return to shore but once a year to breed and nest.

Migratory fowl and other birds such as **loons, grebes, herons, plovers, ducks,** and **geese** are also seen on the islands. Some stop just to rest on their long journeys, while others take time out for nesting and breeding before continuing.

Other inhabitants of the islands include the **Brandt's cormorant,** a powerful web-footed diver that swims underwater after its pelagic prey.

The **western gull,** a noisy old friend seen all over the West Coast, vigorously nests on the Channel Islands high above the sea.

Sandpipers are seen not only on the sandy shore, but also on the rocks and cliffs above, where nature has provided ample food and few predators.

Marine Creatures

An action of the sea called upwelling occurs along the California coast. Actually it happens all over the world, near the equator as well as in the Antarctic. In simple terms, coastal upwelling occurs when water from deeper levels of the ocean is brought to the surface to replace the surface waters when they are moved offshore by heavy winds.

The upwelled water is colder and contains richer nutrients such as nitrates, phosphates, and silicates. These nutrients act as fertilizer for marine plants and ultimately help the fishing industry. Sometimes large areas of the sea become red, green, or brown from the rapid reproduction of microscopic plant and animal organisms called plankton.

During this "plankton bloom," small animals graze upon these tiny organisms. The smaller

TIDEPOOL ORGANISMS

shield limpet	sun star
ribbed limpet	brittle star
owl limpet	green urchin
plate limpet	giant red urchin
horned slipper shell	isopod
black abalone	barnacle
chiton	crab
mussel	shrimp
black turban snail	eel
leafy hornmouth	bristleworm
checkered periwin-	ribbonworm
kle	flatworm
dog winkle	green alga
octopus	brown alga
sea slug	red alga
anemone	sponge
sea star	hydroid

animals are fed upon by larger animals, including fish, which are in turn food for the larger fish. And when the whales graze in these colorful "pastures," they consume up to a ton of plankton per mouthful.

Tidepools

It's hard to describe the myriad marine creatures of the Channel Islands without first mentioning the tidepools that thrive along their rocky shores. A tidepool is a pocket of the sea trapped regularly after the tide has gone out. The miniworlds that exist in each of these tiny pools are replicas of sealife in the larger picture. The fight for existence against such mighty forces as the pounding surf in high tide, drying sun and smothering heat during low tide, ultraviolet radiation from the sun, rain that dilutes the salinity, and constant predators presents ongoing adversity for these sturdy survivors.

One major predator is man. The creatures of the sea have not yet evolved a defense system to fight such calamities as oil spills or chemical pollution. It's up to us to do everything in our power to protect these fascinating creatures. When exploring or studying tidepools, each person has a responsibility to leave it as found. Apparently, it does no harm to the tiny creatures to pick them up (carefully), or turn

them over, or scoop them up in a jar to watch them swim freely, as long as everything is returned *exactly* the same.

Note: Wear sturdy rubber-soled shoes (tennis shoes) that you don't mind getting wet, as most of the rocks around the intertidal zone are slick. Whatever you do, don't wear thongs. Be sure to check the tide table in the local paper or marine store, and keep track when you're meandering at low tide; it could be difficult to return when the tide is barreling back in, especially in a rocky area. The best time of year to tidepool is winter and summer, since they are also the times of the lowest tides.

Intertidal Zone

The intertidal zone is the area between the highest high tide and the lowest low tide. It's created by the coming and going of the ocean current each day. The currents also change with the time of the month, the year, and the quarter of the moon. This creates a continuum of habitats, from high rocks that regularly get the splashing surf at the highest tides to the deepest level of pools that are exposed only during the lowest tides at certain times of the year. All of the species in the zone have learned to live with the ocean and its capricious nature. Those with the least tolerance to atmospheric pressure live at the lowest part of the zone or closest to the sea. Tolerant ones live toward the tops of rocks or reefs. The poor little creatures that would get washed into the sea (and probably eaten) every time a large wave crashes into their rocky homes occupy the protected pockets and crevices on the lee side of the rocks. Nature thinks of everything.

The following intertidal organisms are found along the entire Pacific coast from the top of Alaska to the southern edge of Mexico. For an excellent pocket guide that identifies and explains Pacific tidepool life, get a copy of *Pacific Intertidal Life,* by Ron Russo and Pam Olhausen, Nature Study Guild, Box 972, Berkeley, CA 94701.

Sand Creatures

The smooth sand constantly brushed by the incoming and outgoing sea hides a multitude of organisms. Everyone has seen the tiny **sand crab** burrowing its way into the wet sand of the backwash of each wave, straining for tidbits of food. Other small creatures (all different) come in many sizes and shapes: some have antennae, some hop sideways, some are gray, white, or the color of the sand. At night swarms of tiny sandhoppers leap onto kelp fronds in search of food. These, too, are part of the food chain with their own set of predators.

Marine Flora

Some brown algae (seaweed), called kelps, form large tangled forests consisting of **giant kelp, feather boa kelp, bull whip kelp,** and **elk kelp.** All of these brown algae depend on gas-filled bulbs, called pneumatocysts, to buoy their long, swaying stems, and blades that transfer energy from the sun into the dim depths of the bottom regions of the "holdfasts," which anchor the kelp to the sea floor. These kelp forests are habitats for a great variety of marinelife that depend on them for food and shelter. The fish that live within the forests are colorful and varied.

Among the most flamboyant algae is giant kelp, growing as much as 100 feet from the sea floor to the surface. It grows amazingly fast, as much as three feet a day, fed by the rich nutrients of the colder water brought in by upwelling, and plenty of sunshine. A new plant usually doubles its size every three weeks. The long stems are buoyed by brown, tear-shaped pneumatocysts. From the surface, the kelp resembles a jumbled mass of brown rubbery stems and vines and tobacco-like leaves.

From the diver's point of view, the stems grow a good distance apart from each other on the sea floor and indeed resemble a forest of tall trees. The holdfast is not a root in the sense of a land plant, gathering nutrients from the surrounding soil. It is simply an anchorage. The alga takes nourishment directly from the seawater through all exposed surfaces.

Reproduction is through microscopic cells known as spores, produced by a female plant and fertilized by a male; free-floating spores then germinate and begin to form separate new plants. Some seaweeds produce mini-plants which eventually separate and become new plants. Eventually giant kelp becomes so top-

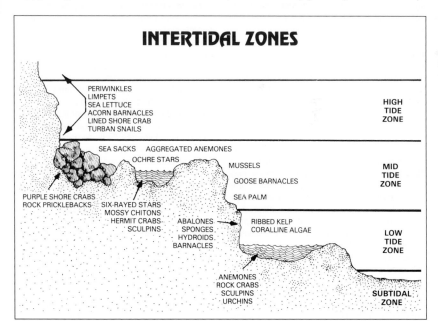

INTERTIDAL ZONES

PERIWINKLES
LIMPETS
SEA LETTUCE
ACORN BARNACLES
LINED SHORE CRAB
TURBAN SNAILS

HIGH TIDE ZONE

SEA SACKS   AGGREGATED ANEMONES
OCHRE STARS
MUSSELS
GOOSE BARNACLES

SEA PALM

MID TIDE ZONE

PURPLE SHORE CRABS
ROCK PRICKLEBACKS   SIX-RAYED STARS
MOSSY CHITONS
HERMIT CRABS   ABALONES
SCULPINS   SPONGES
HYDROIDS
BARNACLES

RIBBED KELP
CORALLINE ALGAE

LOW TIDE ZONE

ANEMONES
ROCK CRABS
SCULPINS
URCHINS

SUBTIDAL ZONE

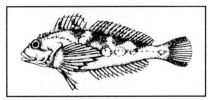

heavy that the holdfast lets go and the entire plant ends up floating on the surface of the sea until caught by a current and thrown in a heap on a beach or rocky shoreline. However, it continues to nurture, harboring a variety of crabs, worms, clams, starfish, and other invertebrates.

Just as tidepool life exists because it can sustain itself despite drying, temperature change, salt level, and tide level, so it is with kelp. One of the more hardy, able to resist and persist, is a green alga called **sea lettuce,** which can lose up to 75% of its tissue water and recoup to fine fetter once in the water again. A brown alga, common **branched rockweed,** can withstand up to 48 hours of exposure without drying out. On the other hand, most red algae are extremely sensitive to heat and light and exist in the low intertidal zone because they cannot survive more than two or three hours of exposure.

Algae Aquaculture

Aquaculture is the farming of aquatic plants and animals and is practiced in many countries in the world. In Japan and other Asian countries it has been a flourishing business for years; approximately 15% of the world's iodine comes from Japan, where it is manufactured from kelp.

In the U.S. aquaculture is still in the developing stages. A multimillion-dollar algae-harvesting business is already very successful here. Algin, a derivative of kelp, is found in many products that you see in the supermarket every time you shop. Next time you buy ice cream, chocolate milk, pudding, salad dressing, cheese, or fruit juice, take a close look at the ingredients. Algae derivatives furnish a gel used to emulsify and stabilize foods. They are used in other diverse ways, in dental molds, beer, fertilizer, animal feed, paint, and cosmetics.

The kelp beds off California are leased out by the state, which accepts bids from companies that do the actual harvesting in specially designed ships that often gather 400 tons of kelp a day. San Diego is a very popular area for kelp harvesting because of good year-round weather. Under the auspices of the Department of Fish and Game, kelp can be cut up to a maximum of four feet below the surface of the water. Opening up the surface directs more sunshine beneath the sea and onto the plants, encouraging new growth. Harvesting is a healthy process.

Seaweed Dishes

Some countries (Japan, China, and the Philippines, plus the state of Hawaii) have recognized the value of eating seaweed for centuries. These algae are nutritious and rich in vitamins A and E. The red, green, and brown algae are also very high in niacin and vitamins C, B-12, and B-1. They contain digestible proteins--highest in the red and green varieties. Three ounces of red algae supplies one-half the adult daily protein requirements. Common sea lettuce is high in iron, protein, iodine, magnesium, vitamins A, B-1, and C, and sodium. Pluck or cut the blades from rocks at low tide, wash well, dry at room temperature, and then use as a soup base.

Be aware that *except* in state parks and reserves, gathering algae for noncommercial use does *not* require a California fishing license or permit. In a state park or reserve, you must obtain a permit from the state Department of Parks and Recreation. In the course of collecting algae in intertidal areas, you will find many invertebrates, including clams, crabs, worms, and snails, living among the seaweeds. You can take these animals only in legal seasons and with a fishing license. Outside of bureaucratic permission, all you need is a sharp knife, a bucket, some plastic bags, and don't forget your rubber-soled shoes. A good guidebook is handy to have along.

The best time to collect is at low tide--tides reach high and low levels twice a day. You can find tidal charts in many beach community newspapers, or check at your local sporting goods store or bait and tackle shop. Rocky shorelines are your best bet for collecting algae; the sides of the rocks are richer in plant life than the tops. To get the freshest seaweed, take it directly from the place of attachment. Don't get lazy and grab a bunch that's been washed ashore--it's seldom fresh and will be full of debris.

MARINE MAMMALS

Marine Mammal Protection Act

More than 25 species of marine mammals inhabit the Channel Islands Sanctuary. After being nearly demolished by the extensive hunting in the 18th and early 19th centuries, seals, sea lions, and a variety of fur seals have made a remarkable comeback. The Marine Mammal Protection Act of 1972 was passed with the intention of protecting the mammals, and management was transferred from the coastal states to the federal government. Many people think this law was enacted primarily to protect whales, but it was written to include all marine mammals--to the dismay of many fishermen.

There's much controversy among fishermen, who say the sea lion and sea otter are interfering with their business. According to divers, the sea otter eats a tremendous amount of abalone each year. Commercial fishermen complain that the growing sea lion population is taking a larger share of fish--often right from their nets--not only creating a decrease in income, but fouling up expensive gear, creating "down time," and worst of all (according to the fishermen), they cannot destroy an animal that persists without first obtaining a special permit from the National Marine Fisheries Service.

Ecologists argue that nature provides its own means of thinning the herds: many newborn pups are trampled to death each season in the rookeries as the herd multiplies. But fishermen are still demanding the right to destroy a seal that is making a nuisance of itself in the nets. Right now, there are no clear-cut answers. The law says it is illegal to harass a marine mammal. Harassment is interpreted as human activity that changes the behavior of the animals. You cannot harm, capture, kill, interfere with or enter a rookery, or closely pursue a whale with a boat.

Pinnipeds

Pinniped means "featherfeet" and refers to the modification of the front and hind feet to form flippers. Many of the seals, such as the **harbor seal,** spend six to eight months at sea. Others, such as the **northern fur seal,** spend considerable time on land. These creatures have thick hides with heavy layers of fat underneath and in some cases fur to protect them from the cold.

CALIFORNIA WHALES

northern right
fin or rorqual
minke
sei
blue or sulphurbottom
finback
humpback
gray
sperm
pygmy sperm
dwarf sperm
beaked or bottlenose
Baird's beaked
Hubb's beaked
Cuvier's beaked
orca or killer

The pinniped family includes two basic groups: the eared seals--**fur seals** and **sea lions**--and the hair seals, or so-called true seals --**harbor seals**, **ribbon seals,** and **elephant seals.** Eared seals have small external flaps for ears. They move rapidly on land since they can turn their hind flippers forward, almost like feet, and they use their large forward flippers to swim quickly in the water. These mammals return year after year to special breeding areas called rookeries, commonly on offshore islands. Breeding season is a noisy, hectic time at the rookery. Males fight for territories and to the victors go groups of 25 or more females, accurately called "harems." Males go more than two months without feeding during breeding time.

Hair seals have no external ears. They have small front flippers, and use their hind flippers for swimming. They cannot turn their hind flippers forward, making them very clumsy on land.

Five species of pinnipeds gather to breed, pup, and nurse their young in the Channel Islands: the **harbor seal, Steller sea lion, California sea lion, northern fur seal,** and **elephant seal.**

Sea Otters

After surviving for at least three million years, the

northern Alaskan fur seal

sea otter was almost annihilated in the middle 1800s. It was quite a thrill when, in 1938, a large herd of 100 sea otters was discovered about 15 miles south of Monterey. This marine mammal, part of the weasel family, can grow to about 4 feet long and reach a weight of 60-87 pounds. Its hind feet are large and webbed, with the fifth digit (comparable to man's little toe) the longest. The tail is used to help guide the animal while swimming, which it can do very efficiently. Its most impressive feature, however, is its beautiful soft fur, which in the past made many coats and nearly caused its extinction.

The otters' front paws are stubby with retractable claws. The animals are quite adept with them, using them much as a human uses fingers. Anyone who has ever tried to remove an abalone attached to a rock knows that it is impossible to do without a metal bar. The otter, however, is quite an accomplished underwater hunter, easily capturing abalone and other shellfish. You'll commonly see it floating on its back with a rock in one paw, holding a shellfish in the other, pounding away at the shell until it frees the flesh, ready to be nibbled.

The otter has no blubber as do seals and sea lions; its fur is not efficient enough to maintain its body temperature at 100° F, so it has a high metabolic rate and must consume large quanti-

ties of food each day. It forages (very efficiently) day and night. As the herds grow, the prognosis is that certain fishing industries will be greatly affected: Pismo clam, abalone, sea urchin, shallow-water red and rock crab, Dungeness crab, lobster, razor clam, and all open mariculture (marine farming) projects. The otter lives about 20 years and produces one pup approximately every two years. Its only enemy (besides man) is the white shark.

The first record of sea otters was made in 1741 after Vitus Bering (the explorer for whom the Bering Sea was named) spotted them in the Commander Islands and eastward in the Aleutians. The famous explorer was accompanied by a German naturalist, George Wilhelm Steller. The group obtained about 800 pelts from Indians, who hunted them for pelts and food in reasonable numbers. Bering and Steller took them home to Europe--the first time Europeans were exposed to otter pelts. In 1778, English explorer James Cook returned home from extensive travels along the north Pacific coast and revealed to the world the potential profit awaiting the hunter. Thus began the sea otter fur trade, which would attract people in ships from many parts of the world, weakening and ultimately loosening the hold of the Spanish flag on California.

Whales
When whales are mentioned, most West Coast dwellers think of the **gray whale,** which is enthusiastically observed as it migrates along the Pacific Coast from the Bering Sea to Baja and back each year. Others remember fondly the fun and games created by "Humphrey the humpback," which led the Coast Guard and many boaters on a romp up the Sacramento River Delta in 1986. But many more species of this usually gentle, giant mammal (part of the cetacean family) live in and around the coast near the Channel Islands. Although we think of all whales as being gigantic, the **pygmy sperm** grows to only 13 feet maximum, and some of the **beaked whales** grow only to 15-17 feet. The **false killer** isn't a true whale, but belongs to the dolphin (Delphinidae) family and gets huge, to 18 feet. The **killer** grows to 31 feet, and the **pilot,** to 22 feet.

Various sources say there are 78-91 species

of cetaceans in the world. The cetaceans store thick layers of blubber under their skins. This provides insulation against cold, and some scientists believe it enables them to go for long periods without food. It's becoming evident that the gray whale feeds heavily during the four months it spends in the Bering Sea and feeds lightly during its eight months of migration to and from Baja. Rather amazing, considering the energy it must take to swim thousands of miles, and on the return, nurse a baby as well (if it's a blue whale, the baby could be 25 feet long and weigh up to two tons at birth!).

Some whales feed on plankton, minute organisms floating in the sea, straining them through baleen plates, the fine netlike apparatus in their mouths. Although the mammoth mammals have been known to snack on passing schools of anchovies or other small fish, they are mainly plankton eaters. So the largest animal on earth feeds on the smallest organisms lowest on the food chain, where the supply is more abundant. In captivity, the animals are fed a variety of soft-boned fish, such as mackerel, and squid.

The killer whale is the only known enemy of the great whales--along with man. But attacks are not as common as some would think. Pods of killer whales have been known in isolated instances to attack a lone whale, but the killer whale's reputation rises mostly from tales related by whalers who have had their slaughtered whales (under tow) attacked by killer whales. The killer is ordinarily a fish eater.

Great whales appear to be unusually healthy animals; the slow movers attract acorn barnacles, which are really just "hitchhikers" and do no physical harm. Parasites on the other hand can be a disabling menace, maybe even causing the aberrant behavior of "beaching." Scientists have found large quantities of parasites on these beached mammals.

Whaling

For centuries the whale has been a source of food and oil (and for a while, whalebone), especially for the polar region natives. Seven thousand years ago, Eskimos on Canada's east coast were using toggle harpoon heads. In the mid-19th century they were "invented" again by the Yankee whaling fleet. Yankee whalers began

whaling off the coast of California in the early 1800s. By the late 1800s, the gray whale was thought to be extinct. Shore whaling (called "whaling by hand") helped shape California's history, and the first whaling station was built in Monterey in 1854. Others were built up and down the California coast and down to Baja but were short-lived. In 1874, Charles Melville Scammon (the whaler who discovered and exploited Scammon's Lagoon in Baja) wrote: "This particular branch of whaling is rapidly dying out, owing to the scarcity of the animals which now visit the coast."

During this time, the Americans dominated the whaling industry. Their chief target was the **right whale,** so called because it was the "right" whale to catch: it was slow moving, didn't sink when killed, contained valuable baleen used for women's corset stays (big business in those days), and of course was a great source of valuable oil used for lamps and smokeless candles. (Petroleum was discovered in 1859 and Edison came through with the incandescent bulb in 1879; otherwise we may never have had the privilege of seeing a whale.) When overhunting pretty well wiped out the right whale, the new target was the **sperm whale;** these were taken for oil and ambergris (used in perfume).

The industry was really making inroads into the whale populations with the development of the explosive harpoon gun in 1868, fast steam-powered catcher boats, and later with the use of floating factory-ships. The whaling industry methodically went about its business, destroying one species of whale after the other. After 1880, whaling was just about finished. However, interest was revived again in the States between 1940 and 1965. Whales were slaughtered and used mostly for pet food until it was no longer economically feasible to hunt them.

Only two nations--Japan and Russia--continue to hunt, and they aim primarily at the sperm whale for its oil. The Japanese eat whale meat but it accounts for only two percent of the fishing industry and is steadily declining. Russia takes a small number each year for the subsistence of Siberian natives. It is illegal for Americans, except for Eskimos, to hunt whales under both the Marine Mammal Protection Act and the Rare and Endangered Species Act. The Fisheries Conservation Act of 1976 prohibited whaling

PACIFIC DOLPHINS AND PORPOISES

common or white-belly
Pacific pilot
Risso's
Pacific white-sided
harbor
Dall
false killer
striped
rough toothed
Pacific bottlenose

within a 200-mile ocean zone off the U.S. coast. The last "killer" ship registered in the U.S. was the *Sioux City,* now used for marine research.

Dolphins and Porpoises
If there were a popularity contest for sea animals, hands-down winners would be porpoises and dolphins. They always appear to have smiles on their faces, their squeaky "talk" is a happy sound, they impart a playful attitude, and certainly their friendly rapport with human beings in marine parks around the U.S. has endeared them to millions of people. Also of the cetacean family, they have many habits similar to those of their big brother, the whale. The terms "dolphin" and "porpoise" are continually confused. Strictly speaking, the dolphin is the long-beaked variety. The porpoise is the snubby-nosed form. Porpoises and dolphins have intrigued man for centuries.

They have been written about, sung about, drawn, and fought over. Aristotle compared them to man: ". . . dolphins are born of a womb, take milk from nipples, breathe with lungs, make a variety of sounds, copulate rather than spawn, and care for their young, often with the help of an 'auntie.'" (When you see "dolphin" on menus, it is not a cetacean, but is actually a fish called mahimahi or dolphinfish.) Around the Channel Islands, it isn't unusual to see hundreds of **white-sided dolphins** cavorting in the wake of a fast-moving boat. The largest herds appear from August to January--or you can see individual performers at San Diego's Sea World.

HISTORY

INDIANS

Canalinos
Humans have been touching these islands for centuries. Remnants of prehistoric man place him here 11,000 years ago. Today, the only people we can learn about are the Chumash Indians, inhabitants of the Channel Islands at the time of the arrival of the Spaniards. The Indians are referred to by several names. Even though their language, based on the original Shoshonean, evolved into many dialects, all Channel Island Indians are known as Canalinos.

These particular Indians are considered to have possessed higher than average technical abilities. They are credited with many contributions to the culture of the time, but the most outstanding was their wood-plank canoe called a *tomol.* Evidence shows that before this boat was developed, the Indians used a primitive craft made from large bundles of tule grass. It had obvious disadvantages: it lasted only one or two times in the sea and could not go long distances.

On the other hand, the *tomol,* a fine wooden craft, was sturdy and fast, had two prows, and sometimes had wing boards as well.

The canoe was constructed of planks split from driftwood logs with wedges made of whalebone or antler (the Canelinos had no metal tools). They drilled and reamed holes with stone drills and strung strong cord made of fiber through the planks to hold them together. They then buried the planks in wet sand and built fires over them, steaming the boards so that they could bend them to the desired shape. They caulked the seams with asphaltum (thick black oil that oozes at certain rocky areas along the Southern California coast, such as Carpinteria), and even then, the craft took on water. But these 12- to 16-foot vessels were more than adequate for taking 12-20 mariners long distances, to the Mainland and from island to island--even though they had to include a youth or two to bail water.

The Canalinos were hunters and fishermen. They hunted sea lions, otters, and seabirds. They fished from their wood-plank boats and used shiny hooks carved from abalone shells that fooled the big fish into thinking the hook was a little fish--the first man-made lure? It apparently worked well, as indicated in the many kitchen middens found all over the Channel Islands; obviously seafood was an important part of the Canalino diet.

The Indians were talented in other areas also. They wove sturdy, handsome baskets from plant fibers, varnishing those they wished to make waterproof. They painstakingly made tiny beads from the marine snail (purple olivella), among other shells. These were strung and valued for trade with Mainland Indians. Besides beads, islanders traded otter skins, seal pelts, shellfish, and carved stone figures (often depictions of whales or seals) used as charmstones. The Island Indians had quantities of stone to work with, as on Catalina where there's an abundant supply of soapstone, steatite, and obsidian. These Island objects were traded for Mainland goods scarce or not available on the islands, such as acorns, rabbits, deer, and a hard rock called chert.

Indian Religion

All the villages of the Channel Islands were independent of each other, each with a *wot* (chief) and a shaman. These two men controlled the life of the Indian villager with rules and ceremonies. The chief depended on the mysterious prowess possessed by the shaman to help him through difficult times, such as drought or eclipse. Important ceremonies consistently held in the village dealt with birth, death, and puberty for both boys and girls. Puberty ceremonies were so universally celebrated among the hunting and gathering Indians that historians believe them to have been brought from Asia itself.

The boys went through a rigorous ceremony,

Canalino Indians built huts from branches and tule grass.

the *toalache,* which involved the ingestion of a narcotic, also called *toalache.* The girls' rite was more in the nature of a debut, a presentation to society of a marriageable young woman. It was a time of moral lectures and a test of virtue. First, the girl swallowed a ball of tobacco in a test of virtue. If she could retain it without regurgitating, she was indeed a virtuous Indian maiden; if she regurgitated, she was considered a fallen woman and held in contempt. Sad for the girl with a queasy stomach! During the three-day rite, some of the old Indian taboos for women remained, such as not eating meat, and using a stick to scratch her head instead of her fingers. But mostly it was a preparation for life as a wife, mother, and efficient member of the community --and for her future health.

These qualities were enhanced by practically baking her in a pit for three days and nights, protected from hot stones only by a mattress of branches from such plants as the California mugwort and the western ragweed. During this time she was the center of attention, and although she did fast from all food, she could drink, was bathed with warm water, and was the central figure in hours of dancing and singing and the distribution of gifts.

After three days, her face was painted by the wife of the visiting official (guests from a neighboring village) in charge of the ceremony. The woman placed anklets and bracelets of (highly valued) human hair and shell necklaces on the girl. A sand painting was made on the ground and the girl was given moral lectures, instructing her on how to act to be socially acceptable. She should be industrious and not a gadabout, bathe each day, be hospitable, have a straightforward manner with no malice in her heart. At the end of the ceremony, she was given a ball of sage meal and salt that she then spit into a hole in the center of the sand painting and she watched as the entire "painting" was brushed into the hole and the earth packed in on top of it--her future was sealed.

The Indians of the Channel Islands were all part of the Chingichnich religion that originated on Catalina Island. The medicine men exercised incredible exploitations of the people. The shaman was considered a wizard, a powerful man deserving of the people's respect. He induced spells, producing items from his mouth that he said were sent to him from the heavens. He would take credit for magically causing the death of an enemy in another village.

The medicine man also explained the signs of nature to the people; a rainbow was a sign of good fortune, while an eclipse was a certain omen of calamity. During an eclipse the people were reduced to shouting and weeping, pounding with sticks on the ground, all to scare away the evil monster trying to steal the moon or sun. The shaman must have been right, since they always managed to scare away the evil monster that was eating their celestial body. Falling stars were children of the moon; the morning and evening stars were the Big Stars, and Polaris was the "star that does not move."

The Advent of the White Man

It appears that life went on among these Indians for centuries with very little outside intrusion. This was to change shortly after the Spaniards declared the west coast of the continent for the king of Spain in the mid-1700s. Shortly afterward, the Russians and Americans discovered that the coast was home to a precious little sea creature, the otter, which had a ready market in Asia and Europe desired for its velvetlike fur. The otter hunts that would change the destiny of a country (Spain) and a culture (the Indians') began. For a while the Russians and Americans were competitors, each trying to outhunt the other. After realizing what was happening,

the Spaniards, too, began hunting the otter, at the same time placing strict embargos on all foreign ships, ordering them to leave the territory. These orders didn't stop the Russians or the Americans, nor, for that matter, ships from other countries that were beginning to enviously eye the beautiful California coast.

The Spanish didn't have the manpower to police the entire Pacific coast--outsiders had their way. The beginning of the end for the Spanish regime was on the horizon; the hunts continued. The otter was slaughtered on a grand scale and soon it was all but wiped out. But neither the Americans nor the Russians considered that, and in fact they ultimately joined forces, employing experienced hunters, the Aleut Indians with their sleek *bidarkas*--kayaks made from seal skins stretched over whalebones. The Aleuts made temporary camps on the islands while they massacred the sea otter for its fur. The hunters found that there was also a market for certain species of pinnipeds and then virtually destroyed the Guadalupe fur seal, northern fur seal, and northern elephant seal, which was prized for the superior lubricating qualities of its oil. One large bull might produce more than 200 gallons of this oil, while his whiskers fetched a handsome return in China as opium-pipe cleaners.

In the midst of all this turmoil, the Channel Island Indians were caught up in the outsiders' frantic search for money. The peaceful Canalino Indians were no match for the aggressive Aleuts. Their women were raped, the men murdered, and entire families commandeered by the invaders from the north while they stayed on the islands. White man's diseases were rampant; syphilis and measles were responsible for the deaths of most of the Indians who weren't murdered. The few that remained agreed to go to Mainland missions. By 1857, there were no Indians left on the Channel Islands. It was the end of an era--the white man's entrance to the California coast was totally destructive.

INDUSTRY

Pioneers

In a different spirit, even the pioneers played havoc with nature's balance. In the latter half of the 19th century, settlers began to arrive with their sheep. What better place? They needed no fences, there were no other farmers to disturb, the grazing areas were massive. These voracious animals were allowed to roam and reproduce freely. Overgrazing destroyed native plants; the introduction of oats and other "exotic" crops further damaged the natural vegetation of the islands. People have tried to tame these bits of land, but in most cases the greatest equalizers of all, nature's elements, have maintained the upper hand. Today, bowing to this natural power, man has wisely chosen to preserve most of these islands as they are and were in prehistoric times.

Chinese

The Chinese were heavily discriminated against during and after the gold rush. They were often smuggled into the country by dishonest sea captains to sell (yes, like slaves) for cheap labor. It was sometimes necessary for these ships from Asia to lay over or hide the Chinese on the Channel Islands so the captain could complete his nefarious dealings and sneak by wary customs agents.

While spending time on the islands, the Chinese discovered the profusion of abalone along the islands' shores. After the sea otter slaughter (sea otters eat thousands of abalone each year) and the destruction of the Indian (who also harvested his share of the shellfish) the abalone was ignored and allowed to replenish for many years. At the first opportunity, the Chinese returned and harvested cove after cove of the delicately flavored abalone meat that had been prized by Asians for centuries. This quietly administered industry (California's first organized fishing industry, if you don't count the Indians') flourished in all of the Channel Islands and by 1879 more than four million pounds a year of dried abalone meat was being exported.

The hard-working Chinese were eventually driven away by other immigrants: Italians, Portuguese, Slavs, and Japanese. By 1890 Chinese fishing villages were nonexistent. Commercial divers during the past 30-40 years have made their dent in the abalone population as well. Abalone has become more scarce each year; now the meat is sold at local fish markets for about $65 a pound!

The First Oil Boom

Southern California's first oil boom took place in the late 1800s. Much like the gold rush, it brought economic rewards to the state, and everyone wanted to get into the oil business. The industry was a baby. It wasn't until much later, in the 1890s, with technical improvements in drilling, storing, and refining, that it became a viable business. As the years passed, Southern California continued to upgrade the industry until it was producing 25% of the world's oil. Offshore leases of the outer continental shelf were first obtained in the 1950s. Today, San Pedro and Long Beach Harbor still bustle with the comings and goings of large oil tankers from all over the world; we all keep our fingers crossed that each year will be "spill-free."

CHANNEL ISLANDS NATIONAL PARK

San Miguel, Santa Rosa, Santa Cruz, Anacapa, and Santa Barbara, the five northernmost of the eight Channel Islands, make up Channel Islands National Park, established on March 5, 1980, when President Carter signed a bill into law creating the National Park and Marine Sanctuary to preserve the area's delicate ecology. The entire Channel Islands National Park is a reserve included in the Man and the Biosphere Program, an international effort to define and solve worldwide environmental problems and issues. National marine sanctuaries fall under the administration of the National Marine Sanctuary Office, National Oceanic and Atmospheric Administration (NOAA), and the U.S. Department of Commerce, and are managed by the National Park Service and the California Department of Fish and Game under an agreement with NOAA. The sanctuary includes the land areas of Anacapa, Santa Barbara, San Miguel, and most recently acquired (1987) Santa Rosa, plus a band of sea extending six miles around each of the five northernmost Channel Islands.

PRACTICALITIES

RECREATION

Camping

Camping is permitted on Anacapa, San Miguel, and Santa Barbara with a free permit from Park Headquarters at 1901 Spinnaker Dr., Ventura, CA 93001, tel. (805) 644-8262. Visitors planning to take their own boats should study U.S. Coast and Geodetic Survey Charts 18720, 18729, and 18756. Anchoring at either Anacapa or Santa Barbara Islands can be hazardous because of sea conditions. A maximum of 30 people per day are allowed to camp at each island and only in designated areas. You must haul in everything for your stay, including water and fuel. When you leave you must take all trash with you.

The facilities at the campgrounds include pit toilets and tables. No open fires are allowed. If you plan to cook you must bring a small stove. The restrictions on using the stoves are meant to control the possibility of a wildfire on the arid islands, which would destroy the years of effort by the National Park Service to restore the land to its original condition. A fire department is nonexistent. Also, discharge of firearms and fireworks is not allowed in the park or within the one-nautical-mile seaward boundary of ocean within the state ecological reserves.

Activities

When you get right down to it, there's not a whole lot to do on the Channel Islands. In fact there are probably many people who wouldn't be interested in this kind of trip at all. Let's find out how you rate. Do you need electronic entertainment, a regular bed, or a close-by fast-foodery to make your getaway worthwhile? If you answered yes to any or all of these questions, cancel your trip to the Channel Islands--*right now*. On the other hand, does the shock of a black velvet sky sparkling with brilliant stars always bring a lump to your throat? Can you gaze fascinated for hours at a time into a small rocky pool filled with the colorful minutiae of marinelife? Do you somehow mistake the sound of the sea crashing onto a rocky shore for a lullaby? If you answered yes to any or all of *these* questions,

you will have the time of your life on the Channel Islands.

All visitors to the Islands should know that most of what you get from a visit is a glimpse of life before the advent of modern man. Because of the importation of domestic animals allowed to overgraze the land and the intrusion of "exotic" plants, including fast-growing grain types such as oats, barley, and sea grasses, the native vegetation was choked out almost entirely. These introduced seeds were broadcast in open plowed fields by well-intentioned farmers, further crowding out the native grasses. This combination of events all but destroyed the original landscape. Today, with a lot of TLC, the native plants are returning. With this in mind, hiking on the Islands (where permitted) is restricted to formal paths.

GETTING THERE

The ocean around the northern Channel Islands can change from placid to rough and choppy very quickly, especially in the afternoon. It's wise to study local conditions and be prepared. Island Packers Boat Company provides regular transportation to Anacapa, Santa Barbara, Santa Rosa, and San Miguel Islands; you should make reservations at least one to two weeks in advance and check seasonal schedules. The office is next door to the Channel Islands National Park Headquarters at 1867 Spinnaker Dr., Ventura, CA 93001; call for reservations, (805) 642-1393, for information (805) 642-7688. Several commercial boat companies operate open-party and charter trips the rest of the year, especially during the whalewatch season, January through March. For more detailed information call Park Headquarters, tel. (805) 644-8262.

Access and Permits

A permit to visit San Miguel is free through Park Headquarters in Ventura. Access is by excursion boat only. For permission to land on Santa Rosa Island, contact Park Headquarters. To visit Santa Cruz, contact the Nature Conservancy, Santa Cruz Island Preserve, 213 Stearns Wharf, Santa Barbara, CA 93101, tel. (805) 962-9111.

For further information write to: Channel Islands National Park Visitor Center, 1901 Spinnaker Dr., Ventura, CA 93001, tel. (805) 644-8262. Boat transportation and package tours are provided by Island Packers, 1867 Spinnaker Dr., Ventura, CA 93001, tel. (805) 642-1393.

Romance and Adventure
Sailing charter trips are available from **Naviga-** **tors Channel Island Cruise,** 1621 Fernald Point Lane, Santa Barbara, CA 93108, tel. (805) 969-2393. Luncheon trips start at $40; overnight island cruises for two are $450 and up. These trips are available April through November. Twilight and sunset cocktail harbor cruises are offered at Captain Jack's Landing, 4151 S. Victoria Ave., Oxnard, CA 93030, tel. (805) 985-8511 and (213) 457-9221.

ANACAPA ISLAND

Anacapa lies 11 miles southwest of Oxnard, 14 miles south of Ventura, and 26 miles southeast of Santa Barbara. Isolated and remote, it stretches five miles across the sea but has a total area of only one square mile. Anacapa is actually three separate islands separated by narrow channels, inaccessible from each other except by boat. West Anacapa, largest of the islands, is punctuated with sea-etched caves and craggy peaks. On Middle Anacapa, surrounded by high cliffs, meadows of green grass display giant coreopsis with their distinctive yellow flowers that, when in bloom (on a clear day), can be seen from the Mainland and from far out to sea.

GEOLOGY

A volcanic rock, Anacapa is riddled with labyrinthine caverns in the submarine lava flow that you can observe at the island's base. Anacapa Island is made up almost entirely of dense deposits of Miocene volcanic rock, lava ash, and breccia (rock consisting of sharp fragments embedded in compacted sand, clay, or lava ash). As time, wind, and sea continue to erode the cliffs, they expose gravel and pebbles of different minerals. Near Frenchy's Cove, look for a large vein of almost-white chalcedony (a translucent quartz commonly pale gray or blue with a waxlike luster), and on the south shore of West Anacapa near Cat Rock the geology buff can spot San Onofre blue-green breccia. While browsing Cat Rock, notice the surge channel and the adjacent blowhole that makes a beautiful photo subject if you have a little patience.

The famous Arch Rock, a natural "bridge" formed by constant sea erosion, lies at the easternmost extension of the island. This is Anaca-

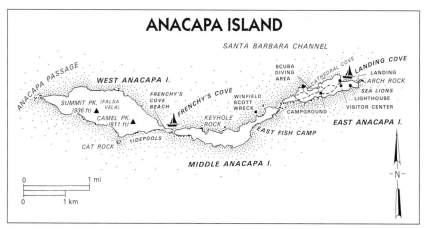

FLORA AND FAUNA

Anacapa has practically no trees. The landscape is reminiscent of California's high desert, with only low-growing scrubby shrubs that include **cholla, dudleya,** and **coreopsis.** The most readily noticed animals are the birds. You'll see **cormorants, scoter ducks, black oystercatchers, western gulls,** and **brown pelicans** gliding low over the sea and high along the rugged cliffs. The once nearly extinct brown pelican uses the slopes and cliffs of West Anacapa as its only large nesting site on the west coast of the United States. Because West Anacapa has been designated a research nature area for the pelican rookery, no landings are permitted without written permission from the superintendent.

Brown kelp hugs the shoreline, providing a haven for a myriad collection of fish, invertebrates, and other curious sea creatures. This is a favorite place for divers to photograph, explore, and to see **abalone, lobster,** and **scallops.** Fishermen (with a valid fishing license) will find **sheepshead, rockfish, perch,** and **sand dabs. Sea lions** and **seals** frolic in the surrounding waters, and the top of the cliff on Middle Anacapa is an ideal viewing location during the Jan.-March migration of the **gray whales** that passes close to the island.

HISTORY

pa's trademark and the sight most people remember after visiting the Channel Islands. James Whistler first brought it to the attention of the public when he sketched it during his time in the Coast Guard. Arch Rock is 80 feet high and the archway is 50 feet high--product and victim of the pounding sea. Along the island's coast, the erosion from the perpetually crashing waves has created blowholes, surge channels, caves, benches; the black sand you see on a few beaches during low tide is actually tiny flakes of the black lava of which the island is made. Earthquake faulting, folding, lifting, and the ancient volcanic eruptions (from a still unknown source) created steep-sided cliffs that fall precipitously into a deep sea. Viewing the rugged splendor of Anacapa is one of those lifetime events not soon to be forgotten.

Indians

Because there is no water source, most historians believe that the Canalino Indians didn't live on the island permanently. Instead they used Anacapa as a hunting ground for shellfish, sea lions, and seals. They also used the ready supply of sturdy minerals to make arrowheads. Many kitchen middens have been found, and other remnants of the past still lie on Anacapa; remember, everything on the islands is protected by federal law, so don't take any souvenirs--whether Indian, animal, plant, or mineral.

Europeans

The first outsiders to see Anacapa were the crew of Cabrillo's ship, which anchored near the small island in October 1542. It wasn't mentioned again until 1769, when Portola made

VENTURA BUSINESS BUREAU

Knowledgeable guides often escort tour groups to the Channel Islands.

notes in his log, calling it Las Mesitas ("Little Tables"). But it was Juan Perez, supply-ship captain of the Portola expedition, who named it Falsa Vela ("False Sail"). This name is still in use for the tallest point on Anacapa. On a clear day seamen have a remarkable view of the 936-foot peak. The island was renamed Anacapa by Captain George Vancouver, sailing under the British flag on his journey down the California coast in 1793.

The closest islands to the Mainland, the Anacapa group was probably the easiest for smugglers to reach in the mid-1800s, along with ruthless sea captains who deposited their deported Chinese slaves here until buyers could be found. As a result, the industrious Chinese gathered abalone, a money-making bonanza that abounded in West Anacapa's tidepools.

Navigational Aids

Historians believe that the Indians traveled between islands in their *tomols* (wooden canoes) at night after the westerly winds calmed down. Indians tended open fires on island promontories as navigational aids. By the early 1800s, the Indians were gone from the Channel Islands,

and Europeans began settling the California coast. As traffic increased, maritime disasters became commonplace. Now, as then, fog appears when least expected and a calm sea becomes a churning chaos--often too quickly for a ship to escape its torment.

Though the Channel Islands lay on the course traveled between New Spain (Mexico) and the Philippines, Spanish galleons soon learned to give these formidable rocky bits of land a wide berth. For years ships went aground around the islands and it was evident that a lighthouse was needed.

The East End Lighthouse

Only after a disastrous accident (December 2, 1853) brought attention to the channel's need for a lighthouse was it seriously considered. A 225-foot sidewheel steamer called the *Winfield Scott* went aground in a thick fog on Middle Anacapa's rocky coast. Two hundred and fifty passengers (and $800,000 in gold bullion) waited eight days on the barren island with virtually no food, water, or shelter before they were rescued. In 1854, a United States Coast Survey team agreed that Anacapa was the ideal spot for a lighthouse, but after careful exploration concluded that it was impossible to build on the steep-cliffed island. Many years passed before something more than talk took place. In 1912, an unattended automatic acetylene beacon was built; in 1932, the present lighthouse was erected by the United States Lighthouse Service (later to become the U.S. Coast Guard).

When first built, the lighthouse was attended by a group of Coast Guardsmen accompanied by their families. In 1969, the light was automated, and at an elevation of 277 feet it's one of the most powerful on the California coast. The catadioptric light boasts 1.2 million candlepower and can be seen 23 miles in all directions. Housed in a traditional white cylindrical structure, a foghorn sounds every 15 seconds in foggy weather. A radio beacon close by transmits with a full range of 10 miles. The Anacapa light on East Anacapa continues to serve as a beacon for the many ships that pass, endangered by the fog that often shrouds these rocky islands. Today the lighthouse is attended by personnel stationed in Port Hueneme on the Mainland coast. A park ranger lives year-round in one of the former Coast Guard houses on East Anacapa, still white with a red-tiled roof. Another house has been transformed into a museum for visitors to the island.

ISLANDERS

The Websters
Anacapa's history includes very few permanent residents. And as on all the other Channel islands, sheep brought the first settlers to Anacapa. In 1907, Heaman Bayfield ("Bay") Webster

visitors en route to Anacapa Island

MEREDITH

(son of the Ventura postmaster of the era), his wife, Martha, and their two young sons, Morris and Harvey, bought the lease to Anacapa from the Department of the Interior for $75. They set up housekeeping and lived on the island for the following 10 summers. They raised sheep and opened a tourist resort, calling it the Webster Sheep Ranch and Fishing Camp. It was primitive--with sand-flushed toilets. (A trapdoor on the windward side of the outhouse received gusts of wind-blown sand--flush courtesy of Mother Nature.) They brought water from the Mainland in five-gallon jugs. With no fresh water on Anacapa, it's curious how the sheep survived; one bit of lore claims that each morning after heavy night fog had soaked their wool, the animals licked the moisture from one another's coats. A good part of their diet was the dudleya, a low-growing succulent that provided some liquid.

Webster instigated one of the first package tourist trips on the California coast. For a budget sum, he brought families to the island in one of his boats, offered them fishing, swimming, hunting, hiking, and Indian artifact hunts; a smokehouse was available for fishermen. Who wouldn't jump at the chance for that vacation on the Channel Islands today! Entrepreneur Bay Webster was way ahead of his time.

Frenchy the Hermit
Born Raymond Ledreaux in Brittany, his colorful past is said to have included a bitter experience of aborted studies for the Catholic priesthood, followed by a seaman's life that took him around the world and, finally, from China to America. Contentment was cut short by the death of his young wife during the 1918 influenza epidemic. Perhaps it was these tragedies that first turned Frenchy to his reclusive life on tiny Anacapa Island in 1928. The Frenchman survived alone during the years through fishing and by using his ever-ready supply of seafood to trade for other necessities with local fishermen and occasional campers. All who knew Frenchy enjoyed a visit to the rocky island, and never arrived without a jug of wine to loosen his tongue. Their evening might include a dinner of cioppino and lobster (he was a good cook), and tall tales of the sea, or perhaps discussions of classic literature and fine music.

Frenchy was a gem, and though he lived a life far from human company (with his crowd of cats), he didn't fit the stereotype of "hermit"; he always welcomed visitors to the island. In 1954, Frenchy turned 68 and the Park Service employees decided he should be moved ashore after 26 years on Anacapa Island. A lovely cove on West Anacapa's north shore bears his name.

GETTING THERE

Being the closest to the Mainland, East Anacapa is the island visitors most frequently see. Channel Islands National Park Service encourages camping, hiking, and picnicking in small groups.

Island Packers, a commercial carrier, provides transportation between Ventura and East Anacapa, with seasonal schedules available. The boating company offers a variety of trips to other parts of Anacapa and to the rest of the Channel Islands. Some are day-trips; some are multiday island adventures. A popular trip takes passengers to Frenchy's Cove Landing on special low-tide days to explore the tidepools for several hours. Island Packers also delivers campers to East Anacapa and makes arrangements to pick them up on a designated day. You can't change your mind--remember, there's no phone on the island! However, the Park Service has a radio for emergencies--only.

For further information, prices, and schedules, contact Island Packers, 1867 Spinnaker Dr., Ventura, CA 93001, tel. (805) 642-1393. For information about other commercial carriers, contact Channel Islands National Park Headquarters, 1901 Spinnaker Dr., Ventura,

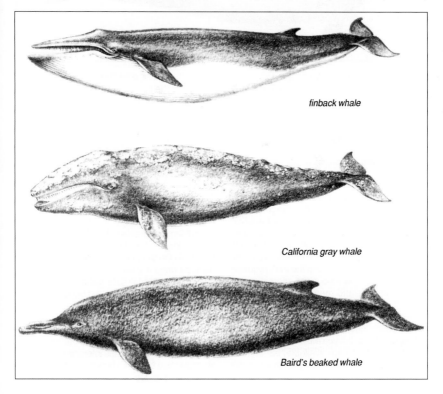

finback whale

California gray whale

Baird's beaked whale

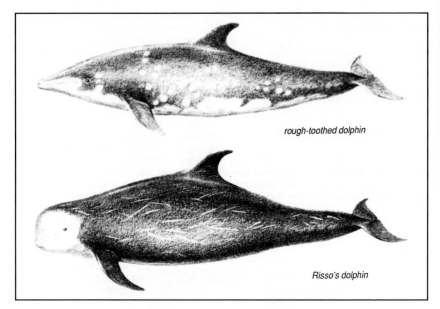

rough-toothed dolphin

Risso's dolphin

CA 93001, tel. (805) 644-8464. Sportfishing and scuba-diving boats frequent the island, and all boaters are invited to anchor offshore.

RECREATION

Hiking on East Anacapa

The first thing you must do when arriving on East Anacapa Island is climb a steep stairway of 154 steps up the side of the mountain; after that you've really arrived. The park ranger is very helpful, and with planning through the Park Service, you may arrange for tours, walks, and other programs. A self-guiding trail acquaints you with the magic of nature on Anacapa. The walk is short (1.5 miles), and the park requests that you stay on the trails in the interest of protecting fragile island resources and for your safety. If you happen to visit on a foggy day and the foghorn is operating, *do not* visit the lighthouse. Severe hearing damage may result. Picnicking is allowed, but you must carry all trash off the island. Latrines are available, but there is no fresh water, so bring along whatever water you'll need.

CAMPING

Anyone wishing to camp on the Anacapa group is restricted to the campground on East Anacapa. It is free on a first-come, first-served basis and limited to 30 people or six groups; therefore, reservations and permits are a must. The permit gives you 14 days on the island; you may not make reservations more than 90 days in advance.

Bring everything you need; there is nothing on Anacapa Island except the artistry of Mother Nature. But travel light; remember, you haul everything up the side of the cliff (shelter, food, fuel, water, etc.) and then walk another quarter mile to the campgrounds. You'll find picnic tables, so bring a portable stove if you plan to cook. Be prepared in case a strong wind comes up (one frequently does), and bring a tent that can be well-anchored.

Note: There's no room to run free, throw a football, or even a Frisbee. Expect to spend your time on Anacapa tuning in to nature and enjoying the solitude, a subtle interaction with what life must have been like hundreds of years ago. This is unique, life on a desert island with its many changing moods and faces. Pets are not allowed.

Weather

The weather is something to consider when planning a camping trip on the Channel Islands because in most cases you can't just pack up and go home. The wind often blows for several days at a time--even in summer--at speeds up to 20-30 miles per hour. Your only protection will be the shelter you bring along. Tube tents are not recommended; a small mountain tent is best. Wet, thick fog can also set in for several days. Spring and winter rains turn the trails into thick quagmires of mud; when the sun shines, there are no shade trees to provide relief. If all of these possibilities don't discourage you, you'll have the time of your life.

What to Bring

Bring an extra day's supply of food in case the weather turns bad and you cannot leave when planned. Plan on a gallon of water per person for each day. Bring an extra change of clothes in case you take an unplanned swim. Bring at least one heavy jacket, a rain poncho (the boat ride can be wet), and a woolly cap is nice. Bring also: a ground cloth, a windbreak, and a medium-weight sleeping bag. A backpacker's stove is necessary. Gathering live or dead plants on the island is prohibited. Use biodegradable soap *only*. Do not pour waste in the ocean or on plants; dispose of it in gravel areas. You'll be glad you brought a brimmed hat, sunscreen, first-aid kit, binoculars, and camera. Bring the usuals: matches, flashlights, etc.

Swimming, Fishing, and Diving

Beaches on East Anacapa are inaccessible, but on hot, still summer days, swimming is great in the landing cove. This means you'll enter the water from the landing dock several feet above the water. Snorkelers will find kelp beds not too far from the dock. A favorite scuba spot, the water is crystal clear, though many areas are thick with seaweed. Here marinelife flourishes with the usual and the unusual darting in and out of the brown leaves and bulbs of the tall kelp forest.

Note: The waters for one nautical mile around each of the park's islands are part of the Cali-

fornia State Reserve. State fish and game laws apply. Some areas in these reserves are available for sportfishing only. Check with your local Fish and Game officer or the park ranger, and remember to come with a valid California fishing license. Spear guns are not allowed.

FOR BOATERS

As your boat approaches East Anacapa and you begin to look for the park entry, watch for a cluster of white buildings on the bluff. A white-painted wall marks a small dent in a cliff used as a landing for traffic in and out of East Anacapa. Though there's room for a good-sized vessel, there's usually a surge. Put on your muscles; a dinghy can and should be hoisted the 11 feet to the platform because the surge and movement from the blowhole will surely bounce the dinghy against the dock. This is the loading area for supplies for the National Park Service personnel. Everything is hauled up the cliff with the help of a crane. Boaters will see two buoys off the dock, but overnight mooring is definitely discouraged.

Cathedral Cove

This cove is considered a marginal fair-weather anchorage but is one of the loveliest coves on the island. Some boatmen leave their boats anchored here when going ashore to the ranger station, a half mile east. Be prepared for thick kelp along the coast. Underwater nature trails are in the planning stages for Cathedral Cove. For adventurers, Cathedral Cave is a multi-chambered sea cave that you can explore by skiff in calm weather; beware of surge.

Frenchy's Cove

Frenchy's Cove is a great beach, a good picnic spot, and an outstanding snorkeling area. And for nature lovers, this is the place to explore the extensive tidepools at low tide. Most sailors agree that Frenchy's is the most sheltered anchorage on Anacapa--in calm conditions. When the sea rises, there isn't a good anchorage on the island. In calm water you can land a dinghy on the beach; there are no facilities. If the sea is surging, landing can be touchy. Frenchy's is popular, not only for its tidepools but also for the caves in the cliffs northwest of the cove. You can explore the vaulted interior of the nearby caves (Frenchy's and Indian Water Cave) by skiff.

The *Winfield Scott*

Close by, divers will find the *Winfield Scott,* a steamer that grounded and sank here in 1853. Clear water in the area makes ideal conditions for good underwater photos. Just take pictures, no souvenirs please!

Cat Rock Anchorages

On the south side of West Anacapa, three-quar-

ters of a mile west of the West Passage, lies Cat Rock. Head at least 200 yards west of that for a safe anchorage. Expect some kelp. East anchorage lies under the lee of the land east of Cat Rock. Pick your way through the kelp and you'll find deep water close to the shore.

East Fish Camp

East Fish Camp is an anchorage popular with fishing boats. Here you'll find protection from west to north winds--but expect an occasional surge in the anchorage. In a calm sea this is an adequate overnight refuge. The East Fish Camp shore is usually thick with kelp.

SANTA BARBARA ISLAND

THE LAND

Of the eight Channel Islands, Santa Barbara is the smallest, roughly one by one-half mile, containing a total of 640 acres. The island lies 38 miles west of San Pedro and 25 miles west of Catalina Island.

The tiny triangle-shaped rock is a remnant of an ancient Miocene volcano and geologically associated with the Guadalupe Islands of Mexico. It's a marine terrace on top of steep, jagged cliffs, some as high as 500 feet. From the cliffs, two peaks gently swell from the center of the island: the highest, called Signal Peak, rises to 635 feet. The second highest, at 562 feet, is North Peak.

The island shares the rough-hewn look of the other Channel Islands with caves, coves, blowholes, rocky ledges, and dramatic drops to the sea.

Climate

Santa Barbara Island's climate is mild, with daytime temperatures varying from 50-80° F. Frost is almost unheard of, but fog is another matter. It often shrouds the island early in the morning and in the evening. As on the Mainland close by, rainfall averages 10-12 inches yearly, falling mostly in the winter. The winds can be devastating, rising quickly and blowing hard across the desolate landscape of Santa Barbara Island.

FLORA

Because of the lack of water and the frequent mighty winds, the island has no trees and only low-growing scrub vegetation. The closest thing to a tree is the **coreopsis** plant, which often grows to 10 feet on the island, showing bright yellow, daisylike flowers across the landscape in the spring. Rabbits have reduced even the coreopsis growth over the years to just a few stands scattered around the island. Other native plants are the **prickly pear cactus** and **sea blite**.

Nonnative plants imported over the years include the devastating **crystalline iceplant** (native to South Africa). No one is certain how it arrived, but since before the turn of the century it's been steadily taking over the terrain. Perhaps a lone seed carried by a migrating bird was the first culprit. Because of its ability to thrive while absorbing salt-laden sea air, it gradually encroached upon the native plants. And when it withers and dies it deposits its salt-loaded tissues into the soil, further destroying the possibility of survival for the native plants.

On the eastern terraces are fields of grasses, including **rye, barley,** and **oats** introduced in the days when farmers tried to tame the wild elements of the island by raising farm animals. Because of the lack of rain and frequent high winds it was not a successful venture. With the protection and care of the National Park Service, native plants are making a slow recovery.

FAUNA

Only two vertebrates live on Santa Barbara, the **night lizard** and the **white-footed mouse.** In the early 1900s a large number of feral rabbits and cats roamed the island. The rabbits furthered the destruction of plants and the cats decimated the bird population. The rabbits proved almost worse than the voracious sheep on other Channel Islands. When the rabbits could no longer reach the leaves, they began nibbling the trunk of the coreopsis, girdling it, which caused the plant to die, leaving a toppled trunk in its wake. But the rabbits are gone, and the cats were rounded up and the last of them shipped off the island in 1978; the result is now a birdwatcher's paradise. The Audubon Society frequently brings groups to the island for a week of observing **barn owls, meadowlarks, burrowing owls, American kestrels, hummingbirds, orange-crowned warblers, island horned larks,** and **finches.** The skies are thick with coastal birds, including a variety of **gulls, cormorants, pelicans,** and the **black oyster-catcher.**

Sea Creatures

The rugged shoreline is surrounded with rich kelp beds that make an ideal habitat for a wide variety of sea creatures, including abalone, lobster, sea urchins, crabs, and myriad varieties of fish. Webster Point cove is a haul-out area for **sea lions** and **sea elephants.** Watching them frolic in the coastal waters is an amusing pastime; bring binoculars and a long lens for your camera. If you spend much time here you'll get used to the raspy bark of these sea mammals and even begin to distinguish whether it's mom calling the pups to come for dinner, or the harsh, commanding call of the courting male.

In early summer you might see pups being taught to swim and fish. They depend on their mothers for food for the first couple of months, but at six or seven months they join groups of the same age and are ready to try their flippers and venture out to sea. Remember, it's against the law to interfere in any way with marine mammals.

HISTORY

The Indians living on nearby islands visited Santa Barbara Island and used it as a campsite while hunting seals and other sealife. Evidence of this lies in several middens scattered around the island. But because of the lack of water there was never a permanent settlement. Explorer Sebastian Vizcaino arrived on the island December 4, 1602, which is the feast day of Saint Barbara--and so this little bit of rock was named Santa Barbara Island. As with all of the islands, it was peaceful and undisturbed by the white man until the mid-1800s, when shipping and otter hunting became common along the Pacific coast.

In the early 1920s, a group of farming families led by Alvin Hyder tried farming on the island. They are responsible for clearing large stands of coreopsis to plant barley and hay used to feed about 200 sheep. They also began raising Belgian hares (all of which were gone by 1940). By the mid-1920s the farming venture failed and the settlers left the inhospitable island.

A story has circulated for years about a bare-footed wanderer who found shelter on Santa Barbara during the Depression. He cared for the wild cats that had been left behind by settlers long gone. The story goes that he eked out an existence by trading fish with passing boats.

BOATING SAFETY

Boating accidents can be avoided with simple education. Boaters in California are urged to look into the many safety classes offered by several statewide organizations. The largest of these are provided by the U.S. Coast Guard Auxiliary and the U.S. Power Squadrons. These classes last six to 16 weeks and include information on aids to navigation, rules of the road, charts and compasses, boating regulations, marlinspike seamanship, marine engines, and boat trailering practices. Call the Coast Guard Auxiliary at (213) 590-2217. A list of boating safety classes in your area is available by writing to: Department of Boating and Waterways, 1629 S Street, Sacramento, CA 95814, tel. (916) 445-2616.

After his departure the island was left to nature's capricious whims until World War II. The U.S. Navy used the island as an early-warning outpost; in the 1950s it was used as a missile-tracking station.

Santa Barbara Island became part of the National Park system in 1938 and was designated part of the Channel Islands National Marine Sanctuary in 1980.

RECREATION

Camping
Camping is permitted on Santa Barbara Island, but it is a trek for the hardy. The camping area is next to the ranger's headquarters; the ranger is on the island most of the year. You debark onto a landing dock and then you must carry all equipment up a steep quarter-mile trail to the campground. Once at the campsite things get a little easier. No more than 30 people are permitted at five campsites. And be warned, your camp will probably be only a few feet from your neighbor; in other words, there's no privacy.

Remember to bring everything you need: drinking water, campstove, charcoal, food, garbage bags (yes, you must haul out all your trash), and clothes for wide variations in weather. The campsite has toilets, picnic tables, and one fire ring and four charcoal grills where charcoal cooking is permitted only when open fires are allowed. In times of heavy winds, and May to October, open fires are prohibited. (See "Anacapa--Camping.") This is camping on the proverbial desert island. Permits (free) are required; you can obtain them from Channel Islands National Park Headquarters in Ventura, tel. (805) 644-8262. Pets, slingshots, firearms, and fireworks are prohibited.

Hiking
Hiking is permitted only on six miles of established trails. Ask the ranger about the **Canyon View Self-guided Trail** and the booklet that interprets much of what you see.

Two trails begin at the campsite. One (to the left) wanders the gentle terrain to a gorge where you can see one of the few stands of coreopsis. This is good birdwatching country; don't forget the binoculars and bird identification book. The second trail eventually leads to Signal Peak, the highest peak on the island. Expect a steady ascent over several hills until finally you reach the summit, with a dramatic view of the sheer drop into the rocks and swirling sea below. From here you can see across the narrow channel to Sutil Island, a huge, barren rock.

Note: Hikers, do not wear Vibram-soled hiking boots, please, as they tear up the fragile landscape.

Water Sports
Access to the sea is at the Landing Cove only. Climbing down the trail from the campsite, you have a choice of a variety of water activities on Santa Barbara Island, such as **swimming** and **snorkeling** off the rocky shore, or from the landing dock. The water is crystal clear and makes for fantastic **underwater photography. Fishing** is permitted off the landing platform; don't forget to bring your fishing gear and license, and note seasonal regulations.

Nature Watching
The best thing to do on Santa Barbara Island is to observe nature. Even if you've never been intrigued with winged creatures before, get out your binoculars, perch on a craggy cliff to view the coastal birds, or hike into the canyon near

sea elephant

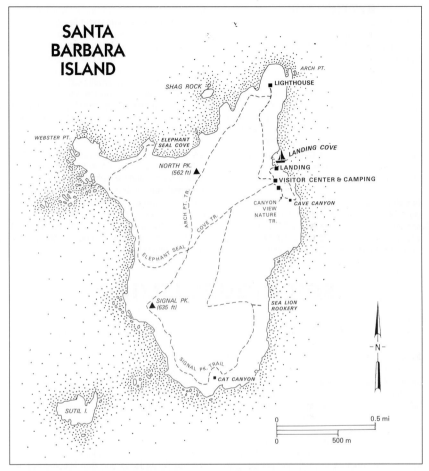

SANTA
BARBARA
ISLAND

ARCH PT.

SHAG ROCK

LIGHTHOUSE

WEBSTER PT.

ELEPHANT
SEAL COVE

LANDING COVE

NORTH PK.
(562 ft)

ARCH PT. TR.

COVE TR.

LANDING

VISITOR CENTER & CAMPING

CANYON
VIEW
NATURE
TR.

CAVE CANYON

ELEPHANT SEAL

SIGNAL PK.
(635 ft)

SEA LION
ROOKERY

– N –

SIGNAL PK. TRAIL

CAT CANYON

SUTIL I.

0   0.5 mi

0   500 m

the coreopsis, and you'll be entertained and ed-
ucated by the antics of these sky creatures. The
best time to watch the birds is early in the morning or at dusk when they're all looking for food.

You can spend hours watching the agile sea
lions jumping the waves, diving, and playing
much like small children at the shore. At certain times of the year the sea elephants join in.
When a seal moves on land it is called "hauling."
The two main hauling areas lie on the southeast and northwest shores of Santa Barbara Island.

Tidepools
At low tide you can explore the tidepools. This is
a mesmerizing activity. No doubt you'll see purple sea urchins, limpets, starfish, and minute
organisms. Please take care not to interfere
with their life cycles; these delicate life forms
are a California treasure that must be guarded
for future generations to enjoy. Wear sturdy rubber-soled shoes (no sandals); the rocks you'll be
climbing around on are very slick. Be aware of
when the tide comes back or be prepared to
swim to shore.

GETTING THERE

Public transportation is available next to Park Headquarters in Ventura aboard one of several Island Packers sail or power boats. Boats leave for Santa Barbara daily during the summer. Day-trips and roundtrip transportation for campers are available. Winter weather gets rather nasty around this outer island, and few trips are scheduled. Write for a yearly schedule: Island Packers, 1867 Spinnaker Dr., Ventura, CA 93001, tel. (805) 642-1393. Private boats travel to the island, but visitors must have a camping permit and reservations before arrival if planning to spend the night.

For Boaters

Boaters planning the trip to Santa Barbara Island should first study U.S. Coast and Geodetic Survey Charts 18720, 18729, and 18756. The trip from Santa Barbara Channel will take you across the Pacific Missile Range, which is often in use. For information about firing times call (805) 982-8841. A Coast Guard lighthouse sits on Arch Point. Anchorage is usually limited to the Landing Cove area, and the dock is not acceptable for boats. Those wishing to go ashore must do so in a skiff or small boat. Be prepared for sudden rising sea and wind, especially in the afternoon and during the fall and winter. If a strong northeast wind is forecast, leave immediately.

A safe daytime anchorage in calm weather lies off the north coast in about 35 feet of water with a sandy bottom. From here you can explore the coastline by skiff and no doubt you'll meet the friendly sea lions that live along the shore. They like to watch you almost as much as you enjoy watching them. A calm day of anchorage offshore Santa Barbara Island can be a soothing interlude between you and Mother Nature's creatures.

SAN MIGUEL ISLAND

THE LAND

The most remote island off the California coast, San Miguel is harassed by northwesterly gales that blast it continuously.

Eight miles long and four miles wide, San Miguel Island encompasses an area of 14 square miles and lies 26 miles from Santa Barbara, the closest point on the Mainland. Two peaks just over 800 feet tall in the center of the island are San Miguel's highest points. Surrounded by treacherous reefs and shoals, San Miguel exhibits a shoreline of gentle sandy beaches and rugged rocky cliffs.

Prince Island, a tiny islet close offshore Cuyler Harbor as you approach San Miguel, has steep-walled canyons that drop straight to the sea, adding to the stark landscape as you approach.

In many places the 10,000-acre island is smothered by sand that all but strangles the struggling plantlife. To complete this moonscape facade is a caliche "ghost forest," where macabre remnants of broken trees line up like white tombstones on the desolate sand-covered surface. The scientific explanation is quite fundamental: caliche is a calcium carbonate sand, composed mainly of the shattered lime skeletons of innumerable sea creatures, that blows inland from the beaches, engulfing the existing vegetation. Organic acids in the plants reacting chemically with the sand cement the fine grains together. After the inner plant decays, perfect castings remain. Some of these strange forms have been standing for thousands of years while others are new--the process continues. These startling caliche forms also appear on Santa Rosa and San Nicolas but are quite rare in other areas of the world.

Climate

This isolated, windswept bit of land lies vulnerable to the capricious whims of nature's violent northwesterly storms, unguarded by the landmass of the Mainland. San Miguel is the westernmost island of the Channel group. Yearly rainfall is about 11 inches, and as on the other islands in this unfriendly channel, fog can descend quickly and unexpectedly. Dress for the wind, whether it be hot or cool.

FAUNA AND FLORA

San Miguel is the California coast's largest breeding ground for six species of pinnipeds (fin-footed mammals), the seals and sea lions. The **California sea lion, Steller sea lion, northern elephant seal, harbor seal, Guadalupe fur seal,** and **northern fur seal** return to San Miguel's Point Bennett to "haul out," sometimes traveling great distances from throughout the northeastern Pacific. In late spring and early summer the cows come ashore at this sandy peninsula to bear their young and then breed again almost immediately. After a gentle summer of mother's nursing and care, the pups learn to fish amidst a rich supply of food. By autumn most are ready to begin their nomadic lives in the sea.

Because of the rugged, isolated cliffs, three major sea bird colonies live here undisturbed. **Auklets, gulls, guillemots, cormorants, snowy plovers,** and many others breed on San Miguel and Prince Island. The few vertebrates on the island include the **island fox** and the **white-footed mouse. Barn owls, peregrine falcons,** and **red-tailed hawks** are common birds of prey.

A few rare plant species grow on San Miguel: the **live-forever, wild buckwheat,** and **rose mallow.** The bright orange bloom of the **coreopsis** appears each spring climbing the hill from Cuyler Harbor. In a wet year San Miguel produces a blazing crop of **California poppies.**

HISTORY

San Miguel appears to have supported a large community of Canalino Indians. Many middens have been discovered on the relatively undisturbed island, and archaeologists hope that some are still undisturbed by pot diggers. Though the wind has been known to unbury Indian graves, someday these pristine sites may reveal more about the long-gone Canalino Indians.

Most historians agree that "Isla de Posesion" was the name that Cabrillo gave to San Miguel on his voyage of discovery in 1542. How tragic that he was never able to boast of his wondrous discoveries--Cabrillo died in January 1543. Historians believe that he died in Cuyler Harbor on San Miguel Island. His fellow voyagers changed the island's name to La Isla de Juan Rodriguez in his honor. Though Cabrillo is reportedly buried on San Miguel, his grave has never been found.

Charts from the later Vizcaino expedition identified San Miguel as La Isla de San Lucas. The final change came in 1770 when cartographer Miguel Costanso changed the name to

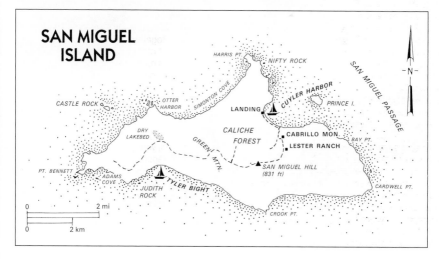

honor himself. In 1793, British Captain George Vancouver traveled south along the California coast and fixed the names of the islands on nautical charts.

The Fascinating People

George Nidever of San Nicolas fame was the first to try ranching on San Miguel Island, grazing cattle, horses, hogs, and sheep in the mid-1800s. After Nidever, a parade of hermits, boatmen, and would-be ranchers came and went, unobtrusively struggling with the land and the tempests. They spent their time building and patching from what they could scavenge from nature's collection of flotsam and jetsam violently thrown on San Miguel's shores.

Captain Waters, a salty character who ranched the island during the late 1800s, declared it a separate sovereignty. Obviously that didn't take hold. The federal government has owned San Miguel since the signing of the Hidalgo Treaty in 1848 and leased it to various ranchers over the years. In 1906, rancher John Russel built a V-shape fenced compound, out-

buildings, and a ranch house from planks, timber, and scraps, much of which was combed from the beach. The shape of the building was to urge the winds to rush by the house and out to sea without damage, similar to the windshields seen today on large trucks. The man was ahead of his time! By 1930 he was gone.

Probably the name that lingers with the desolate little island more than any of the others is the "king" of San Miguel, Herbert Lester, and his family. Lester and his wife, Elise, both New Yorkers, arrived on the island as honeymooners. From the stories that filter from the past, Herbie and Elise learned to love the island and led a blissful life for a long time. Herbie was thrilled when asked to manage the Russel sheep ranch. The couple happily filled their days with the not-so-easy chores of day-to-day living on the little island: gathering firewood, dealing with the water situation, trying to keep the constant wind-blown sand out of the house (would you believe a revolving door?), struggling to make ends meet when there was little money, and very little to make do with. But the Lesters were happy and

BRUCE CRAIG

unearthly-looking caliche on San Miguel Island

PRACTICALITIES

San Miguel Island is managed by the National Park Service and has a resident ranger for most of the year. The island is open to the public on a limited-access basis; camping is allowed by permit. This protects the large seal and sea lion rookeries that are thriving at Point Bennett. For years the island was used as an aerial bombing target, and though all precautions are taken, every once in a while an old bomb shows up. A free permit is required to visit the island and you *cannot* obtain permits at the island. Get your permit from the Channel Islands National Park office in Ventura, 1901 Spinnaker Dr., tel. (805) 644-8262. Public transportation is available aboard Island Packers boats, tel. (805) 642-7688. San Miguel is well worth a visit, especially to see the rookeries and the unusual caliche. A knowledgeable park ranger will guide you around the island; hiking is restricted to the designated trails. No fishing is allowed from shore.

For Boaters

Anchoring overnight is permitted only at Tyler Bight and Cuyler Harbor. Inexperienced boaters should beware the dangers of the unpredictable wind and sea conditions. Cuyler Harbor was named after its original government surveyor and was a favorite anchorage for past explorers. Sand dunes on the south side of the anchorage cover the shore. Cuyler Harbor can be a comfortable and uncrowded anchorage, but it's not unusual for a cranky surge to suddenly appear and for sweeping winds to rage over the cliffs.

San Miguel is an island of great extremes; you can anchor in calm conditions at Cuyler one moment and be taken on a roller coaster ride the next. Take all precautions possible and be alert to the changeable weather.

A government-designated "danger area" marks the eastern half of San Miguel Island. Look into the regulations in chapter two of the *U.S. Coast Pilot.* The coastline at Tyler Bight is covered with large areas of sand dunes. Adams Cove lies at the east end of the sandy beach extending east from the point with an indented cove of sloping rocks and sand. San Miguel is a dangerous destination and only the most experienced boaters should attempt it.

DANA SEAGARS

sea lion pups

ingenious and loved the freedom to explore and enjoy their "island paradise."

Two daughters were born while the Lesters lived on San Miguel. Elise taught the girls, Marriane Miguel and Betsy, in their own small schoolhouse with the help of the 500-volume library she brought with her to the island. It was a life that today many folks would envy. Mostly through the efforts of the Lester family, a small monument was placed on the island to honor the memory of the first visitor to San Miguel--Juan Rodriguez Cabrillo.

The Lesters welcomed many visitors from the Mainland--by sailboat, airplane, fishing boat, and official Coast Guard vessel; Elise kept a guest book and in 12 years recorded several thousand entries. Unfortunately, the story does not have a happy ending. When WW II hit the country, the government began planning to take over the "Lesters' island." Eventually two sailors were put on the island as "guards." Apparently the intruders and the thought of leaving his island was more than Herbert Lester could handle; he ended his life with a gun. His wife and daughters moved to the Mainland and have never returned to San Miguel.

The Navy did take over. It removed the sheep and used the island as an aerial bombing range during WW II and the Korean War. After that it became a missile target area. The bombing of San Miguel was finally stopped in May of 1960 after ecologists protested. The National Park Service signed an agreement with the Navy to preserve and manage the island. The breeding colony of pinnipeds at Point Bennett has increased and multiplied since.

SANTA ROSA ISLAND

THE LAND

Santa Rosa is the second largest of the Channel Islands, about 15 miles long from east to west and nine miles across at its widest point. Its 55,000 acres offer the same rugged landscape as its brother islands but with the soothing touch of gentle slopes covered with grass sprawling to the edge of the sea, some ending in sand, some ending abruptly in rocky ledges and rugged cliffs. Some say that Santa Rosa resembles the Azores in the mid-Atlantic. Fortunately, Santa Rosa has fresh water year-round, which gives it a rosier future than its neighbors. Two high mountains, Soledad Peak (1,574 feet) and Black

Mountain (1,298 feet), rise above the deep canyons and high coastal cliffs that dominate parts of the island.

Climate
Santa Rosa doesn't have as much protection from the Point Conception headland as the islands to the east and south, and therefore winds can be ruthless: 20-knot winds are common, and winter gales have been clocked at 90 knots. By some meteorological quirk, Santa Rosa receives only half the rainfall of the adjacent coastline. But the consistent fog shrouds the island with moisture, which helps to keep the grasses green, in some areas year-round. In a really wet year, the island spring is alive with the color

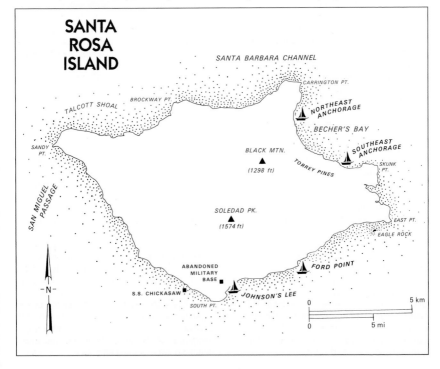

of California poppies and lupine. When planning a visit to the island, be prepared to dress in layers. It can be cold or it can be hot--it really depends on the wind.

FLORA

As with all the other islands, the introduction of alien animals and plants has been hard on Santa Rosa's natural environment. Spanish and Russian sailors left pigs on Santa Rosa for future food sources. Santa Rosa boasts one of only two stands of **Torrey pines** in existence. (The other stand of Torreys grows in the pine groves around La Jolla, a community called Torrey Pines.) Fortunately, the pines have survived the animals' rooting habits. The pigs did just fine,

thank you, and their rooting instinct, which destroys all seedlings, has made it impossible for native plants to survive. Why and how the pines made it are questions that so far have not been answered. The trees survived monumental climatic changes over the years in *only* these two isolated spots. Even the Torrey pines have mutated somewhat to adjust to island living. The tops of the trees, which grow in deep-cut canyons and ravines, are whipped constantly by the wind; maybe that's why they grow only to about 35 feet. **Coastal, scrub,** and **island oak, willow,** and **Catalina cherry** also survive on Santa Rosa Island.

FAUNA

The island supports the usual introduced animals, and the only native mammals left are the **island fox, white-footed mouse,** the **island spotted skunk,** and the **California myotis,** the smallest bat living on the Channel Islands. Other natives include a species of **salamander,** a species of **frog,** and two types of **lizards.** The **harbor seal** and the **California sea lion** make yearly stops on Santa Rosa.

HISTORY

Prehistoric Remains

The remains of a dwarf mammoth (only six feet tall) were found on Santa Rosa in a depression that has been called a "fire pit"; in other words, the little-big beast was barbecued. Radiocarbon tests indicate that this feast was held 29,700 years ago! Some scientists conjecture that this prehistoric cousin to the elephant may have arrived from the Mainland after having been washed out to sea by a torrential storm. By swimming or just keeping afloat (after all, an elephant does come equipped with a built-in snorkel), or perhaps by rafting, it survived until it reached a friendly shore. Another theory is the familiar old "land-bridge" idea. At some point, sections of this bridge to the Mainland along the coastline sank, creating Santa Rosa Island and stranding the elephant-like behemoth, known to have roamed the west coast of the Mainland during the prehistoric era. Being

---

AVOIDING SHARKS

Boaters, swimmers, surfers, and divers by the millions safely enjoy California's beaches and coastal waters. However, once in a great while a shark attack is reported. Be aware of the facts without stressing out while you're in the water of the Pacific. One of the easiest precautions to take is to avoid areas where seals and sea lions congregate. Another place not to go is the location of a previous shark attack. Since 1926, there have been 65 shark attacks recorded off the California coast, 44 attributed to great whites. Two of the attacks were at San Miguel Island, and three were off Point Conception. Most of the other confrontations occurred north of Point Conception, which should help put Southern Californians at ease. Sharks seem to avoid kelp beds, which should make skin divers exploring the beds around the Channel Islands feel a little more relaxed. A few statistics: most attacks on humans occur at the surface (not because the person looks like a seal as some believe, but for territorial reasons); and in Northern California, most attacks took place in clear water under 60 degrees rather than in warm or murky waters.

*Santa Rosa Island's
Carrington Point*

stranded on a small island with limited food sources and interbreeding may have caused stunting. All of this is conjecture; will we ever *really* figure out what happened so long ago?

The Spanish Explorers

Historians believe that the Vizcaino expedition named the island San Ambrosio and that more than likely, Juan Perez, who explored the area in the early 1770s, named the island Santa Rosa.

The Earthquake of 1812

The missionaries had little luck luring the island Indians to the Mainland missions because of the Indians' isolated location. It was not easy for the priests to get to the islands, and the Indians were happy with their lifestyle, at least until the invasion of outsiders hunting the otters. Then in 1812 a destructive earthquake hit the adjacent Mainland and the Channel Islands. Its epicenter lay along the Santa Rosa canyon called Canada Lobo. A tear in the earth 1,000 feet long, 100 feet wide, and 50 feet deep remains as proof of nature's devastating force on that day. Historians say the rumbling earth, crumbling boulders, and mammoth waves crashing onto the coast were the factors that finally led the Indians to the Mainland missions and Christianity.

Settlers

After the Indian era, the island was part of a land grant from the Spanish Crown presented to Don Carlos and Don Jose Carrillo. Don Carlos gave half the island to his two daughters as their dowries when they were married. For many years the families raised sheep on the island and Santa Rosa was known far and wide for the great fiestas at shearing time. Before the turn of the century, most of the sheep were removed by the island's then-new owners, A.P. and W.H. More, and replaced with cattle and racehorse stock. In 1902 Walter Vail and J.V. Vickers bought the island and strengthened the cattle herds, grazing some of the finest cattle in California. Santa Rosa Island does not show the severe abuse that some of the other islands suffered, proving that with balanced grazing, the ecology can be preserved.

In December of 1986 the island was sold to the U.S. Government (for $29.58 million) and it is now part of the Channel Islands Marine Sanctuary. Over time most of the cattle will be removed, but the park's representative says that the sanctuary is planning to keep a small herd in operation so that visitors will understand the importance of the cattle ranch and its effect on the island for so many years. Hopes are high that the island will soon be open to the public for camping, backpacking, and specialized nature treks. The former owners of Santa Rosa, the heirs of Vail and Vickers, have retained the ranch house near Becher's Bay for private use until 2011.

RECREATION

Hiking
A landing permit (free) is required to go ashore on Santa Rosa Island. You cannot get a permit on the island; you must obtain it at the Channel Islands National Park Headquarters, 1901 Spinnaker Dr., in Ventura, tel. (805) 644-8262. A knowledgeable National Park ranger meets visitors and guides them on a three- to five-mile trek with a good historical and geographical lesson. He also points out the interesting facts of the island's flora and fauna. You are not given free run of the island; hikers are restricted to designated paths (dirt roads left over from the former owners) and taken on a sample hike around the lovely, lonely island.

Fishing and Diving
The thick kelp beds and offshore reefs provide a rich haven for scallops, gamefish, abalone, and lobster. The comparatively small number of divers who do brave the poor anchorage find a fish paradise. (Don't forget your license, and note the seasons.) On a calm day the water is clear and underwater photography in the kelp forest can be spectacular. These same reefs have proven deadly for a number of vessels that failed to recognize the danger, where gale-force winds can rise unexpectedly.

BOATING ANCHORAGES

Santa Rosa is without a good natural harbor. Its westernmost extremity is **Sandy Point,** aptly named for the 400-foot white sand dunes that extend from that point inland. **Becher's Bay** is a long open bay four miles across backed by low sandstone cliffs. Though it can be a comfortable daytime anchorage, some sailors describe it as a wild and interesting spot for an overnight stay. The cattle ranch uses a pier at Becher's; landing there is by permit only. **Eagle Rock Anchorage** is considered a temporary anchorage under the cliffs with good shelter. **Ford Point Anchorage** is another temporary anchorage in the lee of a small point. It offers little shelter for anything but a short stay. Note the inviting sandy beach nearby.

thistle

DIANA LASICH HARPER

Johnson's Lee lies immediately northeast of the southernmost point of the island (there's a light at this end). Experienced sailors call it the best anchorage on Santa Rosa; however, spring and winter can be uncomfortable. On the cliffs above the anchorage notice the abandoned military barracks. Beware of the dilapidated Navy pier. The shore is lined with thick kelp beds here. The anchorage is fairly comfortable as long as the weather is good. As many boaters already know, there isn't a good safe anchorage at Santa Rosa in bad weather.

PRACTICALITIES

Visitors go to the island on Island Packers boats (next to the park office in Ventura). For schedules and reservations call (805) 642-1393; fares are adult $60 RT, child $50. Right now, part of the adventure is just getting on the island. A dock has yet to be built, so visitors are landed six at a time from a small motorized skiff launched from the larger boat. Becher's Bay can show a strong, turbulent surf, so it's a given that passengers are going to get a little wet (more than likely *very* soaked). With the proper spirit it's all part of the fun; visitors should bring an extra set of clothing and keep cameras in plastic bags until safely ashore. Be sure to bring food, water, film, towels, or anything else with you. The only facility so far is the portable latrine. You must obtain landing permits (free) from the Channel Islands National Park Headquarters, 1901 Spinnaker Dr., Ventura; tel. (805) 644-8262.

Channel Islands Aviation
You can take a day-trip allowing five hours on Santa Rosa Island via a small plane leaving Camarillo Airport. For more details call (805) 987-1678.

SANTA CRUZ ISLAND

THE LAND

Santa Cruz Island is a verdant surprise compared with the drier islands of the channel. The usually abundant supply of water has given the island the look of a magnificent green paradise. The beauty of this, the largest island, has attracted boaters for generations.

Within its boundaries lie rolling meadowlands, rugged slopes, rivers, waterfalls, sandy beaches, thick stands of pine trees, splashing streams, old wooden bridges, craggy bluffs, deep wooded canyons, and giant caves--a natural wonderland surrounded by the beautiful Pacific.

Santa Cruz is composed primarily of igneous rock from early volcanic eruptions; sedimentary sandstones and shales fringe the island's shores. It boasts gigantic sea caves and its tallest peak rises to 2,450 feet. A few geologists contend that the northern and southern parts of the island originally sat on two different small plates of the earth's crust, the southern part having originated near the San Diego area. The island encompasses 62,000 acres, is approximately 25 miles long and two to seven miles wide. It lies 23 miles southwest of Santa Barbara.

FLORA

Ferns add rich beauty to the **closed-cone pine** forests in the northern and western parts of the island. **Eucalyptus** trees were brought to the island years ago.

With controlled grazing, Santa Cruz seems to have suffered less than some of the other islands. Endemic plants still grow here, even though wild boar and at one time more than 40,000 feral sheep ran free on certain parts of the island. A native plant, the **dudleya,** adds a

touch of gray-green against the stark cliffs. A rainbow of colorful wildflowers covers the rolling meadows in spring, including the **California poppy, blue lupine, thistles,** and many more. More than 600 species of plants grow on the island in 10 different plant communities; 40 species are restricted to the Channel Islands, and eight grow only on Santa Cruz. Some of the more notable examples are **Santa Cruz Island ironwood** and the **island oak.**

FAUNA

Santa Cruz Island fauna is more varied than on many of the other Channel islands except Catalina. Along with 10 species of terrestrial mammals, including the **white-footed mouse** and the **big-eared harvest mouse,** four kinds of **bats,** plus hundreds of **Channel Island foxes,** and the **island spotted skunk,** you'll find two species of **salamanders,** one type of **frog,** three kinds of **lizards,** and a small group of **snakes.** More then 140 species of land birds have been identified, including **quail, pheasant, ravens, meadowlarks, doves,** plus an occasional **eagle.** An example of island endemism is the **island blue jay,** which is larger and bluer than its Mainland cousin.

The 77 miles of shoreline, cliffs, beaches, offshore rocks, and tidepools provide an important breeding habitat for colonies of nesting **seabirds.** Scorpion Rock near the east end of the island has become a popular rookery for the **pelicans** that are coming back strong after a few years' setback during the DDT scare. Hundreds of **California sea lions** and **harbor seals** thrive in the island's isolated coves. In fact, at Painted Cave you will often find a bull sea lion and his harem on the rocks in the last chamber. At one time elk and boar were introduced to the island for hunts; now they are gone.

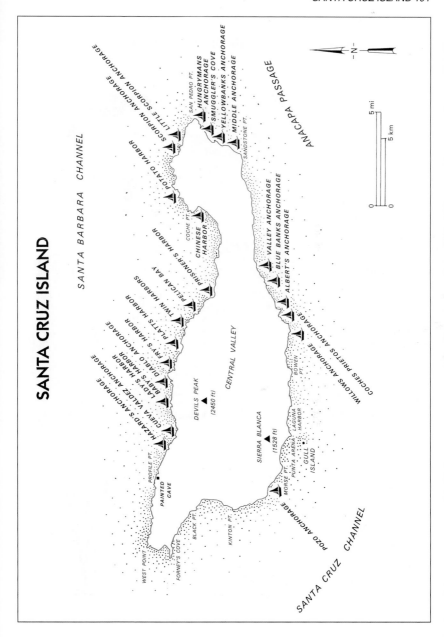

SANTA CRUZ ISLAND

SANTA BARBARA CHANNEL

SCORPION ANCHORAGE
LITTLE SCORPION ANCHORAGE
SAN PEDRO PT.
HUNGRYMANS ANCHORAGE
SMUGGLER'S COVE
YELLOWBANKS ANCHORAGE
MIDDLE ANCHORAGE
SANDSTONE PT.

ANACAPA PASSAGE

POTATO HARBOR
COCHE PT.
CHINESE HARBOR

PRISONERS HARBOR
PELICAN BAY
TWIN HARBORS
PLATTS HARBOR
FRY'S HARBOR
DIABLO ANCHORAGE
BABYS HARBOR
VALDEZ ANCHORAGE
CUEVA VALDEZ ANCHORAGE
HAZARD'S ANCHORAGE
PROFILE PT.

DEVILS PEAK
(2450 ft)

CENTRAL VALLEY

VALLEY ANCHORAGE
BLUE BANKS ANCHORAGE
ALBERT'S ANCHORAGE
COCHES PRIETOS ANCHORAGE
WILLOWS ANCHORAGE
BOWEN PT.

SIERRA BLANCA
(1528 ft)

LAGUNA HARBOR
PUNTA ARENA
MORSE PT.
GULL ISLAND

PAINTED CAVE
WEST POINT
FORNEY'S COVE
BLACK PT.
KINTON PT.

POZO ANCHORAGE

SANTA CRUZ CHANNEL

5 mi
5 km

BROWN AND RED ALGAE OF THE CHANNEL ISLANDS

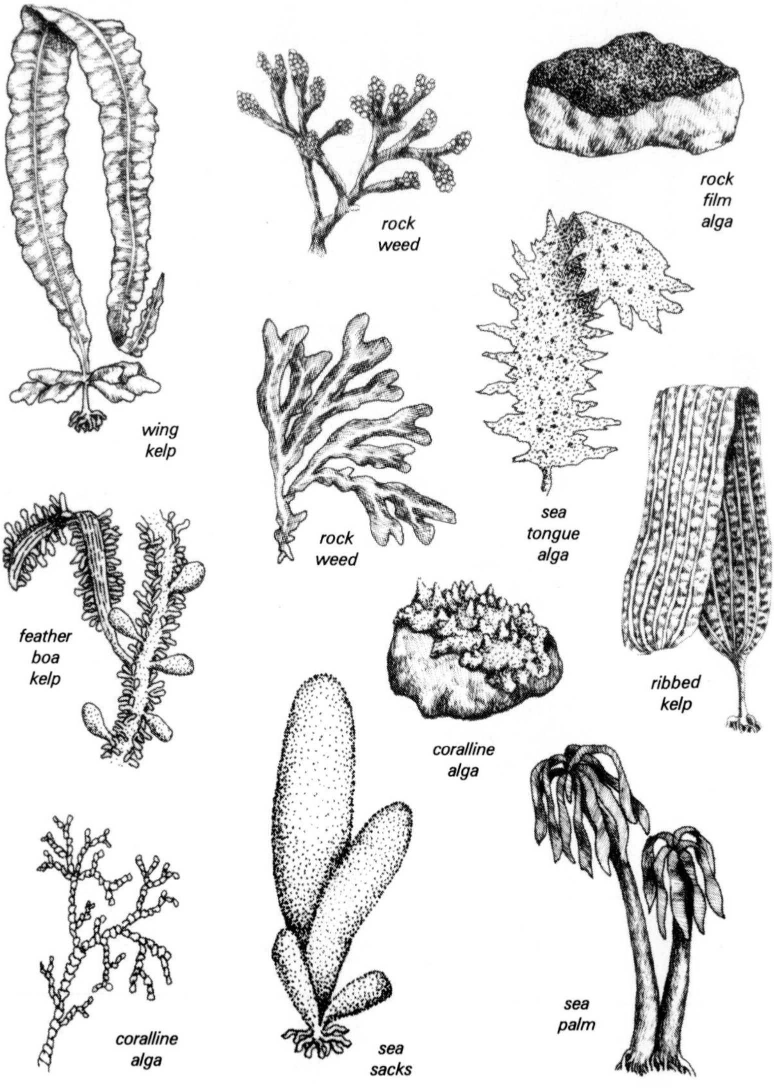

wing
kelp

rock
weed

rock
film
alga

rock
weed

sea
tongue
alga

feather
boa
kelp

ribbed
kelp

coralline
alga

coralline
alga

sea
sacks

sea
palm

HISTORY

Prehistoric Indians

A survey of the Indian sites on Santa Cruz suggests that there are as many as 3,000 undisturbed Indian sites. It seems natural that this would be the location of one of the largest Indian communities because of its size and extraordinary natural resources. (Water, a problem for so many of the other islands, appears to have been abundant on Santa Cruz.) It wasn't unusual for early settlers to run into an interesting piece of Indian stoneware lying on the surface of the ground. Fortunately, the "pot hunters" who destroyed so much archaeological information in the early 1900s did not manage to dig on this island. Today's scientists know the value of approaching the middens slowly and with great care even if it means postponement. Technology keeps improving and one day more light will be shed on Santa Cruz's prehistoric Indians. Many pieces have already been carefully preserved in museums and private collections in Southern California.

The First Spanish Visitors

In 1769, a supply ship traveling north along the Pacific coast from Mexico accompanying the Gaspar de Portola and Father Junipero Serra expedition (of mission fame) got lost and sailed right past San Diego, its scheduled port of call. Ultimately the *San Antonio,* with Spanish Captain Juan Perez at the helm, sailed into the bay of an island occupied by many Indians (scientists estimate the population at the time was between 2,000 and 3,000). As it turned out, these Indians were friendly and curious. Visits were exchanged; the crew went to shore and the Indians came aboard the *Antonio.* The crew gave the islanders small gifts, and the Stone-Age Indians were in awe of everything made of iron: weapons, equipment, chains, and gadgets.

When the time came for the ship to depart, the ship's priest, Fray Juan Vizcaino, realized that he had left his staff (topped with an iron cross) on shore. He presumed he would never see it again, and the crew prepared to hoist anchor. To the priest's great surprise, he saw a canoe approaching the ship. It carried the Indians, returning the lost staff. In honor of the kindness, friendly nature, and honesty of its people, the island was named then and there La Isla de Santa Cruz, Island of the Holy Cross.

Prisoner's Harbor

In 1839, 25 years after the last of the Chumash Indians had left the Island, the governor of California granted it to Andres Castillero. In 1857, the island was sold to William E. Barron, who in turn sold it to Justinian Caire and associates in 1869. The island is the center of many fascinating stories. A legendary or historical anecdote about Prisoner's Harbor has persisted through the years.

In the early 1800s, the Mexican government needed colonists to settle California towns. Other countries had already begun sending ships and casting covetous looks toward this desirable new country. One method of colonization was to release prisoners who would agree to settle in one of the distant communities. In the spring of 1830 a boatload of prisoners was taken to the lovely (but small) town of Santa Barbara and dropped off.

This was not to the townspeople's liking, and after much plotting and planning they suggested to the prisoners that they could begin a cattle ranch on the lovely verdant island of Santa Cruz. Santa Barbarans supplied the convicts with cattle, supplies, seeds, equipment, and transportation to Santa Cruz. The new islanders were dropped off at the cove named in their honor, Prisoner's Harbor.

In the fall, a fire destroyed the colony and all the convicts' hard work. As goes the story, the convicts built rafts from the hides of freshly slaughtered cattle and headed for the Mainland. Now this is where history falters. One version says that the green cow hides attracted sharks, and the prisoners never made it to the Mainland. A more romantic ending has it that they all

---

FUMAROLES

Santa Cruz is the only Channel Island that reputedly spouts active fumaroles along the shale slopes of the Island. Recently, boaters have described these smoky vents shooting fire.

Santa Cruz elephant seal

made it to shore, were eventually assimilated in the community, and lived happily ever after.

Justinian Caire

Justinian Caire, an immigrant from France, was the original developer of Santa Cruz Island. Living in San Francisco about the time of the gold rush, Caire and nine associates bought Santa Cruz Island in 1869. Legend tells us that that was the beginning of a love affair between Justinian Caire and the island. Caire bought his other partners out one by one until, in 1887, the island was all his.

Originally attracted to the island because the climate and territory were similar to those of the islands off the French Mediterranean coast, Caire began to build a small European colony on Santa Cruz. He brought craftsmen from Italy and France and began creating a typical Old World estate in the island's lovely central valley. By the end of the century, close to 100 people lived on the island, mostly French and Italian immigrants. They had planted vineyards and used bricks fired from island clay to build a huge winery. It's said that the winery produced some of the finest wine in the state.

The community boasted two-story French-colonial brick buildings with delicate wrought-iron balconies (made on the island); a tiny brick chapel was complete with stained-glass windows, altar, candles, tower, and bell, and it was always ready for a visiting priest to say Mass. The colony had a bakery, laundry, blacksmith shop, wagon shop, stables, and well-built living quarters. Caire grazed cattle and merino sheep. Olive groves and fruit orchards, including apple, peach, and pear, were established, and rolling hills of barley and oats were raised for livestock. The Caire children and grandchildren enjoyed idyllic summer visits on their beautiful island.

Justinian died in 1897, and his wife in 1911. Prohibition forced the winery to shut down; it operated only a few years after that era. Changes in the ranch operation began after Caire's death, and the colony suffered setbacks during the Depression. In 1936 the family made overtures to the government, offering to sell the island explicitly for creation of a national park. The price was $750,000. It was a sensational idea and the public went for it in a big way. As often happens in bureaucratic affairs, a lot of time passed without a decision. When no offers were forthcoming to form a national park, Los Angeles businessman Edwin L. Stanton bought all but 8,000 of Santa Cruz's 62,500 acres from the Caire estate for one million dollars. An article appeared in the *L.A. Times* on April 24, 1937, lamenting the loss of a possible national park on Santa Cruz Island. The price was *so* right! In 1986, when the federal government bought Santa Rosa Island (similar in size) for the express purpose of creating a national park, the price was $26.58 million.

Edwin Stanton's son, Dr. Carey Stanton, moved to the island in 1957 to run the Santa

Cruz Island Company. In 1975, Dr. Stanton approached **The Nature Conservancy** about a possible joint conservation effort to ensure the preservation of Santa Cruz. With the generous arrangement with Dr. Stanton and tremendous public support, The Nature Conservancy was able by 1978 to acquire a limited interest in the island, which was to mature to ownership of approximately 90% of the island not later than 2008. Dr. Stanton died in December of 1987, the end of an era of family ownership. The Nature Conservancy assumed full responsibility for ownership and management of the western 90% of Santa Cruz.

The island has been touched by a fascinating parade of people over the years, from Charley the Hermit, who lived in an old shack at China Harbor, to the Navy personnel who kept track of the missiles, to Otis Barton, who in 1949 climbed into a strange-looking giant steel sphere he called a benthoscope and sank to 4,500 feet below the ocean's surface. His only connection with the world was a telephone and a cable. Through a small window he saw little in the pitch blackness except occasional streaks of phosphorescence and a few fish he called miter and lantern. After seven minutes in the depths, with 2,000 pounds of pressure per inch closing around the ball, the crew of the barge and tug assisting him in the experiment brought him slowly to the surface. All told he was submerged for two hours and 19 minutes.

DIVING AND CAVING

Diving
Diving is good around the island. Although less kelp grows here than around some of the other islands, you'll find rich marinelife to observe and photograph. At Santa Cruz many coves and bays lie within easy access of the beach, but remember your permit restricts where you may go ashore. Lobster and abalone are very popular game on the island; don't forget your fishing license.

Painted Cave
The immense sea caves in various places around the island are fascinating to visit. Painted Cave just west of Profile Point is best en-

20,000-YEAR-OLD TUSK

A six-foot, nine-inches-long tusk from an imperial mammoth that roamed the continent 20,000 years ago was found in 1984 on Santa Cruz Island. The tusk, found by a young boy, was imbedded in rock. The immense mammoth stood some 14 feet tall at the shoulder and thrived during the late Pleistocene Epoch. It died out as a species at the end of the most recent ice age, about 10,000 years ago. The tusk can be seen at the Santa Barbara Museum of Natural History.

tered in a small dinghy or skiff. (You might want to bring a flashlight or two.) The water is usually placid unless there's a swell. It's an easy boat ride for those anchoring in Cueva Valdez. Painted Cave's walls are approximately 80 feet high at the entrance, and the ceiling rises to over 130 feet inside and then slopes to about 20 feet at the back end. It's easy to see how it got its name: beautiful reds, yellows, and greens glow in the low light as you enter the cave. The first section cuts more than 600 feet into the base of the island; row all the way in and when you reach the back turn hard to starboard, which will bring you into a side chamber, 150 feet into darkness. But here you'll find a beach and rock ledges with seals and sea lions. If you choose to use a flashlight the pinniped tenants will quickly slide into the water and disappear. Three more caves lying 1.1 miles west of Painted Cave are also great to explore. They all have large entrances.

SANTA CRUZ NORTH

Cueva Valdez
Cueva Valdez is a popular anchorage for beach-loving families. A sandy beach is great for the kids, and swimming is good, with just a few patches of kelp here and there. Three-quarters of a mile west of Cueva Valdez anchorage you'll find a sandy beach with limited anchorage at Hazard's Anchorage.

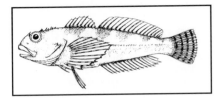

Lady's Harbor

This is really two harbors; one is a small cove, and the larger one is great anchorage for just a few boats. This harbor tends to be crowded on fine summer days. Little Lady's is only a fair-weather anchorage and is much smaller. Boats longer than 35 feet may have trouble turning around once inside the harbor. Landing (with permits) is allowed in both coves. This is lovely terrain with a stream and pools running into the sea.

Diablo Anchorage

Immediately west of Diablo Point you'll find Diablo Anchorage and a half mile east Fry's Harbor. Diablo is rarely crowded and is a good stopover when the weather is quiet.

Fry's Harbor

This is one of the most popular anchorages at Santa Cruz Island and can be crowded. But if you're lucky--maybe in the middle of the week, and it's deserted--you'll find it a beautiful place to be lazy for a few days. The rocky cliff immediately southeast of the beach provided the rock for the Santa Barbara breakwater in 1929. You'll notice remnants of the operation. If you have a choice, the best spots to anchor are tucked in under the west cliff. Take a picnic and make a dinghy trip to the small cove immediately east of Fry's, or explore the cave 600 feet west.

Prisoner's Harbor

Traveling the four miles between Fry's and Prisoner's Harbors is spectacular. More than likely you'll pass a few commercial diving and fishing boats. Along the way you'll see ragged cliffs and sloping hills that become low-lying cliffs, dotted with small coves all the way. Kelp is common for a quarter mile offshore. One of the coves, Orizaba Cove, is a lovely spot in good weather and usually entertains a few harbor

seals in the bay. Another pretty place is Twin Harbors; either makes a good lunch stop. Naturalists, notice the ironwood trees in the wooded canyon of the west anchorage. Along with the rugged cliffs, Prisoner's Harbor offers a pier, tall eucalyptus trees, and a few small buildings. This is the main landing for the Santa Cruz Island Company; freight boats arrive regularly. Please note the signs that say "Landing closed to permit holders." Your landing will be on the beach; wade ashore.

Pelican Bay

Pelican Bay is a large anchorage and will accommodate a good number of boats on a calm, sunny day. In spring the scenery is beautiful with myriad wildflowers in bloom. This is where Ira and Margaret Eaton brought their little girl in 1910 and later operated a resort. The Eatons lived on the island until 1937. You can still see remnants of the once popular hotel. Margaret Eaton tells a wonderful story of her family's life on the island in her book titled, *Diary Of A Sea Captain's Wife* (see book list). This was also a favorite spot for filming movies in the early days of Hollywood. Some boaters prefer Pelican to any other harbor on the island. (Others say it can be bumpy and prefer Fry's.) In calm weather take a dinghy to Tinker's Harbor or Little Pelican (pull your dinghy out of the grasp of the waves and rising tides.) This is a great place to explore the nearby woods and canyons or take a dinghy and investigate the many coves and dents along the coast.

COCHINEAL

The cochineal scale insect is common in Mexico. It was used to make red dye in that country for centuries until synthetic varieties came along. The cochineal will eventually kill the host cactus plant. It was introduced to Santa Cruz Island in 1938 to try to kill out the prickly pear cactus that was rampant on the island. By 1950, the insect scale took hold, and the cactus began to decrease.

Park rangers give visitors an orientation onboard boats headed for the Channel Islands.

Chinese Harbor

This open bay provides little protection for more than a brief stop. If you see smoke rising from the northeast cliff of the anchorage several hundred feet above the beach, don't be concerned; it's a fumarole, the only one on the offshore islands.

Potato Bay

Formerly known as Tyler's, this is a beguiling bay, though narrow and between steep cliffs. It's not recommended for an overnight anchorage unless the weather is very calm.

Scorpion and Little Scorpion Anchorages

Scorpion is the main landing area for the Gherini Ranch. Little Scorpion, with a little better protection, is the favored of the two for anchoring. Explore along the coast in a dinghy in the early morning; you'll see spectacular scenery, including caves, alluring little coves, and ragged cliffs.

SANTA CRUZ SOUTH

In Brian Fagan's excellent boating guide, *Cruising Guide to California's Channel Islands,* a warning states that all south coast anchorages of Santa Cruz are subject to heavy surge from tropical storms off the Mexican coast; they can come in without warning, especially in summer.

Smuggler's Cove

Smuggler's Cove is a large open roadstead where a large number of small craft anchor in calm weather. This is a small bight with Caire's old olive groves and tall eucalyptus trees overlooking the cove. Landing is not allowed because of a hazardous beach break.

Yellowbanks

This is one alternative to Smuggler's Cove either in calm or heavy weather. Yellowbanks is usually not as crowded as Smuggler's.

Albert's Anchorage

This anchorage is a fairly comfortable one in calm weather, with good shelter from west through north. Some boaters complain that the steep cliff to the west shadows the cove in the late afternoon and it can be dark and cool. The view of the island's southeast coast is lovely and you can even see (in the distance) Anacapa Island from Albert's Cove. A small beach lies at the head of the anchorage. Albert's can be bumpy when there's a surge. Landing is on the beach and there's limited access inshore.

Sandstone Point Anchorage

This exposed anchorage is not recommended for an overnight stop.

Coches Prietos

This is another picturesque cove (Coches Pri-

DIANA LASICH HARPER

etos means "black pigs") and some boaters consider this the best anchorage on the south side of Santa Cruz Island. It offers a great sandy beach and good shelter, but it can be crowded with visitors, especially in the summer. This beautiful, semicircular beach extends into an inland valley. Landing is on the beach.

Willow's Anchorage
This is another popular anchorage. It's very pretty but recommended only in good weather. Landing is on the beach.

Pozo Anchorage
Pozo Anchorage has lovely scenery but the unprotected anchorage cannot be recommended for more than a brief stay.

Forney's Cove
Forney's is another of the most popular anchorages on Santa Cruz Island. It's isolated, with breathtaking scenery, great skin diving, and excellent fishing nearby. Landing can be tricky on the beach because of the shallow and irregular surf. Take off your shoes because you'll probably get soaked. Forney's is a boater's paradise, and in the spring the rioting color of wildflowers is intoxicating. You have to see them to appreciate them; bring your camera!

Potato Patch
Beware of the rough area called Potato Patch, which extends two miles west of West Point. The meeting of opposing currents in the Santa Cruz Channel and the main channel causes its rough water. Even in the calmest weather you'll have ripples and mild turbulence.

PRACTICALITIES

Obtaining Permits
Ninety percent of Santa Cruz is privately owned by The Nature Conservancy and visitors are allowed on a limited basis only. You must obtain permits for boats to land on the western 90% of the island in advance from The Nature Conservancy. In Santa Barbara, call (805) 964-7839. You must complete an application and follow island rules. Boaters, for example, must have complete sleeping and cooking facilities on board. Landing permits are for day use only. Permit fees are $15 for 30 consecutive days or $50 for a calendar year. The Nature Conservancy conducts a limited number of day-trips to the island each year for a fee. For information contact The Nature Conservancy, Santa Cruz Island Preserve, 213 Stearns Wharf, Santa Barbara, CA 93101, tel. (805) 962-9111.

Note: Anyone interested in contributing to The Nature Conservancy's Santa Cruz Island Preserve can forward checks to the address above. Your contribution is tax-deductible and entitles you to all regular benefits of The Nature Conservancy, including a periodic newsletter on the Santa Cruz Island Project.

SAN NICOLAS ISLAND

If nothing else, San Nicolas Island's claim to fame is a fascinating story about 1,000 Indians who lived here at one time--and about one Indian woman especially, Juana Maria. Today much of the island appears lonely and desolate, with only a few hardy government people enjoying life on this high-tech, windy bit of land.

THE LAND

San Nicolas Island covers 22 square miles, and lies 53 miles (almost due west of Catalina Island) from the California coast. The island topography is not very spectacular, made up of plateaus, terraces, and a few peaks (its highest is 907 feet above sea level). San Nicolas forms the outer corner of a quadrangle with the other southern Channel Islands, Santa Barbara, Catalina, and San Clemente. Its easternmost point is an ever-changing sandspit. During the last century the continuous attack of the wind and the sea has considerably altered this part of the island.

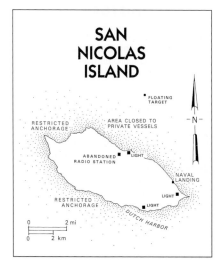

Climate

The climate is temperate, with a mean temperature of 60.4° F, lows and highs averaging within four degrees. Fog keeps the humidity up to about 76%. The winds can rage, with the prevailing northwest winds averaging between 35 and 50 miles per hour almost every day of the year. Sandstorms can happen anytime; the island is often described as a mountain of shifting sand.

FLORA AND FAUNA

Sea Organisms

The western perimeter of the island, called Land's End, is a mass of tidepools alive with **barnacles, snails, sea urchins, limpets,** and multicolored **sea anemones.** Rocky pockets and crevices are a gathering spot for **purple sea grass, sea lettuce, brown sea moss,** and **black sea snails.**

Sea Creatures

The rugged coastline of San Nicolas provides stone ledges and platforms where the **harbor seal,** the **California sea lion,** and the **northern elephant seal** bathe in sun and sea. Elephant seals, almost extinct during the 1800s, inhabit a large rookery on San Nicolas. In 1950, observers counted 168 and the seals have continued to increase their numbers.

Sea Otters

In 1938, when the southern sea otters were presumed to be extinct, a herd of 100 was discovered along the central California coast. Ports at Moss Landing in the north and Port San Luis in the south bracket the otter's 180-mile range. In 1977, the U.S. Federal Wildlife Service estimated that the count had grown to 1,800, and the herd continues to grow. The federal government, under the authority of the Marine Mammal Protection Act, has moved a small population of sea otters from the central California coast to San Nicolas. The motivation is the fear

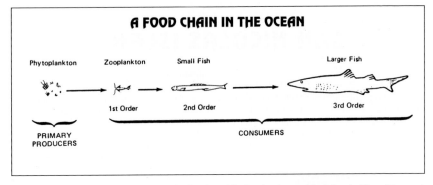

A FOOD CHAIN IN THE OCEAN

Phytoplankton   Zooplankton   Small Fish   Larger Fish

1st Order   2nd Order   3rd Order

PRIMARY
PRODUCERS   CONSUMERS

that an oil spill would wipe out the growing herd, since oil-tanker traffic is heavy along the California coast.

Unlike many marine mammals, the otter does not have a layer of blubber beneath its skin to keep it warm in the chilly waters of the Pacific. Instead, it relies on a blanket of air pockets within its fur. When covered with oil, the fur mats down, destroying the air bubbles and losing its insulating quality. Within 24 hours, the "oiled" otter will die. At present the otter is included in the *threatened* species list, and certain environmentalist groups (Friends of the Otter is one) would like its status to be upgraded to *endangered.*

Commercial fishermen are lobbying for the otters to be relocated north of Point Conception since they believe the otters will spread to other islands nearby, destroying sealife. The otter has a voracious appetite, eating one-quarter of its weight each day. The teddy-bear lookalike dines mostly on the lobster, scallops, and abalone that thrive in the Channel Islands' offshore kelp beds--delicacies of man and a big part of the commercial fishermen's income.

Land Creatures

Despite the construction of a Navy complex on the island, the sturdy animals living on all of the Channel Islands continue to persist on San Nicolas. The few endemic animals include the small **island fox,** the **white-footed mouse,** the **rock hen,** a species of small **lizard,** and a type of **beetle.** For some reason the fox grows slightly longer than related foxes on the other islands, and its coloring is somewhat different. The San

Nicolas fox has a black back. The skies and cliffs are rampant with **ravens, seagulls, cormorants,** and **horned larks.**

Over the years, the last of the sheep have been removed from the island and the land is beginning to recover. With the help of high humidity from intense fog that prevails much of the time, spring flowers once again cover the landscape. The blue coastal **sage** blossoms and the yellow **coreopsis** brighten the otherwise dismal panorama. Native plants are regaining the land with the absence of the constantly foraging sheep. Firmly established plants also lessen the erosion and blowing sand.

HISTORY

Indians

It's not certain whether San Nicolas Island was sighted by the Cabrillo party in 1542 or not. In 1602, Spaniard Sebastian Vizcaino followed Cabrillo's path and claimed San Nicolas on December 6. (This is a presumption by historians but seems plausible since the 6th is the feast day of St. Nicolas.) Early sea logs report that the island supported a large Indian population. The arriving padres named these Indians Nicolenos. Some scientists theorize that the Nicolenos were more peaceful than the other Channel Island Indians because they found so few arrowheads.

Many middens and burial sites have been found, however. Another fascinating remnant left behind on the south coast of San Nicolas was a sample of the Nicolenos' artistic talent; petroglyphs--large inscriptions of the sea and whales (some as long as six feet)--were discovered in a cave nicknamed by early ranchers the "Cave of the Whales." So many questions--and so few answers. Was there some religious significance to these large whale drawings? Why weren't others found? We'll probably never know. Part of the wall fell in 1961 and was given to the Southwest Museum in Los Angeles by the United States Navy.

The Nicolenos led peaceful lives and seldom saw visitors. (It's questionable whether the Spanish actually got off their ships and *explored* the island, since there's very little good anchorage for vessels.) The island's extensive kelp beds, rich with sealife, were overrun with otters. Then the otter hunts began, and almost the entire population of Nicoleno Indians was ravaged and murdered--the plight of all the Channel Island Indians--by hunters for the Russian and American traders. In 1835 the few remaining Indians were taken to Mainland missions.

The Abandoned Woman of San Nicolas

In 1835, the priests discovered the population had fallen from more than 1,000 to 17-20 people. The Franciscan padres commissioned a vessel, *Peor Es Nada,* to relocate the remaining Nicolenos. When Captain Charles Hubbard arrived at San Nicolas to remove them, without warning a gale riled the sea. The small schooner bobbed on its anchor as the crew, in haste and confusion, rounded up the remnant group of Indians (mostly women and children) and their modest belongings. The rising sea forced the captain to leave as soon as possible. As the

ship was about to set sail with all Indians aboard, a young woman noticed that her child was not among them. She leaped into the agitated sea and swam to shore to search for the child. The captain, fearful for the safety of his crew, passengers, and ship, scurried for the Mainland-- without the Indian woman or her baby.

Captain Hubbard told his story to the padres at San Gabriel Mission and expressed his intention to return for the woman after he completed a voyage to San Francisco. As it turned out, the trip to San Francisco was the last for the *Peor Es Nada.* Less than a month after the trip to San Nicolas the schooner sank, and Captain Hubbard with it. More than a few Mainland people had heard the story of the woman left on San Nicolas, but no one ever tried to do anything about it. Years passed, and the occasional hunter or fisherman mentioned signs of someone living on the island. No one was ever seen so no one investigated, convinced the woman couldn't possibly have survived alone all that time.

In 1850, George Nidever and Thomas Jeffries sailed with a crew of Mainland Indians to San Nicolas to hunt otter and, if possible, find the remains of the Indian woman and her child and return them to the Mainland mission. They remained on the island for six weeks, hunting and preparing the otter and seal hides. One night, an Indian working with Nidever hiked around the island and was convinced he saw a running figure some distance away. He tried to catch up with this surprise visitor, but was unsuccessful. His report put Nidever on the alert, and each

sea otter

DIANA LASICH HARPER

time he visited the island he searched for the phantom.

Three years later, he and his hunting companions, including Carl Detman, stumbled on a basket filled with a feather dress. Nidever was determined to find the woman this time, and he and his companions conducted a thorough search, cave by cave, beach by beach, every inch of the island. Finally, several days later, Detman followed fresh footprints to one of the high peaks and a grass shelter.

Found at last--it was almost unbelievable. The woman appeared to be about 50, healthy and active. She was in a beautiful dress of shiny green cormorant feathers matching the one the men had stumbled upon earlier. Through sign language the men learned that her child had not survived; in fact she had found it dead the day she swam ashore. She had managed quite well over the years, surviving on birds, fish, abalone, seal blubber, and roots. After her early experiences with the vicious hunters who had wiped out most of her people, it was no surprise that she was fearful of the otter hunters she observed on the island occasionally, and did her best to remain hidden.

After gathering her few possessions (including bone needles and feather dresses that so impressed her discoverers) into a basket, she joined the men and journeyed to the Mainland. She was welcomed into the home of Captain Nidever. The shy woman appeared quite pleased with her new world and enjoyed the many wondrous things that she was introduced to. The rest of her people had been taken 18 years earlier either to Los Angeles or San Gabriel missions, yet it was almost impossible to find anyone left who could speak her language. Finally, after much searching, an old Indian at Santa Ynez was brought to meet Juana Maria (a name not given to her until she was baptised on her deathbed).

After 18 years of desolation, loneliness, and a struggle for survival, Juana Maria was being cared for. The story goes that she liked the variety of foods that were new to her, including hardtack bread, fresh fruit, and (especially) sugar. Some blame the foods for her death, but who will ever know? She was treated very kindly, but despite everything, was dead within seven weeks of her rescue, marking the end of five

civilizations on San Nicolas Island. She was buried in the graveyard at Santa Barbara Mission; a plaque erected in her memory in 1928 reads:

> *Juana Maria*
> *Indian Woman Abandoned on*
> *San Nicolas Island eighteen years*
> *Found and brought to*
> *Santa Barbara*
> *by*
> *Captain George Nidever*
> *in 1853*
> *Santa Barbara Chapter*
> *Daughters of the American Revolution*
> *1928*

Legend says that the local priest sent her feather dress and possessions to Rome, but no one knows where any of these things are today. In 1957, archaeologist Arthur R. Sanger of Los Angeles, who searched the Channel Islands for 30 years collecting Indian artifacts for the Museum of the American Indian in New York and the Los Angeles County Museum, was certain he had found the skeleton of Juana Maria's child. He said that this particular infant skeleton was found buried much deeper than the others, and that beads buried with the child were imported in the 19th century. Anything is possible. An exceptionally fine children's book called *Island Of The Blue Dolphins,* by Scott O'Dell, gives a fictional account of Juana Maria's years alone on the island.

Ranching

In 1857, only four years after Juana Maria's removal from San Nicolas, the first rancher, Captain Martin Kimberly, brought in sheep, whose descendants defoliated the island for the next 84 years. San Nicolas didn't go through the line of private ownership as did most of the other Channel Islands. However, it was leased to a variety of ranchers--Howland and Vail, L.P. Elliot, Roy Agee, and Martin Kimberly, running thousands of sheep and continuously planting grasses that would survive in the salty, windy environment.

Over the years overgrazing was a way of life. In 1840 the island boasted trees, brush, and moss, but by 1900 San Nicolas was devastated.

At one time, the smallest fully accredited school in the county with a full-time teacher (Miss Alma R. McLain) was conducted on San Nicolas Island. The entire student body of San Nicolas Elementary School consisted of two students, Frances Agee and John Scrimiger.

Navy

In 1933 President Hoover gave jurisdiction of San Nicolas to the Navy. After the army temporarily administered it from 1942 to 1947, Point Mugu regained administrative control of the island for the Navy. Since then it has been closed to the public and used for various training programs. Now part of the Pacific Missile Test Center's Sea Test Range, San Nicolas maintains a far different landscape from that of the other Channel Islands. The multimillion-dollar government complex includes a 10,000-foot runway that accommodates supersonic target aircraft and planes from the Mainland during weapons tests. San Nicolas offers an unobstructed area over which the Navy can test its new airborne weapon systems. The tests are conducted over a rectangular plot of ocean 200 miles long and 80 miles wide, between San Nicolas Island and Point Mugu on the Mainland. The entire program, including sophisticated missile-tracking devices, is closely coordinated with those at Point Mugu. White telescope domes dot the plateau, and approximately 180 military and civilian technicians live on the windswept island.

Management

A joint agreement between the Department of the Navy, Department of the Interior, and California Department of Fish and Game provides for the care, management, and protection of the flora and fauna, and recovery of the land, on San Nicolas. Indian artifacts are protected by the Antiquities Act, which governs historic and prehistoric remains. Excavation and collection of these is controlled and must be approved by the Department of the Interior. A Project Review Board reviews proposed scientific research to determine scientific merit, justification, and impact on the environment. The uncontrolled "pot hunters" of the last century inflicted much damage and destroyed archaeological treasures that could have helped in learning more about the original inhabitants of San Nicolas. These government agencies are making certain that history does not repeat itself.

PRACTICALITIES

San Nicolas and San Clemente islands are off-limits to the general public, as they are military reservations. If you want to visit either, you must adhere strictly to government regulations regarding each island, which you can obtain by writing Naval Air Station, Point Mugu, CA 93042, or call (805) 982-7567.

Boating

Boaters interested in San Nicolas should check out Chart 18755. The restricted naval area extends three miles around the island. An aerolight rises 981 feet above the east end. Marine lights shine from white pyramid-like structures on the south, east, and north sides of the island. A lighted buoy sits 1.3 miles southeast of the east sandspit. Another landmark to beware of is **Begg Rock,** 15 feet high and eight miles northwest of the west point of San Nicolas Island. A reef extends north and south of the rock more than 100 yards in each direction. The rock rises abruptly from depths of 50 fathoms and can disappear into a foggy day. A lighted whistle buoy sits 500 yards north of the rock. Anchorage around San Nicolas is usually uncomfortable, and in many cases restricted.

SAN CLEMENTE ISLAND

THE LAND

The grass-covered promontories and ragged cliffs of volcanic rock give San Clemente an arid look most of the year. Only in early spring is there a fresh green coverlet on the island. Even that lasts only a short time. Twenty miles long and two to four miles wide, San Clemente is the fourth largest of the Channel Islands, covering an area of 56 square miles. Its highest peak rises 1,965 feet. The island is a labyrinth of caves; at least one of them reaches up two stories. The shoreline shows masses of bubbled rock formed from ancient volcanic eruptions of sizzling lava hardened by the cooling sea into strange forms. Not far from the shore at West Cove are dozens of steep sand dunes (300 to 1,000 feet high).

FLORA AND FAUNA

Flora

Ten endemic plants grow on San Clemente, more than on any of the other islands. Scientists believe that **stipa**, an endemic bunchgrass, was probably the island's main ground cover in the past. Bits of it still grow on the weathered side of the island in deeply cut canyons. In spring, the island boasts myriad wildflowers, including mountains of succulents called **dudleya**, the orange flowers of **mimulus, prickly pear cactus, wild cucumber, coastal sage, poppies, San Clemente larkspur, San Clemente Indian paintbrush, San Clemente island bush mallow, San Clemente broom, thistles, lupine, white morning glories,** and **cholla cactus; ferns** and **moss** thrive at the bottoms of sheer-walled canyons hung with long trails of **snake cactus.** But the colorful flowers last but a brief time. The Navy's Natural Resources Program Office has started trying to restore the previous balance with a native plant nursery that includes about 50 species.

Fauna

The most abundant animals are the feral **goats** that have all but taken over the island. They run free into deep canyons and along ribbon-size paths, easily outwitting the intermittent hunters that the government allows and would like to see succeed. One program traps the goats and releases them in Mainland areas, but the goats multiply and replace the departing animals faster

the barren coast of
San Clemente Island

FRANK SILKY

than the trappers can keep up with them. Certain groups of animal lovers have complained loudly about any massive hunts that would thin out the goats, even though the animals are destroying the flora on San Clemente.

The **island fox,** two species of **island mice,** and four types of **bats** still live on the island. An occasional **osprey** flies high over the mountains, along with **mourning doves, hummingbirds, San Clemente Island sage sparrows, finches, meadowlarks,** and **ravens.** The seabirds include **pelicans, gulls,** the **black-footed albatross,** and many more varieties. **Seals, sea lions,** and **elephant seals** don't seem to mind the Navy bombardments, since their numbers are growing. As many as 300 elephant seals use San Clemente as their hauling ground.

HISTORY

Historians presume that what Cabrillo's party first called La Victoria on Oct. 7, 1542, was indeed San Clemente. Vizcaino, during his travels along the west coast in 1602, also sighted the island and renamed it San Clemente.

Indians
Although archaeologists have not conducted as many investigations on San Clemente as on some of the other Channel Islands, archaeology classes from local Mainland colleges have uncovered more than 1,000 midden sites. The Indians used the huge caves scattered around the island as living quarters. San Clemente Indians traded widely with the other islands and with the Mainland; many artifacts from neighboring Catalina Island have been found on San Clemente, along with other proof that these Indian mariners traveled the channel extensively. San Clemente Indians suffered the same indignities at the hands of the Aleut otter hunters as did the rest of the Channel Islanders. Only after the populace had been devastated did the Indians move to the Mainland in the 1820s to San Gabriel Mission.

Island People
The island was largely uninhabited over the years, but a variety of people have touched it in

some way. Documents indicate that a Spanish land grant was awarded to Pio Pico. However, he never claimed the grant. Several ranchers with interests on the other Channel Islands also used San Clemente to raise sheep, but the island's single owner has been the U.S. Government since the Hidalgo Treaty in 1848. The Chinese collected abalone from San Clemente, dried them, and shipped them from about 1890 to 1910.

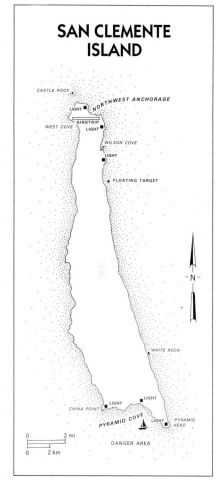

After the Indians were gone the island was used at various times as a hiding place for pirates and then by bootleggers who hid their illegal liquor in the many caves along the shore. Later a number of hermits found the island soothing for short periods of time, but those who stayed the longest were the sheep ranchers.

Navy

In 1934, the U.S. government assumed management of San Clemente Island. During WW II the island, under Navy jurisdiction, was used as a fleet training base and artillery target.

PRACTICALITIES

Boating

You'll find anchorage at Pyramid Cove, but as it's part of the Navy target area, it's off-limits to boaters during periods of bombardment, usually every Tuesday, Wednesday, and Thursday. For detailed information, contact the Commander, Amphibious Force, the Pacific Fleet, Naval Amphibious Base, Coronado, tel. (619) 437-2231, or the 11th U.S. Coast Guard District, 400 Oceangate, Long Beach, CA 90822.

Fishing

Thick kelp beds grow directly off the lee side of the island, where steep cliffs drop to the sea. The ocean bottom deepens quickly here. Sportfishermen and divers as well as the commercial fishing fleet come together at these rich fishing grounds. The Navy allows fishing and diving except in target areas but prohibits landing on any part of the island. Undersea caves hide abundant sealife, including swarms of gamefish and elusive lobsters that have managed to stay away from the ever-present lobster traps of Mainland fishermen.

A CHRISTMAS POEM

In the mid-1950s, an old sheepherder's shack was torn down and two Navy men found a fascinating piece of parchment with the following message:

At Christmas time when gifts are sent
They're from the saint, a kind old gent.
On an isle which bears his name
Is treasure, hid for you to claim
In an iron chest so strong
Buried where the land is long.
If you walk where the tides do meet
You will find it at your feet
Coins so rare, coins so old
Coins of silver and of gold.
If he who finds it is my friend,
All my fortune he may spend.
If he who finds it is my foe,
Curses, misery and woe.

This fascinating ditty should whet the appetites of treasure hunters; or is this just a practical joke perpetrated by a bored sheepherder spending a lonely night on windblown San Nicolas?

KATHY ESCOVEDO-SANDERS

MAINLAND SIDETRIPS

Catalina's fast-moving **Catalina Express** boats take passengers to and from the Island in no time--figure dock to dock about an hour and 10 minutes. Many visitors come to Catalina from distant parts of the country; those interested can take sidetrips to nearby Mainland ports.

NATIVE AMERICANS OF SOUTHERN CALIFORNIA

HISTORY

The prehistory of the southern California coast is much the same as the early history of the Channel Islands. The Indians about whom we know the most are the Chumash. As was the case with all of the Spanish missions, the Europeans, seeking to convert the Indians to Christianity, managed instead to destroy the culture that had existed for thousands of years.

Cradle of California Civilization

San Diego is sometimes called the Cradle of California civilization. Juan Cabrillo's discovery of San Diego in 1542 was the beginning of the Spanish influence that has always been part of California's modern way of life. Mission San Diego de Alcala, built in 1769, was the first in a chain built by Father Junipero Serra and the beginning of the Camino Real ("Royal Highway"). Ultimately 21 missions were built, each a day's walk from the next on the route from San Diego toward Northern California.

The peaceful Pacific Coast Indians were content with a productive life of fishing in a generous sea. The first Europeans were so amazed at the quantities of sardines, tuna, and swordfish the Indians caught so easily that they thought there was enough seafood to support a rich economy with the fishing industry alone.

The Second California Mission

Mission San Luis Rey, the second mission, was constructed in 1798 in nearby Oceanside. A large group of Native Americans called this area home. The missions were generally built near large Indian villages since the object was to convert them to Christianity.

Gabrielino and Juaneno Groups

California Chumash Indians of the Gabrielino and Jauneno groups lived along the coast of what is now Orange County for hundreds of years before the coming of the Spaniards. San Juan Capistrano, several miles inland from the ocean at San Clemente, was the seventh mission (circa 1776) to be built along the California coast. This mission and its priests, along with all the other missions established up and down the coast, drastically changed the lifestyle of the Indians.

Because of this cultural change and the exposure to unknown diseases brought by the outsiders, most of the Indian population didn't survive very long after the coming of the Europeans, with one exception. A small group of Juaneno Indians still lives in Orange County. Not too many years ago, a few archaeological artifacts dating to the first Juanenos were found at the site of the new Crystal Cove State Park.

Canalinos

The long beaches of Santa Barbara's southern neighbor Carpinteria (in Spanish meaning "carpenter's shop"), were alive with energetic Canalino Indians industriously building their wood-plank canoes, or *tomols*. In fact, two explorers (Cabrillo in 1547 and Portola in 1769) were so impressed with the boat-building abilities of the area's Indians that even though more than 200 years passed between visits, both chose names in remembrance of the Indian canoe building. Cabrillo's name was Los Pueblos de Canoas ("Cities of Canoes"), while Portola chose to honor the carpenter with Carpinteria.

Oil Country

Near the present-day city of Ventura, Mission San Buenaventura was founded in 1782 and many of the Indians were enlisted to do the menial work of the padres. Here the Spanish witnessed the Indians use the asphaltum that oozed from the earth in isolated places along the shore to seal their *tomol* canoes and to waterproof their basketry.

The Chumash

North along the coast, beneath the Santa Ynez Mountains in what today is the Santa Barbara area, lived some of the largest communities of Chumash Indians. In 1782 Father Junipero Serra and Captain Jose Francisco de Ortega founded a military presidio to defend against Russian explorers. In 1786, Mission Santa Barbara, the 10th mission under the Spanish flag, was built.

As time went by Indian country became white man's country. The few remaining Indians became ranch hands and were gradually assimilated into the population.

COASTAL CITIES TO THE NORTH

Southern California is an exciting area to visit. There's something to do for everyone. Some of the finest museums in California lie along the coast, famous recreation parks are nearby, and

naturalists will find tidepools to explore, wetlands to observe, and bird sanctuaries of immense proportions. Sunworshipers have myriad choices. And that's just the beginning.

SANTA BARBARA AREA

Sights
The Spanish influence in Santa Barbara lingered longer than in other parts of the West Coast. You can still see many historical buildings from the Spanish era by taking a walk through "old California" on Santa Barbara's "Red Tile Tour." Just follow the red tiles (a brochure is available at the chamber of commerce office at 1330 State Street). The self-guided tour takes you to the Hill-Carillo Adobe built in 1826, the 1827 Casa de la Guerra, (center of Santa Barbara social life made famous in *Two Years before the Mast*), and the Casa de Covarrubias (1817), where the last Mexican Assembly met in July of 1846.

Along the often rough Santa Barbara coast, a 2,364-foot breakwater was built in the 1920s. It covers 84 acres, creating a safe harbor for fishing boats and pleasure craft alike. Santa Barbara's Stearns Wharf, established in 1872, is touted as the oldest operating wharf on the West Coast. In the early days the wharf was used for steamers going up and down the coast; a trip by ship was the quickest way to get to San Francisco or San Diego. Today it's fun to walk on the restored wharf, eat at one of the restaurants, buy fresh seafood at the fish market, take pictures of the town and coastline, or just watch the gulls screech and dive when a fishing boat docks alongside.

A stop at the Santa Barbara Visitors Bureau at 1330 State St., tel. (805) 965-3021, will get you good information and maps of the town. If you plan to visit the Santa Barbara area in August, do stay for the Old Spanish Days Fiesta. This is a citywide good time of five days celebrating the city's Spanish heritage with parades, dancing, flamenco and concert music, an arts and crafts show, rodeo, barbecues, theatrical performances; everyone dresses in the Spanish costumes of early California. Other busy times are during Semana Nautica Regatta (great sailing races) and the Santa Barbara to King Harbor

Race, one of the most popular sailing races of Southern California.

Museums
The **Museum of Natural History,** on Puesta del Sol Rd. (two blocks north of the mission), tel. (805) 682-4711, features a planetarium along with exhibits on mammals, birds, fish, reptiles, plantlife, and geology of the Channel Islands. Also of interest is a diorama of prehistoric Indian life and a 72-foot blue whale skeleton in front of the museum; guided tours are available, small admission fee.

At the **Historical Museum,** 136 E. de la Guerra St., tel. (805) 966-1601, you'll see treasures from Santa Barbara's colorful past: documents, paintings, costumes, and many rare mementos from three eras, Indian, Mexican, and American. Admission is free; call for hours.

Fernald House and Trussell-Winchester Adobe, 414 W. Montecito St., P.O. Box 578, Santa Barbara, CA 93102-0578, tel. (805) 966-1601, charges no admission, but donations are appreciated. Tours are Sunday 2-4 p.m. The Trussell-Winchester Adobe is a 19th-century adobe with authentic furnishings. Timbers from the shipwreck of the *Winfield Scott* were used in construction.

Museum of Art, 1130 State St., tel. (805) 963-4364, is one of the nation's outstanding regional museums, with important holdings of American art. Admission is free Thursday and the first Sunday of the month.

Santa Barbara Mission, at the upper end

of Laguna St., tel. (805) 682-4713, is called the "Queen of the Missions" because of its graceful beauty. It's still in use as a parish church. Take a self-guided tour of the museum, garden, chapel, cemetery, and the remnants of the original water system on the hill north of the mission. It's open daily 9 a.m.-5 p.m.; small admission fee.

Nature Treks

At the **Botanic Garden,** 1212 Mission Canyon Rd., tel. (805) 682-4726 (1.5 miles north of the mission), wander through 65 acres of native trees, shrubs, wildflowers, and cacti in natural settings, or explore the five miles of easy-to-walk nature trails. Visit the historic dam built in 1806 by Indians under the supervision of the mission padres. It's open daily 8 a.m. until sunset.

You'll find the **Santa Barbara Zoological Gardens** at 500 Ninos Dr. off Cabrillo Blvd., tel. (805) 962-6310. In a garden setting, the zoo features a delightful variety of elephants, monkeys, lions, sea lions, exotic birds, and other animals. It's great for children of all ages with a miniature train ride, playground, farmyard petting area, and botanical gardens. It has a snack bar and spacious picnic area and is open mid-June to Labor Day.

Santa Barbara is home to the **Moreton Bay Fig Tree** on Chapala St. and Highway 101. The tree, native to Australia, is the largest of its kind in the States. A pioneer family planted it in 1877

and legend says that more than 10,000 people could stand in its shade at noon--the branches spread more than 160 feet.

Anyone interested in tidepools should go to Carpinteria Beach during the once-a-day low-low tide. Visitors can view the constant battle for survival by nature's feisty organisms. Where shore and sea are tangent, the tidal ebb and flood probably sustains more life per square foot than any other natural ecosystem. Remember, California's aquatic life, plants, and animals are protected by law; especially prohibited is the taking of specimens. Tidepooling is a recreation of looking and learning.

VENTURA AND ENVIRONS

In the mid-1800s settlers from the East and Midwest began to discover the fertile valleys of Ventura County, and farming became the number one economic activity. Close behind, another industry cropped up. From as early as 1896, oil has been removed from offshore wells. The oil business continued to grow and though the economic rewards of the industry along the California coast are great, ecologists are greatly concerned about the damage that the occasional spill causes the wildlife of the Pacific.

Sights

One of the most important stops in the area is the **Channel Islands National Park Building,** across from the ocean at 1901 Spinnaker Dr.,

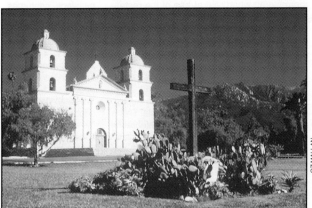

Santa Barbara Mission

OZ MALLAN

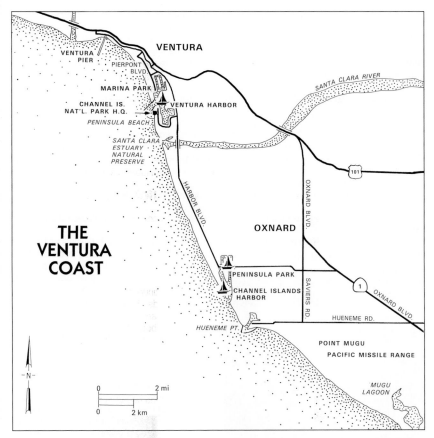

THE
VENTURA
COAST

VENTURA

VENTURA
PIER

PIERPONT
BLVD.

MARINA PARK

CHANNEL IS.
NAT'L. PARK H.Q.

VENTURA HARBOR

PENINSULA BEACH

SANTA CLARA
ESTUARY
NATURAL
PRESERVE

SANTA CLARA RIVER

HARBOR BLVD.

101

OXNARD

OXNARD BLVD.

PENINSULA PARK

CHANNEL ISLANDS
HARBOR

SAVIERS RD.

1

OXNARD BLVD.

HUENEME RD.

HUENEME PT.

POINT MUGU
PACIFIC MISSILE RANGE

MUGU
LAGOON

-N-

0   2 mi

0   2 km

Ventura, CA 93001, tel. (805) 644-8262; the visitor center is open year-round, summer 8 a.m.-5:30 p.m., fall/winter 8 a.m.-5 p.m. The visitor center offers a well-stocked bookstore with a good collection of books concerning the area, the Channel Islands, history, and the sea. Exhibits introduce the visitor to the Channel Islands National Marine Sanctuary--what it does and what its goals are for the Channel Islands.

Also available to the public are excellent films about the Channel Islands and tidepool exhibits where children (and adults) experience a hands-on introduction to the small creatures of the sea. The Island's precious resources have been misused in the past but now the federal govern-

ment is ensuring the Islands will be preserved. The exhibits show us what California must have been like when the first white man arrived. The Channel Islands National Park Center is the best source of information for travelers interested in visiting the Channel Islands; that goes for campers, who must obtain a permit.

Island Packers (authorized concessionaire to Channel Islands National Park) next door offers transportation to and from the Channel Islands on a variety of boats from motor launch to sailing vessels for daytrips and/or to drop off campers. It offers swim and snorkel days, tidepool exploring, whalewatching, camping trips, and special group trips. See individual island chapters for more information. Reservations are necessary, call (805) 642-1393; for information call (805) 642-7688.

Museums
The **Albinger Archaeological Museum** is downtown at 113 E. Main St., tel. (805) 648-5823. The **Olivas Adobe Historic Park** at 4200 Olivas Park Dr., tel. (805) 644-4346, an early California adobe built in 1847, offers a glimpse into the early days of California living. The grounds are open daily, the house is open Tues.-Sunday. Free weekend tours begin at 11 a.m. and 1 and 2 p.m. A 12-minute video on the ranchos of California is offered free on weekends. The **Ortega Adobe Historic Residence** at 215 W. Main St. (downtown), is an 1857 middle-class home. **Ventura County Museum of History and Art,** 100 E. Main St., also downtown, is open Tues.-Sun. 10 a.m.-5 p.m., closed New Year's, Thanksgiving, Christmas.

interpreter at Channel Islands Visitor Center

Nature Treks
For those interested in nature, a visit to the **Santa Clara Estuary Natural Reserve** is well worth the time. It's accessible from Peninsula Beach to the north or McGrath State Beach to the south. This marshland wildlife preserve sits at the mouth of the Santa Clara River. North of the river along Spinnaker Dr. the wastewater lagoons are fenced off, making an outstanding habitat for migratory waterfowl. This is a must for serious birdwatchers.

A larger spot (1,800 acres) is the **Mugu Lagoon,** the largest between Morro Bay and San Diego County. The lagoon lies entirely within the grounds of the Navy's Pacific Missile Test Center. To see the lagoon, you must make reservations. Public access is limited to weekend interpretive tours; call the Public Affairs Office, tel. (805) 982-8094.

Seaside Wilderness Park is a small park of palm trees and Monterey pines where the birdwatching is good. The only way to get there is by a three-quarter-mile walk from **Emma Wood State Beach** in the north. Continue along the beach and sand dunes west of the railroad tracks.

LOS ANGELES COUNTY COASTAL AREAS

In 1860, Los Angeles had a population of 4,355. By 1870 it had grown to only 5,728. Then in 1876, the transcontinental railroad was completed, and things started to move a *little* faster. By 1890 the population had grown to more than 51,000. It's been growing rapidly ever since. Today the population of Los Angeles County has passed 10 million.

Los Angeles Harbor is one of the largest man-made harbors in the world. It engulfs 7,000 acres of land and water and boasts 28 miles of waterfront. The largest commercial fishing fleet in the U.S. calls Los Angeles Harbor home. Fish canneries thrive and cargo ships from all over the world include Los Angeles Harbor as a port of call. The pleasure boater has all that he could want--except isolation. The waterfront has been spruced up in recent years; many of the old ports such as San Pedro and Long Beach have undergone complete face-lifts. Modern hotels, convention centers, and restaurants have been

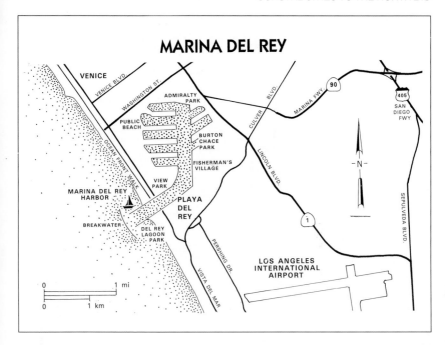

MARINA DEL REY

VENICE

VENICE BLVD.

WASHINGTON ST.

ADMIRALTY PARK

CULVER BLVD

MARINA FWY

90

405

SAN DIEGO FWY

PUBLIC BEACH

BURTON CHACE PARK

LINCOLN BLVD.

FISHERMAN'S VILLAGE

SEPULVEDA BLVD.

VIEW PARK

-N-

OCEAN FRONT WALK

MARINA DEL REY HARBOR

PLAYA DEL REY

BREAKWATER

DEL REY LAGOON PARK

PERSHING DR

1

LOS ANGELES INTERNATIONAL AIRPORT

VISTA DEL MAR

0   1 mi
0   1 km

built next to new state-of-the-art marinas with quaint fishing villagelike complexes and shopping centers to attract out-of-town visitors--as well as local boaters.

Part of the greater Los Angeles Harbor, Marina del Rey is the largest artificial small-craft harbor in the world. Built in 1960, it accommodates more than 6,000 pleasure boats and there's a waiting list! Special events include the Christmas Boat Parade, the California Cup, free summer concerts in the park, July 4 fireworks, and the annual In-The-Water Boat Show.

Catalina Boat Terminal
Boats to Catalina Island leave from Catalina Landing in downtown Long Beach and from San Pedro at the Catalina Air and Sea Terminal under the Vincent Thomas Bridge, daily, year-round. For complete information see "Getting There."

Cabrillo Marine Museum
The original **Cabrillo Marine Museum** at 3720

Stephen M. White Dr. was begun in 1920. It was rather a casual affair instigated by a local lifeguard, John Olguin, who collected sea specimens in mayonnaise jars and exhibited them in an old bathhouse. For years John's collection intrigued children and their parents. Eventually, the museum grew up and John's energetic enterprise hired a curator with a degree. John might still be around as curator emeritus. The new, large museum includes an auditorium, classrooms, laboratories, an exhibition hall with interpretive displays, touch tanks, and aquariums containing marine flora and fauna. The **Gift and Book Shop** is open 12:30-3:30 p.m. The museum is open Tues.-Fri. noon-5 p.m., Saturday and Sunday 10 a.m.-5 p.m. Call (310) 548-7562 for information (a recorded message) regarding guided tidepool tours at the Point Fermin Marine Life Refuge. The museum also sponsors whalewatching tours, trips to the Channel Islands, grunion run programs (a grunion is a small fish that spawns at night along the beach), and Cabrillo Day celebrations.

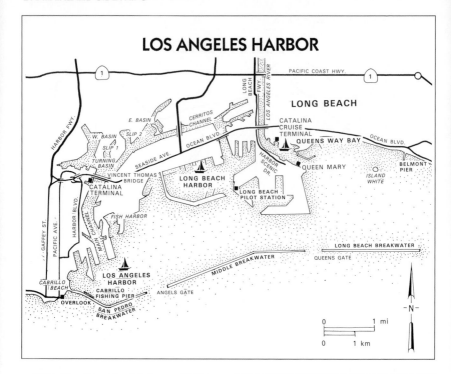

LOS ANGELES HARBOR

Note: The city parking lot charges $5.50 because of beach access.

Ports O' Call Village and Whalers Wharf
A favorite for out-of-towners is to stroll through the "re-created" atmosphere of Ports O' Call, an old California seaport, and then into Whalers Wharf, a 19th-century New England seaside community. Both offer shops, restaurants, harbor excursions, and a view of the main harbor channel.

Abalone Cove Ecological Reserve
Investigate the tidepools. **Point Fermin Lighthouse,** closer to the harbor, was built in 1874. Visitors are not allowed into the lighthouse, but the park and grounds surrounding it are a perfect spot from which to watch the whales during their yearly migration. Along with picnic areas, playground, and small amphitheater, you'll find the **Cetacean and Community Building.** The

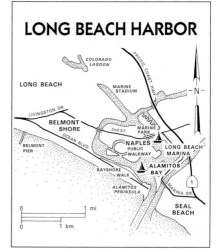

LONG BEACH HARBOR

whale station offers a free 20-minute movie; it's open Saturday and Sunday 9 a.m.-4 p.m.

Queen Mary Complex
Anyone visiting Long Beach for the first time should by all means take an afternoon and visit the *Queen Mary,* or spend the night; an entire section of former staterooms is operated as a hotel with restaurant on board.

The *Queen* was originally engaged in crossing the Atlantic between Europe and the U.S., and she's a grand example of luxury liners of the past. Watch the bungee platform and if you hear a loud horn, look up; you may see a daredevil jumping way up there. Want to try it? All you have to do is pay the fee, $50.

LONG BEACH PRACTICALITIES

Accommodations
Because of Long Beach's proximity to the Catalina Terminal, a sightseeing trip there, either before or after a trip to Catalina Island, is quite convenient. The **Hyatt Regency,** 200 S. Pine Ave., Long Beach, CA 90802, tel. (213) 491-1234, is a handy stopover. The modern hotel is close to the major sights along the waterfront, including the *Queen Mary.* It's across the street from **Shoreline Village** and its trendy shops and restaurants. Transportation is available from the hotel to Disneyland, Knott's Berry Farm, and many other Southern California attractions. Room rates are $130 s, $150 d.

On Queensway Bay, at 700 Queensway Dr., Long Beach, CA 90802, tel. (310) 435-2471 (for reservations from U.S. and Canada call 800-255-3050), TraveLodge Hotel Resort and Marina is a modern, world-class hotel. The hotel is a five-minute walk from the *Catalina Express* boat and close to many other attractions.

Parks and Recreation
Everywhere you look you'll find trendy shops and outstanding restaurants as well as overkill-fast-foods. Visit the **Burton Chace Park** for a nice change of pace. You'll find an eight-acre park with a great view of the main channel, plus transient docks, fishing dock, picnic area, and

COURSES FROM MARINA DEL REY

To:	Magnetic Course	Reverse Course	Distance in Nautical Miles
Pt. Conception	271	91	100
Anacapa Light	260	80	44
Santa Cruz Light	254	74	67
Santa Rosa Light	252	72	82
Begg Rock	225	45	70.5
San Nicholas Island, West End	219	39	68.5
Pt. Vincente	155	335	13.5
Santa Barbara Island	209	29	39
Osborn Bank	203	23	45.5
Tanner Bank	189	9	82
Bishop Rock	184	4	96.5
Catalina Island, West End	179	359	29
Catalina Island Isthmus	166	346	30

COURSES FROM LONG BEACH HARBOR

Long Beach Breakwater To:	Magnetic Course	Reverse Course	Distance in Nautical Miles
Avalon, Catalina Island	183	3	23.5
Isthmus, Catalina Island	208	28	22.5
Horseshoe Kelp	194	14	4.5
14-Mile Bank	140	320	21.5
San Clemente Island, East End	174	345	54.5
Newport Bell Buoy	105	285	17.5
San Diego Entrance Buoy	130	310	81
Catalina Island, West End	220	40	26
Santa Barbara Island	236	56	44.5
San Nicolas Island, East End	229	49	68
Point Fermin	236	56	5.5
Long Beach Marina East Breakwater Light To:			
Oceanside	116	296	48
San Diego, Entrance B	131	311	80
N. Coronado Island	136	316	87
45 Fathom Bank	157	337	64
14-Mile Bank	145	325	21
209 Fathom Bank	145	325	40
San Clemente Island, East End	176	356	55
Catalina Island, East End	183	3	26
Avalon, Catalina Island	187	7	24.5
Isthmus, Ship Rock C.I.	213	33	24
Catalina Island, West End	223	43	28
Santa Barbara Island	238	58	47
San Nicolas Island, East End	229	49	70
Osborn Bank	229	49	50

watchtower. Free parking on weekdays.

Emergency Services

Sheriff's harbor patrol offices lie adjacent to the Department of Beaches and Harbors Administration Offices at 13837 Fiji Way. Harbor patrol offices are staffed 24 hours, every day of the year, and you can reach them by calling (310) 823-7762, or 911 (emergency) to report a fire or to request the paramedics.

REDONDO BEACH AND KING HARBOR

Redondo Beach's King Harbor continues to

grow more popular and more crowded each year. Between boaters and visitors to the Redondo Municipal Pier, the International Boardwalk, and Monstad Pier, King Harbor attracts thousands of people, especially in the summer. It has four marinas.

ORANGE COUNTY COASTAL AREAS

HISTORY

Settlers

The first Americans settled in Orange County about 1859 in the Anaheim area. Inland farmers, away from the swampy coastal regions, were successful raising orange trees, peanuts, barley, corn, pigs, and sheep. From there the colonists spread out and it wasn't long before they settled a small dusty village called Newport next to the sea. It was tough going for the adventurous settlers during those early years. The landscape provided few natural materials to help them establish a town. (The Indians had solved the housing problem by building their oval-shaped huts from branches and tule grasses found along the rolling hills that bordered the Pacific.) The settlers brought everything overland in crude, wooden wagons.

Newport

With the advent of the railroad, the quiet little village of Newport began a transition that would ultimately make it a popular resort destination. A moderate year-round climate attracted people from all over California to its long white beaches, craggy cliffs, and beautiful clear ocean.

For years outlying acreage in Orange County remained untouched. In the mid-1950s an American with great foresight gambled millions of dollars to build an amusement park in Anaheim, many miles away from Southern California's established business centers. The man was Walt Disney.

Mr. Disney at Work

Since Disneyland was built, Orange County has developed into a thriving metropolis. Hundreds of thousands of people and many big corporations left busy inner cities for the sunny countryside. The close-by coastal areas were also af-

fected--new ports and marinas are added each year, with Newport the oldest and perhaps the queen of the Orange County coast.

SIGHTS AND RECREATION

Marine Events and Attractions

Visitors to the **Orange County Marine Institute** get an opportunity through classes and talks to view and understand the natural marinelife of this coastal area. Young people spend a day and night aboard the brig *Pilgrim* learning history and basic shipboard tasks and standing watch. The ship is a replica of the brig that carried Richard Henry Dana to these waters in 1834. Dana's experiences are recounted in his classic, *Two Years Before the Mast*. Another educational program is held onboard the tall

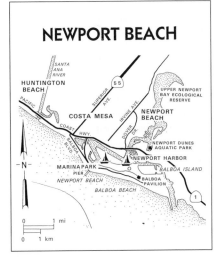

NEWPORT BEACH

ship *Californian,* a replica of a 19th-century revenue cutter.

The **Nautical Heritage Society Museum** offers seamanship training for young people ages 16 to 25. The focus is on California maritime history.

If you happen to be visiting during whalewatching season, the **Festival of the Whales** begins mid-February and continues for a month. Daily whalewatching cruises offshore, lectures, movies, displays, and demonstrations are open to the public.

Amphitheaters
Fine year-round entertainment is presented at many open-air amphitheaters. Check the schedules for **Festival of Arts of Laguna Beach,** 650 Laguna Canyon Rd., Laguna Beach, mail-

ing address P.O. Box 37, Laguna Beach, CA 92652, tel. (714) 494-1145.

This is the home of the summer presentation **Pageant of the Masters.**

The **Pacific Amphitheatre,** corner of Fair Dr. and Fairview in Costa Mesa (next to the Orange County Fairgrounds), tel. (714) 546-4875, seats 19,000; it's the largest outdoor amphitheater in California and presents concerts and big-name entertainment.

Special Attractions
Along with the old favorites, **Disneyland** and **Knott's Berry Farm,** visitors like to stop at **Balboa Island,** a picturesque community on a small island with trendy shops and specialty restaurants reminiscent of the New England coast. And the favored way to get there is onboard the

COURSES FROM NEWPORT BAY

To:	Magnetic Course	Reverse Course	Distance in Nautical Miles
Dana Point	121	301	11
San Diego Bell Buoy	136	316	66.2
60-Mile Bank	170	350	56.3
14-Mile Bank	192	12	13
San Clemente Island, East End	192	12	52.5
San Clemente Island, West End	213	33	50
Tanner Bank	214	34	83.2
Catalina Island, East End	216	36	27
Avalon, Catalina Island	222	42	26.4
Gallagher Cove, Catalina Island	225	45	26.9
White's Landing, Catalina Island	229	49	27
Lone Pt., Catalina Island	230	51	26.4
Isthmus Cove, Catalina Island	239	59	31.5
Emerald Cove, Catalina Island	242	62	33.5
Catalina Island, West End	244	64	36.6
Santa Barbara Island, North End	249	69	58.2
Pt. Fermin Buoy	272	92	21.5
San Pedro Breakwater	276	96	20

OZ MALLAN

Balboa Pavilion

Balboa Island Ferry. This is a small ferry for a short trip, holding only three cars, passengers, and bikers traveling between Balboa and the "fun zone" of the Balboa Peninsula.

Step into the past with a visit to **Mission San Juan Capistrano.** If it happens to be March 19, you'll witness the annual return of the swallows; the Mission is only 10 minutes east of Dana Point.

Nature Treks
Explore the **Corona del Mar tidepools** at Big Corona State Beach and Little Corona Beach. It's one of the few places in Orange County to observe firsthand the intriguing organisms of the sea. Or visit the **Orange County Marine Institute,** 24200 Dana Point Harbor Dr., Dana Point, CA 92629, at the far end of Dana Point Harbor.

Birdwatchers, check out the **Bolsa Chica Ecological Preserve** and **Upper Newport Bay**

Ecological Reserve (see map). The Bolsa Chica Ecological Preserve consists of 1,200 acres of marshland. From two parking lot viewing areas you may see three birds on the endangered species list: **the clapper rail, California least tern,** and the **savanna sparrow.** Take the loop trail across from the beach entrance; interpretive signs are posted along the way.

Note: Most of the marsh is private land, so stay within the viewing areas; you'll find one at Pacific Coast Hwy. across from the main Bolsa Chica Beach entrance, and the other at Pacific Coast Hwy. and Warner Avenue.

The Upper Newport Bay Ecological Reserve is an estuary. Contact **Friends of Upper Newport Bay,** P.O. Box 2001, Newport Beach, CA 92663, which offers interpretive bird tours Saturday during the winter. Not too far from Dana Harbor, take a walk to the northern end of the harbor to the jetty and offshore **Dana Point Marine Life Refuge.**

Events along the Orange County Coast
Around the Bay in May, tel. (714) 644-8211, celebrates the coming of summer with 10-mile jogging/running races around the Newport Beach area.

The **Baroque Music Festival** celebrates the musical heritage in Corona del Mar each June. Also in June, the **Newport Beach Bike Tour,** tel. (714) 650-1000, is a six-mile ride around the back bay, returning to East Bluff Park (and a picnic).

It's fun to play in the sand in October's **Sandcastle Contest** at Big Corona Beach in Corona del Mar. Here you'll see some fabulous sand sculptures created by individuals and by groups. Each December brightly decorated boats follow an eight-mile parade route through Newport Harbor nightly for two weeks in the middle of the month; the event is called the **Festival of Lights Parade.** For details about getting your boat into the fun, call (714) 644-8211.

DANA POINT

Once a major port for square-rigged ships, this harbor was named for Richard Henry Dana, author of *Two Years Before the Mast.* The classic novel is an account of the adventures of a young man from the U.S. East Coast working onboard a merchant ship that plied the waters of the West Coast in the mid-1830s. It depicts the flavor of early California very realistically. Richard Henry Dana would be amazed and proud if he knew this harbor had been named in his honor. It isn't only a gathering spot for modern pleasure boats, but also is a popular dock for whale-watching excursions and research vessels. Scientists at Dana Point accomplished significant fact-finding on the subject of whales' voices and underwater communication. One of the largest and most popular waterfront festivals in Orange County, the **Tallships Competition,** is held here each year; what a beautiful sight!

SAN DIEGO COASTAL AREAS

SIGHTS

San Diego was organized as a town in 1834, and by 1850 was incorporated as a city. San Diego Harbor is considered one of the finest natural harbors in the world. For years the biggest fleet was that of the U.S. Navy. Today, the biggest fleet is the pleasure boats that fill the many marinas in San Diego. Vessels vary

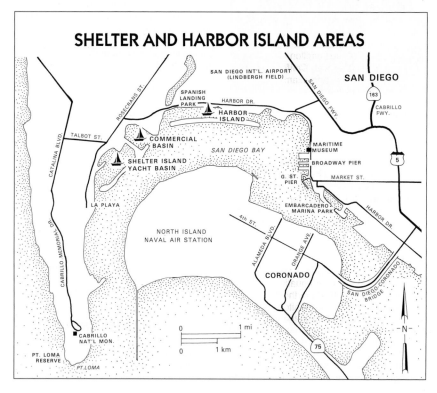

from simple and small to luxurious and large. The temperate climate is perfect for the sailors to whom San Diego is either home base or just a favorite port of call.

Balboa Park

It's possible to stay in San Diego for a month and take in a different outstanding attraction every day (if you don't run out of money first!). Balboa Park, in the heart of the city, boasts 1,074 acres of museums, art galleries, theaters, sports facilities, and one of the world's largest zoos. What's left over is green grass and tall trees. The park's museum and gallery complex is amazing. Within walking distance you find the **Reuben H. Fleet Space Theatre and Science Center,** the **Hall of Champions, Museum of Man, Natural History Museum, San Diego Museum of Art,** and the **Timken Art Gallery.** Most of the Spanish/Moorish buildings in the park were originally part of the Panama-California Exposition of 1915-16 and the California-Pacific International Exposition of 1935-36. Every day the 100-bell carillon chimes each quarter hour from the lovely **California Tower,** another city landmark and example of Spanish/Moorish architecture.

Cabrillo National Monument

The Cabrillo National Monument overlooks what Juan Cabrillo called San Miguel Bay and what today is called San Diego Bay. The monument was established in memory of the first European to visit the entire California coast; he began his quest in 1542.

Stop by the visitor center for an exhibit on Cabrillo's explorations and discoveries. Programs about the monument are presented daily.

Sea World

A desolate marshland several miles north of downtown San Diego has been brilliantly transformed into a 4,600-acre aquatic playground called **Mission Bay Park.** In the heart of this complex, Sea World offers visitors one of the finest marinelife attractions in the world. Along with a high-flying killer whale named Shamu, you'll see the Penguin Encounter in a 5,000-square-foot re-created Antarctic neighborhood behind a 100-foot viewing window, a 28° F home for more than 400 penguins. In the California

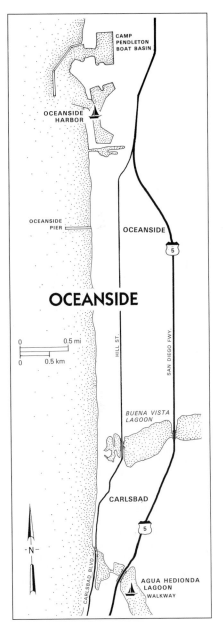

MISSION BAY AREA

Tidepool exhibit, visitors may pick up and examine starfish or sea urchins, or wander around to see dolphins, sea lions, otters, and even a walrus. The whole family will find plenty to see and do.

Gaslamp Quarter
Step back in time to the 1890s and one of San Diego's historic districts. You'll absorb the sights, sounds, and feeling of a bustling California waterfront before the turn of the century with restored Victorian homes. One of the best ways to learn about the Quarter is via walking tours offered every Saturday from 10 a.m.-noon and 1 p.m.-3 p.m. You can arrange custom tours by calling (619) 233-4694.

Animals
For the animal lover, a trip to **San Diego Wild Animal Park** at 15500 San Pasqual Valley Rd., Escondido, CA 92027, tel. (619) 480-0105, is well worth the time. You'll find 2,200 acres of simulated natural habitats for more than 3,000 animals roaming free as they would in their birthplaces. The park, 30 miles from downtown San Diego, includes an African village as well as a five-mile, 50-minute monorail trip (with narrator-guide) that glides silently through expansive Asian and African enclosures. Don't miss the Nairobi Center with its lowland gorilla colony. Along with its Animal Care Center, the park has achieved national acclaim with its condor program. This is one of the few preserves in the

world where the animals run free and the people are contained! The park is open every day of the year; admission is $16.50 adult, $9.50 child (3-15).

Closely related in operations is the **San Diego Zoo** at Balboa Park in downtown San Diego. One of the highlights is the Children's Zoo. Double-decker buses with narrator-guides take vis-

itors on a 40-minute trip through three miles of safari land, including sprawling canyons and mesas. It's open daily.

More Attractions
Old Town is the site of the first European settlement in California. In 1967, the state provided $2 million to buy six blocks in the heart of Old

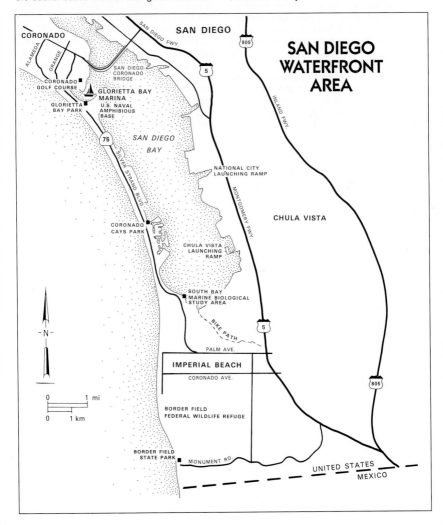

Town. It has been restored and the State Park Old Town Historical Society offers walking tours led by park rangers at 2 p.m. daily from the **Machado y Silvas Adobe** across from the plaza. For more information, call Old Town State Park, tel. (619) 237-6770.

The **Maritime Museum** is a trio of ships, each telling its story of the past. The most familiar, the *Star of India,* is the oldest merchant sailing vessel afloat. The steam-powered ferryboat *Berkeley* was the first successful propeller-driven ferry on the West Coast and was responsible for carrying thousands to safety during the 1906 San Francisco earthquake. The 1904 steam yacht *Medea,* built for a wealthy Scot and later owned by members of Parliament, served in both World Wars. Moored on the Embarcadero, the "fleet" is open daily from 9 to 8; small admission fee.

MEXICO

The Mexican border at Tijuana is a 25-minute trip on the trolley from downtown San Diego. From the border it's another 20-minute walk to Avenida Revolucion in downtown Tijuana, where you'll find dozens of shops. No passport or visa is required of U.S. citizens for a stay of less than 72 hours within 75 miles of the border. You may bring $400 in retail value of duty-free goods back into the States. A good destination for visitors to Tijuana is the **Cultural Complex,** where, in the Omnimax Theater, you relive Mexican history. On the grounds also visit the **Anthropological Museum** and the **Performing Arts Center.** The sports fan can enjoy **horse racing, jai alai, and bullfighting** in season.

HEALTH HINTS

Sunburn

Sunburn can spoil a vacation more quickly than anything else. Approach the sun cautiously. Expose yourself for short periods the first few days; wear a hat and sunglasses. Use a good sunscreen and apply it to all exposed areas of the body (don't forget your feet, hands, nose, backs of your knees, and top of your forehead--especially if you have a receding hairline). Remember that after every time you go into the water, you must reapply sunscreen lotion. Even after a few days of desensitizing your skin, wear a T-shirt in the water to protect your exposed back if you're spending a day snorkeling, and thoroughly douse the back of your neck with sunscreen lotion.

If you still get a painful sunburn, stay out of the sun. Cover up with clothes if it's impossible to find protective deep shade (as in the depths of a dark, thick forest). Even in the shade (such as under a beach umbrella), the reflection of the sun off the sand or water will burn your skin. Reburning the skin can result in painful blisters that easily become infected. Soothing suntan lotions, aloe gel, coconut oil, vinegar, cool tea, and preparations such as Solarcaine will help relieve the pain. Drink plenty of liquids (especially water) and take tepid showers. The best cure is just spending a couple of days out of the sun.

Self-Help

The smart traveler carries a first-aid kit of some kind. If backpacking, at least carry the following:

    alcohol
    adhesive tape
    aspirin
    baking soda
    bandages
    cornstarch
    gauze
    hydrogen peroxide
    iodine
    insect repellent
    Lomotil
    needle
    pain pills
    antibiotic ointment
    pain killer
    sunscreen
    tweezers
    water purification tablets

Even if you're not out in the wilderness, you should carry at least a few bandages, aspirin,

SIMPLE FIRST-AID GUIDE

Acute Allergic Reaction

This, the most serious complication of insect bites or stings, can be fatal. Common symptoms are hives, rash, pallor, nausea, tightness in chest or throat, trouble in speaking or breathing. Be alert for symptoms. If they appear, get prompt medical help. Start CPR if needed and continue until medical help is available.

Animal Bites

Bites, especially on face and neck, need immediate medical attention. If possible, catch and hold the animal for observation, taking care not to be bitten. Wash the wound with soap and water (hold under running water for two to three minutes unless bleeding is heavy). Do not use iodine or other antiseptic. Bandage. This also applies to bites by human beings. In case of human bites the danger of infection is high.

Bee or Wasp Stings

If available apply cold compresses quickly.

Try to remove stinger by gentle scraping with clean fingernail and continue cold applications till pain is gone. Be alert for symptoms of acute allergic reaction or infection requiring medical aid.

Bleeding
For severe bleeding apply direct pressure to the wound with bandage or the heel of the hand. Do not remove blood-soaked clothes, just add others on top and continue pressure till bleeding stops. Elevate bleeding part above heart level. If bleeding continues, apply pressure bandage to arterial points. Do not put on tourniquet unless advised by a physician. Do not use iodine or other disinfectant. Get medical aid.

Blister
It is better not to open a blister if you can rest the foot. If you can't, wash foot with soap and water; make a small hole at the base of the blister with a needle sterilized in alcohol or in a match flame; drain and cover with a bandage or moleskin. If a blister breaks on its own, wash with soap and water, bandage, and be alert for signs of infection (redness, festering) that call for further attention.

Burns
Minor burns (redness, swelling, pain): apply cold water, or immerse burned part in cold water immediately. Use burn medication if necessary. With deeper burns blisters develop. Immerse in cold water (not ice water) or apply cold compresses for one to two hours. Blot dry and protect with sterile bandage. Do not use antiseptic, ointment, or home remedies. Consult a doctor. With very deep burns skin layers are destroyed; skin may be charred. Cover with sterile cloth; be alert for breathing difficulties and treat for shock if necessary. Do not remove clothing stuck to burn. Do not apply ice. Do not use burn remedies. Get medical help quickly.

Cuts
Wash small cuts with clean water and soap.

Hold wound under running water. Bandage. Use hydrogen peroxide or other antiseptic. For large wounds see "Bleeding" above. If a finger or toe has been cut off, treat severed end to control bleeding. Put severed part in clean cloth for the doctor (it may be possible to reattach it by surgery). Treat for shock if necessary. Get medical help at once.

Diving Accident
There may be injury to the cervical spine (such as a broken neck). Call for medical help. (See "Drowning" and "Fractures" below.)

Drowning
Clear airway and start CPR even before trying to get water out of lungs. Continue CPR till medical help arrives. In case of vomiting, turn victim's head to one side to prevent the inhaling of vomitus.

Food Poisoning
Symptoms appear a varying number of hours after eating and are generally like those of the flu--headache, diarrhea, vomiting, abdominal cramps, fever, a general sick feeling. See a doctor. A rare form, botulism, has a high fatality rate. Symptoms are double vision, inability to swallow, difficulty in speaking, respiratory paralysis. Get to emergency facility at once.

Fractures
Until medical help arrives, do not move the victim unless absolutely necessary. Suspected victims of back, neck, or hip injuries should not be moved. Suspected breaks of arms or legs should be splinted to avoid further damage before victim is moved, if moving is necessary.

Heat Exhaustion
Symptoms are cool moist skin, profuse sweating, headache, fatigue, and drowsiness, with essentially normal body temperature. Remove victim to cool surroundings, raise feet and legs, loosen clothing, and apply cool cloths. Give sips of salt water--one teaspoon

of salt to a glass of water--for rehydration. If victim vomits, stop fluids, and take the victim to emergency facility as soon as possible.

Heat Stroke
Rush victim to hospital. Heat stroke can be fatal. Victim may be unconscious or severely confused. Skin feels hot, is red and dry, with no perspiration. Body temperature is high. Pulse is rapid. Remove victim to cool area, sponge with cool water or rubbing alcohol; use fans or air conditioning and wrap in wet sheets, but do not overchill. Massage arms and legs to increase circulation. Do not give large amount of liquids. Do not give liquids if victim is unconscious.

Jellyfish Stings
Symptom is acute pain and may include feeling of paralysis. Immerse in ice water for five to ten minutes or apply aromatic spirits of ammonia to remove venom from skin. Be alert for symptoms of acute allergic reaction and/or shock. If this happens, get victim to hospital as soon as possible.

Motion Sickness
Get a prescription from your doctor if boat travel is anticipated and this condition is a problem. Many over-the-counter remedies are sold in the U.S.: Bonine and Dramamine are two. Medication administered in adhesive patches behind the ear is also available by prescription. If you prefer not to take chemicals or get drowsy, try the Sea Band, a cloth band that you place around the pressure point of the wrists. It works through acupressure, without drugs. For more information write: Sea Band, 1645 Palm Beach Lake Blvd., Suite 220, W. Palm Beach, FL 33401, tel. (305) 684-4508.

Muscle Cramps
Usually a result of unaccustomed exertion. "Working" the muscle or kneading with hand relieves cramp. If in water head for shore (don't panic--you can swim even with a muscle cramp), or knead muscle with hand. Call for help if needed.

Mushroom Poisoning
Even a small ingestion may be serious. Induce vomiting immediately if there is any question of mushroom poisoning. Symptoms --vomiting, diarrhea, difficulty breathing--may begin in one to two hours or up to 24 hours. Convulsions and delirium may develop. Go to a doctor or emergency facility at once.

Nosebleed
Press bleeding nostril closed, pinch nostrils together, or pack with sterile cotton or gauze. Apply cold water to nose and face. Victim should sit up, leaning forward, or lie down with head and shoulders raised. If bleeding does not stop in ten minutes get medical help.

Obstructed Airway
Find out if victim can talk by asking, "Can you talk?" If he can talk, encourage him to try to cough obstruction out. If he can't speak, a trained person must apply the Heimlich Maneuver. If you are alone and choking, try to forcefully cough object out. Or press your fist into your upper abdomen with a quick upward thrust, or lean forward and quickly press your upper abdomen over any firm object with rounded edge (back of chair, edge of sink, porch railing). Keep trying till the object comes out.

Poison Oak
After contact, wash affected area with alkali-base laundry soap, lathering well. Cortisone creams are helpful when itching and blisters develop.

Puncture Wounds
They often do not bleed, so try to squeeze out some blood. Wash thoroughly with soap and water and apply a sterile bandage. Check with doctor about tetanus. If pain, heat, throbbing, or redness develop, get medical attention at once.

Rabies
Bites from bats, raccoons, rats, or other wild animals are the most common source of ra-

bies today. If bitten try to capture the animal (avoid getting bitten again), so that it can be observed; do not kill the animal unless necessary and try not to injure the head so the brain can be examined. Even if the animal can't be found, you must see a doctor, who may decide to use antirabies immunization. In any case, flush the bite with water and apply a dry dressing; keep victim quiet and see a doctor as soon as possible.

Scrapes
Sponge with soap and water; dry. Apply antibiotic ointment or powder and cover with a non-stick dressing (or tape on a piece of cellophane). When healing starts, stop ointment and use antiseptic powder to help scab form. Ask doctor about tetanus.

Shock
Can be a side effect in any kind of injury. Get immediate medical help. Symptoms may be pallor, clammy feeling to the skin, shallow breathing, fast pulse, weakness, or thirst. Loosen clothing, cover victim with blanket but do not apply other heat, and lay him on his back with feet raised. If necessary, start CPR. Do not give water or other fluids.

Snakebite
If snake is not poisonous, toothmarks usually appear in an even row. Wash the bite with soap and water and apply sterile bandage. See a doctor. If snake is poisonous, puncture marks (one to six) can usually be seen. Kill the snake for identification if possible, taking care not to be bitten. Keep the victim quiet, immobilize the bitten arm or leg, keeping it on a lower level than the heart. If possible, phone ahead to be sure antivenin is available and get medical treatment as soon as possible. Do not give alcohol in any form. If treatment must be delayed and snakebite kit is available, use as directed.

Spider Bites
The black widow bite may produce only a light reaction at the place of the bite, but se-

vere pain, a general sick feeling, sweating, abdominal cramps, and breathing and speaking difficulty may develop. The more dangerous brown recluse spider's venom produces severe reaction at the bite, generally in two to eight hours, plus chills, fever, joint pain, nausea, and vomiting. Apply a cold compress to the bite in either case. Get medical aid quickly.

Sprain
Treat as a fracture till injured part has been x-rayed. Raise the sprained ankle or other joint and apply cold compresses or immerse in cold water. If swelling is pronounced, try not to use the injured part. Get prompt medical help.

Sunburn
For skin that is moderately red and slightly swollen, apply wet dressings of gauze dipped in a solution of one tablespoon baking soda and one tablespoon cornstarch to two quarts of cool water. Or take a cool bath with a cup of baking soda mixed in the water. Sunburn remedies are helpful in relieving pain. See a doctor if burn is severe.

Sunstroke
This is a severe emergency. Skin is hot and dry; body temperature is high. The victim may be delirious or unconscious. Get medical help immediately. (See "Heat Stroke," above)

Ticks
Cover ticks with mineral oil or kerosene to exclude air from ticks and they will usually drop off or can be lifted off with tweezers in 30 minutes. To avoid infection, take care to remove the whole tick. Wash area with soap and water.

To Save a Knocked Out Tooth
Rinse tooth in cool water. Do not scrub tooth. If possible, replace tooth in socket and hold it in place. If this cannot be done, put the tooth under the tongue, or wrap it in a wet cloth, or drop it in a glass of milk. See a dentist immediately.

and an antibiotic ointment, powder, or both. Keep wounds as clean and dry as possible. If you're planning to backpack in the interior, another great addition to your kit is David Werner's book, *Where There Is No Doctor*. You can order it for $8.39 from the Hesperian Foundation, Box 1692, Palo Alto, CA 94302. Werner drew on his experience living in Mexico's isolated backcountry to create this practical, informative book. Make sure your tetanus vaccination is current before you leave home, especially if you're backpacking in isolated regions.

KATHY ESCOVEDO-SANDERS

BOOKLIST

Dana, Richard Henry. *Two Years Before The Mast.* New York: Airmont, 1965

Davis, Charlie. *Hook Up.* California: Charles Davis, 1977.

Eaton, Margaret Holden. *Diary Of A Sea Captain's Wife.* Santa Barbara: McNally & Loftin, 1980.

Fagan, Brian M. *Cruising Guide To California's Channel Islands.* California: Western Marine Enterprises, Inc., 1983.

Hillinger, Charles. *The California Islands.* California: Academy, 1958.

Holder, Charles F. *The Channel Islands of California.* McClurg, 1910.

Johnston, Bernice Eastman. *California's Gabrielino Indians.* California: Southwest Museum, 1962.

Kallman, Robert and Eugene Wheeler. *Shipwrecks, Smugglers, and Maritime Mysteries of the Santa Barbara Channel Islands.* Santa Barbara: McNally & Loftin, 1984.

Kroeber, A.L. *Handbook of the Indians of California.* Dover Publications, 1976.

Landberg, Leif C.W. *The Chumash Indians of Southern California.* California: Southwest Museum, 1965.

Moore, Patricia Anne. *The Casino.* California: Catalina Island Museum Society, 1979.

Overholt, Alma. *The Catalina Story.* California: Catalina Island Museum Society, 1962. Edited and updated by Jack Sargent, 1971.

Udvardy, Miklos D.F. The Audubon Society Field Guide to North American Birds, Western Region. New York: Knopf, 1977.

Windle, Ernest. *Windle's History of Santa Catalina Island.* California: Catalina Islander, 1940.

INDEX

Page numbers in *italics* indicate information in charts, maps, photos, or special topics.

ABOUT THE AUTHOR

Chicki Mallan never forgets that she is one of the "lucky people" from Catalina Island. Growing up on a small island is an experience that has colored her entire life. Traveling since childhood, Chicki has logged thousands of miles around the world, first with her parents, then with her own large family. Chicki and children have lived in the Orient and Europe, but she still counts Catalina as the number one island in the world. When not traveling, writing, lecturing, or giving slide presentations, Chicki and husband Oz, live in Paradise, a small community in the foothills of the California Sierra Nevada. Between books, she does what she enjoys most, writing magazine articles. In June of 1987, Chicki was awarded the *Pluma de Plata* ("Silver Pen") writing award from the Mexican government for articles she had written about Mexico.

She and husband Oz and their publishing company, Pine Press, are proud to announce Guide to Catalina as their first title. Chicki continues to be associated with Moon Publications. Other books Chicki has written and published by Moon Handbooks include Yucatan Handbook, Cancun Handbook, Belize Handbook, Central

ABOUT THE PHOTOGRAPHER

Oz Mallan has been a professional photographer since his graduation from Brooks Institute of Santa Barbara in 1950. Much of that time was spent as chief cameraman for the *Chico Enterprise-Record*. Oz's work has appeared in newspapers across the country via UPI and AP, magazines as well as many travel books. He travels the world with his wife, Chicki, handling the photo end of their literary projects as well as lectures and slide presentations. The photos in *Guide To Catalina* were taken on the many trips to Catalina and the Southern California coast.

ABOUT THE ILLUSTRATORS

The banner art at the start of the chapters was done by Kathy Escovedo-Sanders. She is an expert both in watercolor and this stipple style, which lends itself to excellent black-and-white reproduction. Kathy is a 1982 California State University, Long Beach, graduate with a BA in Art History. She exhibits drawings, etched intaglio prints, and woodcut prints, as well as her outstanding watercolor paintings. In the April 1982 issue of *Orange Coast* magazine, a complete photo essay illustrates Kathy's unique craft of dyeing, designing, and etching eggs. Her stipple art can also be seen in Chicki Mallan's *Yucatan Peninsula Handbook, Cancun Handbook, Central Mexico Handbook, Mexico Handbook,* and Belize Handbook.

CARTOGRAPHER

After receiving a BA in Art in 1974, map maker Bob Race earned an MA in Painting and Drawing one year later. For the next 14 years he taught fine art at the college level, and in 1989 he began working at Moon Publications. Bob has always been interested in maps, especially the techniques and materials used to draw them. He is currently exploring cartography applications via computer.

-notes-